THE ORIGIN OF A LEADER

THE ORIGIN OF A LEADER

Transforming Family Patterns into Leadership Power

Pam Manfredo Curtis, PhD

SIMON ACUMEN

New York Amsterdam/Antwerp London
Toronto Sydney/Melbourne New Delhi

SIMON ACUMEN

An Imprint of Simon & Schuster, LLC
1230 Avenue of the Americas
New York, NY 10020

First Simon Acumen hardcover edition September 2026

SIMON ACUMEN and colophon are registered trademarks of Simon & Schuster, LLC

Interior design by Renato Stanisic

Manufactured in the United States of America

1 3 5 7 9 10 8 6 4 2

Library of Congress Control Number: 2026938981

ISBN 978-1-6680-6638-6
ISBN 978-1-6680-6639-3 (ebook)

To . . .

My mom and dad, Roberta and Nick,
for creating my childhood home, one filled with high expectations,
the importance of family, and unconditional love.

My husband, John, for striving with me to create a
loving and real home for our children.

Our children, Christopher, Ryan, and Adriana,
who we hope and pray will create a home for their children
of real conversations, strong relationships,
and unconditional love.

Contents

Introduction ix

Prologue: Fine Is Not a Feeling xxiii

Act I: The Roles You Were Born Into

Chapter 1: Don't Fear Your Feelings. Mine Them. 3

Chapter 2: Meet Your Childhood Cast 17

Chapter 3: Envision Your Childhood Setting 31

Chapter 4: Were You Raised in a Home of Stability? 35

Chapter 5: Were You Raised in a Home of Complexity? 61

Chapter 6: Were You Raised in a Home of Trauma? 81

Chapter 7: Were You Raised in Multiple Home Environments? 101

Act II: The Roles You're In

Chapter 8: The Implications of Your Childhood 111

Chapter 9: What's Stopping You? 129

Chapter 10: How to Confront—and Maybe Even Forgive—the Ones Who've Hurt You 143

Act III: The Role You're Destined For

Chapter 11: How to Have a Real Conversation 165

Chapter 12: Create Psychological Safety 171

Chapter 13: Listen Empathetically 187

Chapter 14: Engage in Constructive Conflict 209

Chapter 15: Provide Constructive Feedback 227

Chapter 16: Real Conversations in Action 245

Exit Stage Left 253

With Gratitude and Love 257

Appendix: The Emotions Library 263

Notes 265

Index 269

Introduction

I'm positively beaming as I drive along Sunset Boulevard in Hollywood, California. On that road, in that weather, it's hard not to feel like all is well. But I'm more excited about the reason for my drive. In fact, I'm so elated (and admittedly nervous) that I nearly miss my exit.

I quickly veer into the short lane on my right and spy a small neon sign that reads *Garage Chateau Marmont*. I stop, hand my keys to the waiting valet, then take a deep breath. I'm about to meet with a C-suite executive in the entertainment industry. It's not the first time we've met, but it's the first time we've met at this historic location. The renowned Chateau Marmont has served as a sanctuary for celebrities, providing them the privacy that artists of all sorts have sought while navigating their careers. I call this a safe space.

I notice that I am grinning ear to ear and feel warmth in my cheeks. I am ready to share my new learnings and insights about who this executive is as a leader. I can't wait! But to do it in a place like this? Whoa!

I wasn't surprised that my client insisted on meeting there. We needed a safe space to talk through what their company was facing and how they could inspire their sizable leadership team into an unknown future. (Hint: It starts with them!) Plus, the discussions I have with my clients go deep. We don't just talk about their business. We discuss their life. And I'm not afraid to ask the hard questions, even of these leaders who may hear yes too often. Privacy and safety are paramount for such vulnerability.

These one-on-ones bring me so much joy because of the mutual vulnerability and meaningful conversations that occur between us. I am deeply grateful that they trust me so much that our conversations lead to emotional breakthroughs and new possibilities in both their personal and professional lives. I do not take this for granted.

Feeling joyful, I walked through the restaurant by a couple of well-known celebrities. (Yes, I did a double-take because I couldn't believe it. Could it get any better?)

Then, bam, a flash of a sweet memory washed over me.

I'm five or six, standing at the front of my class, nervously pressing down the hem of my pastel floral dress and waiting for my cue. My heart beats fast . . . I've never done this before, but I feel ready.

Like I was born for this.

My music teacher, Mrs. Nadler, sits at the piano, tells me to sing my favorite song, and plays the first few notes of the melody. I wait just a few seconds and then hold my first public performance. My voice is timid at first, but when I get to the chorus, I belt it out. So do my classmates.

"It's a Small World" has that effect.

That was the day I became a performer and had the first clear intimation of what I wanted to do for a living. While the twists and turns of life took me down another path, I can still see the seeds for the origin of my leadership capabilities. If I could command the attention of a room with my voice, if I could vulnerably open myself up such that others felt safe to sing along with me, I could transform the world around me. Aside from the singing—which I still do with a few of my clients—that's not far off from how I coach leaders. In a safe space, I speak from my head and my heart to help leaders who've lost touch with who they were so they can discover who they can become.

I carry that beloved childhood memory with me into every client meeting, a constant reminder that the girl I was shaped so much of the woman I am.

Every day, I can't believe my fortune in growing from a small-town performer with stars in her eyes to a big-time executive coach with stars for clients. I'm excited that you'll meet a few of them in this book, many of whom I also interviewed on my radio show. (Note: Some names have been changed for confidentiality purposes.)

For more than thirty-five years, I've worked with some of the country's most well-known executives to transform their leadership. I've observed them in every setting imaginable, from their senior management meetings to large presentations to my favorite one of all: one-on-one coaching sessions where they share some of the most intimate details of their life and leadership struggles. I've witnessed how they deal with conflict (or not). I've heard when they lean in to challenging conversations. I've seen their eyebrows rise or a wry smile form when they receive constructive feedback. And I've been overcome with pride when the changes we've worked so hard to enact become real and start inspiring their team. Their success is my success.

What's more, through the process I lead them through, these driven leaders have also realized success outside of their work. In other words, what I do with my clients isn't just about their business. It's about their lives. So, yes, while our work starts in the business world, my approach is most importantly about becoming a better human being. You're about to take the same journey. It will make you a better leader, a better partner, a better parent, a better friend, and a better community member. I've witnessed tremendous results in my clients' leadership *and* personal lives. This process works, and you'll see that over and over in the stories to come. I promise!

However, it's not easy.

The challenging heart-and-mind work I conduct with my clients is a chief reason why I'm a huge proponent of creating *safe environments*. Honestly, that's my secret sauce. (Don't tell anyone!) Because we get into the nitty-gritty of their lives, and particularly their childhoods, my clients have to feel secure with me during our meetings. To feel safe, they need to trust me—both me as a person and me as an experienced, qualified, proven executive coach. Because I will see you as one of my valued clients throughout our time together in this book, I want you to feel the same kind of safety. I want you to know that I'm in this with you and I'm *for* you. I know you can change your leadership and your life for the better if you'll trust me and the journey I'm about to lead you on.

So, reader, I'm Pam. It's a pleasure to meet you.

Welcome to My Office

The truth is, I grew up leading. President of student council. Director of plays. Starring roles in shows. Yet I didn't realize that I loved helping company leaders until my first job out of college. After working for one manager at a market research firm, I was quickly transferred to support the company's president. That's how my deep and lifelong calling began.

I learned my craft working within IBM, PepsiCo, and Unilever, helping leaders transform their companies. I helped PepsiCo's CEO transform their well-known brand from "just a soda company" to a total beverage business. I partnered with the senior team at Unilever to integrate three of their brands into an entirely new company. And I thrived being the head of Leadership and Organizational Development for Unilever Home and Personal Care.

I wanted to help even more leaders, those who genuinely wanted to grow and change, so I founded my own company, Manfredo Curtis Associates, LLC, in 1999. We step in when a leader is preparing to become a CEO, when teams need to become high performing at the executive level, when organizational cultures need transformation, and when leaders of all kinds need to become authentic, learning how to articulate who they are and inspire people to follow them. We've since worked with General Motors, Harley-Davidson, Cummins, Diageo, and more. I also hosted *Corner Office Confidential*, on SiriusXM, an hour-long show of intimate conversations where I interview C-suite leaders for their best leadership lessons.

Since starting my business and working with the most senior leaders of organizations, I've designed, implemented, and redesigned our executive coaching, authentic leadership, high performance teams, and Peak Performance Coaching models, among others. I've tested them continuously and implemented them successfully across numerous organizations. Bringing the science and practice of industrial/organizational psychology and statistics together has been my proving ground.

I've also spoken in front of rooms of a range of sizes and purpose, from executive team rooms of twelve to hundreds or thousands at education events across the globe, on issues like high performance teams, authenticity, organizational change, psychometrics, and the how-tos of facilitating interpersonal dynamics. In all my speaking, teaching, and consulting, I strive to create psychologically safe places for real conversations to take place. I want the smartest people in the room to also become the most emotionally adept because I've seen just how powerful deep life change can be, for my clients, for those they influence, and for those they love.

Those are my bona fides.

But I know it takes more than facts to make a person trust you.

Your Solution Is in Your Past

Where does a leader begin? When they get the corner office? When they first become a manager or their title finally has "Senior Vice President"? When at least one person reports to them?

The origin of a leader happens much earlier than that—and much earlier than most of us would expect. In all my research and decades of coaching high-level CEOs, I've discovered that the most significant predictor of how you show up in your interpersonal interactions as a leader—and as a human—is your childhood.

Consider it this way: What if your present-day leadership limitations aren't a result of a lack of critical thinking skills, knowledge, or experience? What if your inability as a leader to connect with others lies in your past? What if what you learned and practiced as a child has a much deeper influence on you than you realize?

The thought is heavy yet freeing. It's heavy because you may need to consider a past you wanted to forget. Or you may need to become more self-aware than you think you have time for. Yet it's also freeing because you've identified an untapped strategy for growing as a leader and as a person. You may have hidden strengths that originated in your childhood and that you've yet to fully realize. If you've felt plateaued, this is what you've been missing. You've been so busy looking at your future that you've forgotten about your past. And it's in your past that you can discover your personal blueprint for a better tomorrow. Consider the possibilities!

I know I can help you elevate your leadership and your life because I've witnessed incredible changes in high-level CEOs. These men and women were already leading—or would soon be leading—world-class companies. From any outsider's perspective, they were the epitome of success. However, they knew something needed to change in order for them to achieve their next level. Maybe that meant becoming the big boss. Or dealing with a crisis. Or getting their team to align for once. Or overcoming an obstacle in their non-work life that was negatively affecting their work life.

You may be facing similar problems. And regardless of the size of your company, organization, or your projected revenue, you want to follow in those high-level CEOs' footsteps to experience transformative change in your leadership and your life.

Regardless of your specific problem, I believe the solution is the same:

- Deeply diving into your childhood backstory
- Remembering the supporting cast who most influenced you while you were growing up and what they role-modeled for you
- Identifying the specific type of home setting in which you thrived or were stifled

All of this still affects your leadership strengths, development areas, needs, and more today.

Now, are you nodding your head? Or did you just roll your eyes?

I'm only asking because some of my clients have had the latter reaction. One said he was skeptical about meeting me for a "weird Freudian thing."

I get it. I really do.

Traditional leadership development is about strategies and tactics and game plans and blueprints. Tangible steps you can take to accomplish what needs accomplishing. Rare are the leadership coaches who begin their sessions with "So, tell me about your childhood." But I'm not afraid to bring the therapist's couch to the corner office. When a leader and I are deciding whether we will partner, I don't sugarcoat my approach. This process can take up to two years, it's hard, and it doesn't work unless you're all in. The work we embark on together is about real conversations. It's about getting beyond saying "I am fine" or "good" or "okay." Rather, together, we deeply investigate their feelings going back to childhood. They must have a sincere willingness to accept and explore feedback. And must strive to create a safe, intimate space for vulnerability and growth.

We laugh, we cry, and everything in between. The goal is to profoundly build the leader's self-awareness. I help leaders answer the question "Why do you want to do this work now?" I'm purposefully selective too. I will not partner with leaders unless they agree to be truly committed to transformational change.

Are you committed?

I will give you steps and processes, but the weight of the work is on your shoulders.

A Question of Power

While you may grow up, you will never grow *better* until you understand how deeply your childhood has affected you. Who you are today is a direct result of who you were as a child. When you understand how your childhood impacts your leadership and who you are as a human being, you can't help but see how it affects every part of you *and* how it enhances or detracts from the one essential you need as a leader: power.

Now, some people see power as bad, even corrupt. For others, the more power they have, the more successful they feel. For some, it's of no interest. In reality, wisely leveraging your power can lead to greater effectiveness as a human being, but you need to know what kind of power most moves the needle. The biggest mistakes I see my clients make are trying to use power they don't have, using the wrong kind of power, and not using the power they do have. So what's the "right" kind of power?

I define power as the ability to change others' behavior, to cause others to perform actions that they might not otherwise carry out. On the whole, when people think about "power," they think about formal power. This is often experienced as coercive power (you fear losing your job), reward power (you work for a bonus), or legitimate power (you're the boss).

Informal power holds more influence. Informal power bases have a greater capacity to affect overall employee satisfaction and performance, as well as making a noticeable difference in the home. Informal power is seen in expert power (your skills and knowledge draw others to you), connection power (you know the right people), or referent power (you're trusted and respected). You gain referent power when others trust what you do and respect you for how you handle situations. For example, an HR leader with referent power has employees who open up to them because the employees know the HR leader treats everyone fairly and that they'll come to the rescue of anyone being treated unfairly.

In fact, referent power may be the secret superpower held by the world's top leaders. However, you don't have to be in a leadership or senior-level role to attain this kind of power. Anyone can enhance their referent power. This book is all about increasing your referent power through clearly understanding your childhood and transforming family patterns that may be preventing you from obtaining that kind of power. It's also about harnessing what's already wonderful about you, the strengths you acquired in childhood. In brief, increasing your referent power means learning how to authentically and vulnerably speak your truth, how to build relationships to have real conversations by creating psychological safety, and how to listen and engage in constructive conflict and feedback.

Now is the time for you to start claiming your referent power, to take up more space as a leader, and to make great things happen in your world. Today is the day you begin to discover who you were so you can find who you're meant to be.

The Role You Were Born to Play

Since I'm going to be asking you deeply personal questions that have the potential to unearth troubling answers, I'd like you to consider this approach: Don't think of yourself as *I*. Think of yourself as an actor on stage.

Stick with me here.

When you see your life as a play on a stage, you can take a more objective view of what happened to you and around you than if you see your life history from your first-person perspective. In other words, you can achieve some emotional distance that may help you make better judgments about yourself and others. (Eventually, you'll have to get back to being yourself and learning how to sit with your emotions, something I'll cover in Chapter 1.)

Right now, the curtain's about to part and the play of your life is about to begin.

I've modeled this book after the essentials of a three-act play.

- **The prologue** provides context for what you're about to see. In my prologue, you'll meet Tom, a well-respected and highly regarded leader who was shocked to learn he still had ample room for growth in both his professional and personal lives.
- **Act I** is the setup. You meet the cast, see the settings, and receive information you need for the rest of the play. In my Act I, you'll chart the highs and lows of Act I of your life—e.g., your first eighteen years. You'll recall your own "supporting cast" (or "opposing cast," depending on your childhood!). And you'll self-assess your "setting"—e.g., the kind of home you grew up in. Act I is all about remembering who you were and seeing what was role-modeled for you.
- **Act II** brings in change. In my Act II, you'll consider the implications of your childhood, which will provide deep insights that will illuminate patterns for you. It may also reveal inner confusion, discomfort, and pain. You'll chart Act II of your life, from age eighteen to your current age. Have you experienced anything hard in that act? (That's likely, and unfortunately, a rhetorical question.) You'll also discover if some person or event is blocking you from being the best version of yourself, and how to overcome that block. Act II is all about seeing how your childhood affects your present leadership and life.

- **Act III** offers resolution. My Act III offers proven strategies for having higher-level conversations, increasing your referent power, and inspiring others to follow you. In this final act, you'll learn exactly how to have real conversations that can transform the world and the lives of those around you, from the boardroom to the living room.

If Shakespeare was right and "all the world's a stage, and all the men and women merely players," you have the leading role in your life. So the question you have to ask yourself, especially if you're a leader or a leader in waiting, is this: When all eyes are on you, who will you be?

How to Prepare for Your Leading Role

The best actors consider more than just their script. They want to know their character's backstory, motivation, and who the character is emotionally—everything they can possibly know in order to make the character more believable. So they strive to get in touch with their head, their heart, and their hands.

In their role at any given moment, they must ask themselves:

- **Head:** What am I thinking?
- **Heart:** What am I feeling?
- **Hands:** What do I need to do?

I use this head, heart, and hands method in every meeting with my clients. I want to know what their mindset is and whether they're ready to get to work so they can fully engage in what we're there to do. Plus, I want to help them tune in to their visceral responses, the ones that are tied to their heart's reaction. Since you're now one of my valued clients, I'd like us to go through it. I'm going to ask you to conduct this check-in a few times throughout this book, and I believe it will help you see your progress—even if you're, let's say, emotionally inarticulate.

Here's how to conduct a head, heart, and hands check-in:

1. Check Your Head

Ask yourself, "What am I thinking *right now?*"

Not yesterday, not last weekend, but right now.

For example, my answer is: "I'd like to know if you like my writing style and if my words pull you in." My clients often answer, "My mind is swirling. I have three deadlines within the next two days, and I don't have time to sit in this room and talk about leadership behaviors."

Don't think too hard about it. Just share what is top of mind. And just be honest with yourself.

Right now, what are you thinking about?

The goal for checking your head is to release any positive or negative baggage from your mind. This check-in also helps the many leaders who tend to live solely in their heads, clearing their mental pathway for the second step.

2. Check Your Heart

Ask yourself, "What am I feeling?"

In order to appropriately answer this question, you must slow down, move from your head to your heart, and tune in to your visceral reactions, like tension in your stomach. In reading this chapter, what are you feeling?

Now, why are you feeling that way? It's important to include the why of your feeling. Explaining the "because" is critical to understanding where that emotion came from.

When I check in with my heart right now, I feel nervous about writing this book for you because this is my first book.

For help naming your emotions, see the emotions library in the appendix. And know that *good*, *great*, *bad*, *okay*, and *fine* are not emotions.

Also, a word of warning: If you default to "I feel that . . ." or "I feel like . . . ," you've returned to your thinking domain. Remember, you're checking in with your heart.

In this step, be patient with yourself. Choose to actually feel your feelings.

3. Check Your Hands

Ask yourself, "What do I need to do over the next few minutes or hours in order to focus on myself?"

What *distractions* might keep you from doing your best work? What *physical ailments* might make it uncomfortable for you to concentrate?

As I write this, I'm thinking about an important conversation I need to have with my son Christopher. If he walks in and he's ready to have it, I'll pause my writing immediately. By checking in with my hands, I'm telling myself that this kind of interruption is okay.

Maybe you're expecting a call from a doctor with medical test results. Or the babysitter will come through the door with your kids soon. Physically, your back may hurt, so you'll need to stand or walk around every twenty minutes. Yet maybe you feel completely free and there is nothing distracting you. "No distractions" is a legitimate answer when it's the truth.

The goal is to eliminate (or accept) what could distract you from truly checking in with your full self. For example, if you're feeling anxious, take a walk. On the other hand, you may need to handle a distraction—like getting a call from a doctor—so that you can deepen your self-awareness without distraction. Throughout this book, I will give you several opportunities to check in with yourself. Please take advantage of those chances! I will ask you questions like: What memories are you recalling and thinking about? What emotions are you feeling and why? When I do, make sure you use the list of the emotions in the appendix to inspire you.

When you clear your head, open up your heart, and free your hands, you're making space for possibility. Our childhood influences run deep after all.

Like a roller coaster, the journey you're about to take will involve emotional highs and lows. When you truly take the time to investigate your childhood for its hidden and not-so-hidden patterns, you will experience a gamut of emotions. Since I can't physically be in the room with you to provide a safe environment during these moments, I'd like you to make one commitment to me and to yourself as you read this book: Don't run away from your emotions.

As you'll soon read, your emotions are data to be mined for essential information about who you are and who you could be. But all of us—even the world's most renowned leaders—allow our heads, hearts, or our hands to distract us from discovering the gold mine of that data. So when emotions you may have not felt in quite some time descend upon you in this process, and they will, don't fear them. Don't escape them. Don't negate them.

Learn from them. Your emotions have so much to teach you if you'll just listen. My goal, just as with all my clients, is to help you listen better to your feelings.

If you can commit to that, I can commit to sharing with you what I've taught the best leaders in the world—and what they've taught me.

Today is the day you begin to embrace new possibilities for your leadership and your life.

Prologue: Fine Is Not a Feeling

Tom Linebarger's best day at work led to his worst day with me.

He was first hired at Cummins as an intern. The hundred-plus-year-old company was—and still is—the largest independent manufacturer of diesel engines in the world. When I met Tom, he was the president of Cummins's Power Generation business. His ascent from intern to president was a testament to his drive and his dedication. Tom loved the company, the work he got to do every day, and the people with whom he worked. You could see it in his buoyant energy.

On a momentous day in 2007, Tom's boss Tim Solso approached him with unexpected news. "I think you can be the next leader of Cummins, and I'd like to advocate for you to be CEO at the board."

Tom was floored. Of course he wanted the job, yet he'd never really given much thought to the possibility coming true. Now a moment he'd only dreamed about was becoming a reality. He was also elated because he deeply respected his boss, who'd recently been voted a top CEO of the decade. That vote of assurance buoyed Tom's confidence. As Tom would later tell me, he "floated most of the rest of the day a few inches off the ground."

That wasn't the only unexpected news. Tim later asked him, "Why don't you talk to a few members of the Board of Directors? I think they have some feedback for you so you can be ready to be CEO." With his head soaring in the clouds of possibility, Tom didn't think too much about his boss's request, at least until he woke up in a cold sweat the next morning thinking, *What did he mean by* some *feedback?*

Tom found out soon enough.

The next day, he spoke with board members Alexis Herman and Will Miller. (Will also happened to be the founder's son.) Because they cared about him and wanted him to succeed, they leveled with him. They each said he was smart and clearly hardworking. They recalled how often he'd said, "Hard work and effort is the greatest reward." However, they were both concerned about his CEO potential. They felt he was emotionally distant and cold. Alexis wondered about his emotional intelligence. He didn't listen well. And he came across as arrogant.

Tom wondered if his dream was over before it had even begun.

Despite their critical feedback, Alexis and Will wanted to see Tom ascend to the highest level of leadership at the company, but not until they saw a noticeable shift in his attitude and behavior. So Alexis, a former board member with Coca-Cola, referred Tom to a friend and colleague of mine, Martha Morris Graham, who had been doing some coaching work at Coke. Martha lives in London, so she recommended me. That's how I met Tom, a longtime client whom I now call a friend.

As I begin with all of my clients (and as I began with you), I showed my cards up front. The foundation of our work together is whether you believe that your childhood is the most significant contributor to how you lead today. It's okay if you don't fully believe it at first. I just need you to consider the possibility that it's true.

Tom didn't.

He didn't tell me this until much later, but when I told him my views on how our childhood still affects us, he thought, *What a load of gobbledygook!* And I know my next step didn't help matters. In fact, it was the next step that led to Tom's worst day.

Once a client has decided to work with me (some would say has been forced to work with me), I have a systemized process to learn four essentials about them: Who are they? How do others see them? What aspirations do they have? And what if anything is getting in their way from being their best selves?

With Tom, we started on Step 2 because his boss specifically wanted to know how other people perceived him. So I conducted a *360 feedback assessment*, which gathers data on what a client's bosses, peers, direct reports, and yes, even their spouse and family truly think about that person's strengths and development areas, plus whether they're ready to take on a bigger role. Part of the assessment means I interview many people in their life so I can discover a few simple truths: What makes you wonderful, how do we harness that, and how can you improve?

For CEOs and other high-level executives who've experienced years if not decades of success, this question seems rhetorical. *I'm already improved. Can't you see what I've achieved?* This is exactly how Tom felt. In his words, "I was in my mid-forties, I'd been leading for twenty years, and I was already a very accomplished leader."

On Tom's worst day with me, I handed him his feedback report. He described it as "not quite a New York City phone book," but one that was just as weighty. We spent four hours walking through each and every quote. Within its many pages sat the blunt truth about Tom from his most trusted bosses, coworkers, and, most importantly, his wife, Michele.

When I was out of the room, he likely scanned the opening pages first, the ones that lauded him for his intelligence, his strategic thinking, and his drive. One of his direct reports even said, "I am a Tom champion. I hope he gets to be CEO. It would be a good thing for Cummins." Tom's strengths are many, and his assessment revealed that. Yet I also imagine that Tom heard screeching brakes when I began walking him through the page titled "Development Opportunities." The first line, from a board member, zeroed in on Tom's major deficit: "He's great, but there is one huge gap—interpersonal skills."

Regarding his impatience, arrogance, and his inability to listen well, one peer said that "he puts a lot of emphasis on being right. He wants you to have the same right answer as him." A direct report said, "He talks more than he listens." Another said, "He tires you into submission." And in a damning report on his emotional intelligence, multiple direct reports said effectively the same thing: "Does he care enough about people, or are they only there to help him succeed? I just don't know."

Tom thought, *Can I really have this much wrong with me? Are there really this many things that people don't like about me? At this stage in my leadership? And is it too late to change any of it?*

He was no longer floating above the ground.

He felt six feet under it.

I'm a tough-love coach. Because I care for you, I will tell you the truth, even when it hurts. This has helped me in my work with some of the world's most high-powered CEOs. They want to get to the point; so do I. But here's where we differ: They want to immediately *think* about what problem needs to be solved, and then, with their *hands*, they just want to get stuff done. They want to fix it. For many of them, this has proven to work time and again. Why mess with success? Yet so many of them fail to realize that their current ceiling could be their new floor. That by adding one more check-in, they could ascend to the kind of leadership and life they've only dreamed of.

I want to get these leaders to the point of aligning their head, *heart*, and hands. More often than not, they forget that central and most essential part of the equation: How do you feel?

Like these leaders, you may also need to significantly build your self-awareness so that you can enhance your leadership. This requires tuning into your heart and your emotions.

Can you hear my tough love?

So I'm not shy about digging into the pain points of a new client's 360 feedback assessment. If their wife said they're mean or if their boss said they're cocky, we're going to talk about it, along with all the other pieces we do at the start. And not only are we going to discuss how their shortcomings are currently and negatively impacting their leadership, we're also going to discover the origins of those shortcomings so they can overcome what's likely been holding them back for decades.

To move forward, you have to look back.

Your childhood is the most significant predictor of how you show up in all of your interpersonal interactions as a leader and a human being.

Why do I believe this? I have interviewed thousands of leaders about the details of their childhood. I have asked them to describe the house or houses they grew up in, the characters of their life and how they acted, and key events, from joyful to sorrowful, that were significant to them. We've discussed their beliefs about their capabilities, values, and principles. I have analyzed their personality profiles, which capture their needs, strengths, and developmental areas. I have conducted countless 360 feedback processes. I have coached them through challenging issues leading their teams, colleagues, and organizations, or getting along with their families and friends. Through all of this, I have constantly examined the patterns I am hearing about and witnessing. It's like a big jigsaw puzzle with no box top.

In my experience, the patterns of behavior we learn from others when we're children account for the majority of who we are as leaders. In fact, I would argue that as high as *80 percent* of who you are today is a direct result of your childhood. Some of my colleagues cringe when I say this number, but I believe it to be true. How those closest to you treated and engaged with you early in life impacts how you appear, interact with, and treat the people in your life at work and at home. In your early years, you were taught and you practiced how to conduct conversations, listen, develop relationships, solve problems, and cope with feedback and disappointment—all skills every leader needs in abundance.

Your performance at work (and what makes you uniquely you) is dictated by your thoughts, feelings, and actions. These are informed by the strengths you've honed *and* the development areas you haven't yet conquered. And these were shaped by your childhood environment. If you want to become more effective at connecting with and inspiring others, you must understand how your strengths and development areas are rooted in your childhood environment. Then you must determine what you are willing to change.

This is true for everyone whose roles require them to inspire others. Whether you run a business, coach a sport, or volunteer for your local PTA, you're serving in a leadership position. If you're a parent, you're a leader, too. You will become a better leader by understanding how you practiced interacting with others when you were young.

By taking an objective and vulnerable look at the home environment you grew up in, you will learn so much about how you show up as a leader—both good and otherwise. You might have been raised in a psychologically safe home filled with unconditional love where you were encouraged to achieve. Or you may have learned to navigate a dysfunctional home filled with discord or even trauma. Taking this journey with me and analyzing your childhood isn't about passing judgment or thinking that great leaders only come from specific environments. Even people who grew up amid horrific circumstances develop strengths that help them excel at inspiring others. And even those from idyllic homes have areas in which they can improve.

The real breakthrough to leading better—as a parent, volunteer, coach, or executive—is looking for the origins of the behaviors that you never fully understood but that might be holding you back. To do so, you must become more self-aware. Your ability to understand the people you lead is limited only by how well you understand yourself.

Tom didn't have a clue about himself.

Tom's memory of our first meeting might ring a little too true for you.

I asked him, "How are you feeling?"

He answered, "Good! I'm feeling fine."

I gently reminded him, "Fine's not a feeling."

He was making the mistake I hear so often, when leaders give pat answers to questions about feelings because they're so focused on what they need to *do*. (Who has time for feelings?)

I let my reply sit with him for a moment before I continued. "What are you thinking about? And how are you *feeling*?"

Recalling this moment, Tom later told me, "I remember looking inside and it was just blank . . . I could see everything in the room. I could see the lights and they were fluorescent, and I could see the room size and that the chairs were covered with fabric and a little bit too short and uncomfortable, and I could experience everything in there—except what was inside."

In fact, we'd likely met at least eight times until we had a breakthrough.

I opened that meeting with the question he knew was coming. "How do you feel today, Tom?"

"Pam." He paused.

I held my breath.

"Pam, I'm feeling . . . sad."

"That's wonderful!"

That wasn't my actual reply, but that's what I felt. Not because he was sad, of course, but for the simple fact that he was finally opening up.

I actually replied, "Tom, that's a feeling!"

He laughed.

Tom isn't an outlier.

We have an abundance of severed-heart leaders. They lead well with their heads but move so quickly that their feelings can't catch up. Or their feelings were never invited into the office in the first place. We shouldn't be surprised by this. Our culture applauds and rewards leaders for their critical and analytical thinking, problem-solving ability, intellect, speed, and drive for results. Tom is a prime example. "I always showed up ready to go, ready to do things, ready to make decisions, ready to analyze things. . . . My greatest strength coming up through the company is I got stuff done. I was really good at solving problems, but that's an energy that's all about moving forward, going fast."

Too many leaders rely on thinking through their challenges while ignoring any of the emotions that may be stirred up in themselves or others.

And if these leaders could just access their emotions—their true and deep feelings—without giving up their analytic prowess, they could experience a tenfold or even hundredfold gain at their job and in their life.

Most leadership coaching models focus on what you do or how you do it. They help you learn new skills or proficiencies, rather than helping you show up differently as a human being. In my work with leaders like Tom, I focus on *why* people show up the way they do, because the solution is different based on the answer. The more alert you are to how you are showing up and why, the more insight you'll gain into how you can adjust your behavior toward becoming an authentic and courageous leader who speaks in a voice that is true to yourself and who acts on principles that are important to you.

In my work with Tom, I had to help him overcome his faulty belief that emotions should not be discussed at work. I also encouraged him to develop his self-awareness, which he needed in order to achieve his next level as a leader. He didn't think he was all that self-aware before we met. As he told me, "I misunderstood both how important self-awareness was to my performance as a leader and my overall happiness. I underestimated how bad I was at it and what it was costing me."

To help him become more self-aware, to help him see the true costs of unwittingly living his life based on his family patterns, I needed him to trust me enough to become vulnerable and tell me about his childhood. In other words, I wanted the unfeeling ascendant CEO to tell a stranger the most emotional stories of his life.

After just one in-person meeting, Tom was ready to talk about his Emotional Timeline. We jumped in. Tom opened up to me about his childhood in California. In his earliest memories, his parents are fighting. They would divorce soon after, when Tom was six. He recalls feeling almost relieved that they split, as if a new calm descended on his life. Yet, for the next few years, he was shuttled between two homes—two very different environments with very different people.

He lived with his mother most often, but she worked full-time and went to school in the evenings to finish her degree to get a higher-paying job. He calls her a "determined bootstrapper," a strong woman who always figured out how to make Tom and his brother's life better with each passing year. This determination often left her tired and irritated when she returned home. So Tom learned to avoid upsetting her and to be self-sufficient.

His father's house was very different. He would have been considered a hippie. Marijuana plants were always growing in the backyard. He worked as a commercial painter. He was also temperamental, stubborn, and "very macho." For example, Tom remembers being bullied as a kid and his father telling him, "The next time someone does that to you, look up and hit him as hard as you can." When he was given that advice, Tom was five. He described his father's house as one with "not a lot of supervision or caring moments. It wasn't mean. Just not caring."

You'll read more details about Tom's family when we discuss the nine different childhood settings, at least one of which will cover most everyone's upbringing. For now, these are the broad strokes of his tumultuous childhood, which are also fairly typical for men and women of his generation.

Over time, Tom saw the long-invisible threads that tied his present-day leadership problems to his childhood. For example, his father was intelligent and well-read. Consequently, Tom learned to argue his points and never give up against his dad because his father would argue and not lose. What other people perceived as Tom's arrogance was really his performance anxiety. Tom was a pleaser and wanted to always do well in his father's eyes, so he would show his father and others earlier in his career how much he knew.

- Both his intelligence and his arrogance had origins in something his father drilled into him: "Being wrong is not a possibility."
- His lack of listening skills derived from a learned and reinforced necessity for self-reliance.
- His ability to handle high amounts of responsibility came from a long history of watching his mother take care of him and his brother.
- His problem-solving capabilities derived from often being faced with surprising difficulties that he had to figure out how to overcome, like,

as a latchkey kid, taking care of his younger brother, who didn't want to do chores or homework.
- His inability to access his feelings came from a long history of stifling his emotions in order to appease anyone and everyone near him.

Although Tom's issues had many contributing factors, pinpointing where and when they started helped him see how these issues continued to unknowingly plague him in his leadership and in his life (at least until a rude coach dropped a critical assessment on his desk). However, let's not forget that, even in the hardness of his dual-family home, Tom also learned many valuable life lessons that contributed to his strengths as a leader. He'd leaned on those strengths for decades because they'd gotten results. However, to ascend to his next leadership role, one where the fate of the company would rest on his shoulders, he'd have to become stronger than his strengths. He'd have to face his long-ignored development areas head-on.

At his core, Tom had lost touch with his authentic self. I define a person's authentic self as someone who is genuine—the real deal, no masks, all truth. You speak in a voice that is true to yourself and you act on principles that are important to you. This allows you to lead more passionately because you genuinely believe the things that you say and do. Living authentically reduces performance anxiety. You can recognize your strengths and don't have to be perfect anymore. You realize no one is perfect. Believing you need to be perfect creates a higher level of stress, which actually decreases performance.

When you learn your development areas, you realize that everyone else already knows these things about you—and still thinks you're a decent person and leader, so your stress reduces. Becoming more comfortable and relaxing leads to behaving better as a leader. As a result, you actually become more confident about what you do and therefore more passionate as a leader and a human.

Arguably, Tom had never discovered his authentic self. In the two different family models in which he grew up, he was never given the opportunity to truly discover who he was. As you'll read in the chapters on childhood settings, some homes are better than others for nurturing a more developed sense of self. Tom wasn't granted that chance. (If you feel similarly, take heart. It's never too late to discover who you are.)

Tom recognized that he was not in tune with himself, and he wasn't happy with how he was showing up at work—especially after reviewing his assessment. That's what the board and his colleagues recognized. To get beyond his default mode of being—to stop being cold and arrogant—he needed to experience a behavioral shift. When faced with the negative but constructive feedback of his peers, Tom had to get real with himself.

"I learned a lot of things as a kid that were kind of just in me," Tom told me. "I didn't know that those boundaries or those instincts existed until I self-examined them. They were and still are impacting things that I think I do subconsciously or unconsciously. So, understanding my childhood and what makes me tick has been incredibly important."

As Tom patiently went through the process that I will soon lay out in this book, his results at work spoke to his resolve to see his behavior change for the better. Of course, he eventually became CEO. Arguably, that wasn't even his greatest achievement at work. After he retired, he told me what I hope I can say about my own work on my retirement day: "I felt like I had completed my task." He'd set out to strengthen the company, to make it more prosperous, and to ensure that all of its leaders were performing at their highest levels. He accomplished those goals by developing new strategies, by elevating everyone's performance, and by building a leadership culture that was strong and consistent with the company's values and aspirations.

He can also proudly look back on a host of accompanying accomplishments—namely, "promoting women and people of color, standing up for what is right; contributing to communities in remarkable ways that literally saved people's lives; creating jobs in communities all over the world that helped build families; serving customers well (even when they were difficult); building relationships with leaders in government, large companies, communities, etc., that will serve the company well for years to come; and treating people with dignity and respect and love everywhere I went."

Despite those impressive and well-earned achievements, I'm personally prouder of Tom for what he accomplished outside of his working hours. The change he'd sought at work ultimately changed the man he was at home, a place where he had long put on airs of perfection.

And there's proof.

Tom is six feet, three inches. He seldom realized how much his height and loud voice could intimidate his introverted wife and his young daughters. "Whenever I got angry at home, the volume of my voice and my energy level increased," Tom said. "I became big, and loud, and scary. Yes, I was upset with something my wife or daughters did, and I wanted them to change their behavior. But I didn't want to scare them into doing it. So, that became something I wanted to change about myself to become a better husband and father."

When Tom committed to change himself, he wasn't sure he could. Changing our behaviors is extremely difficult, especially when it comes to behaviors we've been practicing since childhood. Yet Tom's first major breakthrough came when he saw the connection between using his height and voice to get attention and how his angry and frustrated mother had modeled that for him. Once he discovered that, he saw how he could change his behavior. More than that, he *believed* he could change his behavior.

Tom later said, "I had difficulty knowing my own emotions. We talked about my lack of self-awareness. And so when I would be frustrated and I didn't recognize it, I would act out because I wasn't aware of my own emotions that brought me into the situation. If I could be self-aware of where my emotions were, I could calm myself down and then approach it the way one should."

A few years after Tom had undergone this transformation at work and at home, his wife, Michele, gave him this unforgettable Christmas card: "Dear Tom, You have become an even more wonderful husband and father as a result of the leadership work you have done. I am proud of you and love you so much."

The story gets even better.

On a long stretch of highway during his commute to Cummins's headquarters one day, Tom heard a story on NPR told by a mom in similar circumstances to his. She wanted to tell her college-bound son all the most important lessons she'd learned in life before he left home for good. She'd written a long speech, and she'd planned a dinner for just the two of them on the night that she would move her son into his new dorm. But the son, who didn't know the mom's intent, canceled on her because he wanted to go to the dorm's BBQ.

As the mother recounted this story on air, she wept.

So did Tom.

The man who once couldn't access his emotions cried so much that he had to pull off the highway. With a daughter, Alex, about to go off to college and another one not far behind, he could only think, *I can't let this happen to me*. He'd tried to have important talks with his daughters before, but the busyness and mundanity of life always seemed to intervene. He knew he couldn't wait any longer. He was running out of time, and his girls weren't getting any younger.

That day, he chose to write *25 Things I Hope I Told You*. He wrote another edition two years later for his younger daughter, Emily. In those pages, he told his girls what he'd always hoped he'd modeled but wanted to ensure that they fully knew, like advice on finding the right partner and chapters titled "Tell me when you need me" and "I love you unconditionally."

They later told him it was the nicest gift they'd ever received.

Arguably, Tom's worst day with me led to his best day with his daughters.

Thankfully, Tom's forgiven me. We still discuss our respective leadership challenges. For as much as he's said that I've helped him, I've been just as encouraged by the changes he continues to make in his life that are still rippling out.

Now that you've seen what kind of change is possible when you do the hard work of looking back on your childhood, let's discover what your first eighteen years reveal about you, both your strengths and your areas for development.

You may be surprised at what you discover.

ACT I

The Roles You Were Born Into

Whether you realize it or not, Act I of your life—from the time you were born until you turned eighteen—still impacts your behavioral choices and decisions today. To better understand who you are now, you must come to a greater understanding of who you were as a child. This involves remembering the events that shaped you, the people who influenced you, and the home environment that formed you.

In the following pages, you'll be asked to recall those details. Don't worry. Even if it's been years or decades since you've remembered the boy or girl you once were, I'll guide you through bringing your past to the center stage of your mind. Some memories may fill you with joy, others with sorrow or even anger. Through it all, I encourage you to keep exploring—and to pay special attention to your emotions. They will lead you to what's formed you and what could propel you into the next stage of your leadership and your life.

[1]

Don't Fear Your Feelings. Mine Them.

Imagine that you're, say, a twelve-year-old girl in a Long Island suburb in the 1970s. Every night at dinner, your family goes around the table and shares what happened during their day. Then, without fail, your school psychologist mom asks her follow-up to everyone: "How do you feel about it?" I don't have to scrutinize my past too much to know why I am the way I am. For as much as I might have rolled my eyes as a teenager, I remain grateful for my upbringing in such an emotionally intelligent and open family.

My father modeled emotional health too. He was a flight attendant supervisor at United Airlines. He understood the importance of building relationships and tuning in to what his team members needed. He had such empathy for his people. He deeply cared for them because they lived on the road away from their families, flying multiple daily trips and, if they were lucky, long international flights. And honoring each other's emotions didn't stop with my immediate family. My grandmother and godmother were always interested in hearing how I was and how I felt about events in my life. Even at a young age, I looked forward to talking to them because I knew they really cared about me.

As far back as I can remember, I breathed emotions in and out like air. If you identify with that, you can leverage your emotions into growth opportunities. If, on the other hand, emotions were never discussed at your childhood dinner table, you can rediscover, and even resurrect, your feelings. Either way, coming to terms with your emotions, both in your present and in looking at your childhood, is foundational to my proven process. As I like to say, "Emotions are data." By that I mean this: When you discover what you feel and where those feelings are coming from, you'll better understand why you do what you do. Then, in time and with practice, you can change how you feel in order to change your results for the better.

A Quick Aside About Emotions

Beneath all emotions is love or fear. Joy, happiness, and contentment come from love. Anxiousness, hatred, and loneliness come from fear. Do you tend to live on one side more than the other? Do you experience both? If you operate out of love, you may give yourself and others grace and forgiveness. If you operate out of fear, you may have something important or uncomfortable to tackle. No matter the origin, each emotion has something important to teach you. You just need to pay attention to how you're feeling. There is always something to be learned. To help you define what you're feeling, the appendix includes an Emotions Library arranged on a spectrum from fear to love.

Emotions play an invaluable role in helping you figure out who you are and what determines your true sense of self. When your principles and beliefs align with how you show up behaviorally, you'll feel happy. Conversely, when you feel challenged emotionally, you may become frustrated with yourself. The intensity of the emotion also helps guide you. For example, when I speak, I feel alive and vibrant. I'm passionate. Yet when I'm writing, I feel frustrated and become more introverted because I struggle to get my voice onto the page. I wither. Each emotion tells me more about who I am.

Often, the challenge is accepting that whatever you're feeling is okay; there are no "good" or "bad" emotions when it comes to the core memories of your life. After all, those moments helped shape who you've become. Please know that whatever you feel is valid, and all of your emotions *matter*. If you don't allow yourself to feel sad, embarrassed, or angry—especially when you look back at your core memories—you aren't allowing yourself to be really authentic, honest, or healthy. I want you to embrace your emotions!

Remember: Take this slowly. Don't run away from what you feel. To truly determine what a key event from your life means to you, tune in to the visceral reaction it creates. It's data to mine, not fear.

So let's get to deciphering your data by creating your Emotional Timeline.

How to Create an Emotional Timeline (and Why You Should)

When I begin coaching a leader, I first want to understand the interplay of emotions sparked by their life events, so I ask them to draw an *Emotional Timeline* (ETL). Since you're my client now (thanks for reading the book!), let's create your ETL.

The ETL is *foundational* to everything else this book offers. In brief, it charts your emotional highs and lows from birth to the present day. Before we create your Emotional Timeline, let's study an example. I'll tell you what goes through my mind when I review ETLs, then I'll lead you through forming your own.

Meet Sam:

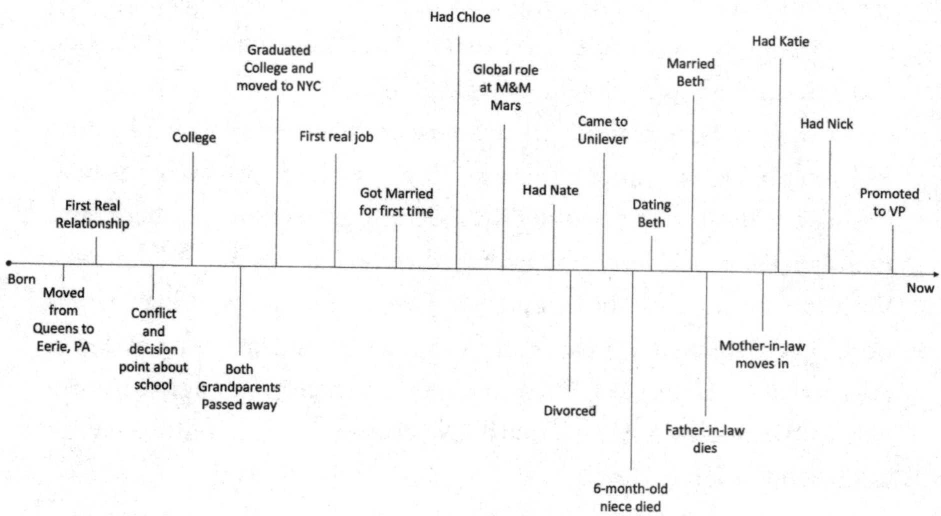

The first revelations I often notice about ETLs are what emotions are displayed and how they're spread across a person's timeline. For example, you can readily see that Sam's life has had a wide range of emotional highs and lows by examining the height of the lines. Many events are above the line, representing moments of joy. In contrast, seven events are below the line. They're all quite sad, and he is able to assign different line lengths. From that, I can assess that Sam easily differentiates his levels of joy and sadness, which leads me to believe that he is self-aware about his feelings. His emotional intelligence is reasonable, if not even high.

Zooming in, I notice a series of interesting event patterns and emerging emotions. Sam's first negative event was moving from Queens to Erie. Clearly, that saddened him. Why? Did he leave friends behind? Was he afraid of something?

His first positive event is meeting someone important. Yet that's followed by a low point filled with conflict and a tough decision about college. Are those events related? Was he scared to leave someone he cared about? He had just moved away from other people in his life.

When I see concurrent events that often tell a deeper story, I can hear my mom's curious and reflective voice echo in my head: "You need to understand what is happening for him." So, in reviewing Sam's ETL, I'd first explore those kinds of questions with him, to seek out what he was feeling and why during these pivotal moments of his life.

I also see a pattern about his romantic relationships. He met his first wife after being in a different relationship. He rated both events as relatively positive—but not that highly. After his divorce, he met Beth, and then *BOOM!* He is very, very happy when he marries her. I'm curious: What did he learn about picking partners and ensuring valuable relationships? Sam also has children from his first and second marriages, events that he ranks the highest of all. Do his kids get along? What did he and Beth do to build relationships between all the children? What lessons did he learn?

I also notice a group of losses and tough challenges. A few too many at one time, in fact. His divorce, his six-month-old niece dying, his father-in-law dying, and then his mother-in-law moving in. That's a lot to deal with!

The final pattern that jumps out at me is the emotional flow of his career progression. Going to college, getting a first-time job, and then getting into a company well known for its famous candy all progressed to slightly higher emotional joys. Yet when he became a VP, which I'd think is a big deal, he didn't rank that very highly. Why? Was it anti-climactic? Or, after all the losses he'd experienced earlier in his life, was it just not as big of a deal as he may have once thought?

Now, grab a piece of paper and a pencil and create your own Emotional Timeline. Then we'll discuss it.

Note: You will need time and both mental and emotional energy to do this. It's okay to read through these steps and tackle this later, but promise me you'll complete your ETL within a week. I typically tell my clients to take thirty minutes to complete their ETL, but you can take longer if necessary. Regardless of how long you take to create it, give yourself time to reflect on it. And if you find it upsetting, take a break. I'll be asking you to reflect on it throughout this book.

Here's How to Create Your Emotional Timeline

1. Grab a pencil and a blank white piece of paper.
2. Set the paper down horizontally so that it's wider than it is tall.
3. Across the middle of the page, draw a line from left to right.
4. On the left-hand side, write the date and place of your birth.
5. On the right-hand side, write today's date.
6. Then, going from left to right, plot out your life's most impactful events *and* assign an emotional value to each event. Events above the line relate to positive emotions. Events below the line bring up negative feelings. For example, your wedding might be plotted one inch above the line. The birth of a first child might be two inches above. A job loss might be one inch below. The passing of a parent might be two inches below.

Not so easy, right?

That's why I recommended a pencil. You may find yourself recalling your significant life events and questioning the emotions they bring up, as well as how each ranks against your other life events. Don't overthink. You know your major life events. And try to let your natural feelings come to the surface for each event.

Take your time. Let yourself feel what you need to feel.

If You Need More Help

If you're tempted to skip this step, draw your Emotional Timeline for just twenty or thirty minutes. To help jog their memories, some of my clients have found it helpful to imagine a director wanting to create a movie about their life, a life filled with so many interesting characters and events. What scenes would that director include?

You may also set aside different times and focus on just one part of your ETL. Your ETL is like a three-act play:

- **Act I** covers your first eighteen years of your life, your most formative years.
- **Act II** occurs after you've turned eighteen, from that point until your present day. It reveals how Act I has influenced who you've become and whether there's a block you need to overcome.
- **Act III** starts when you realize your referent power by improving your relationship-building and conversational skills. As a result, you become a more inspirational leader because you're a more fulfilled human being.

The ETL focuses on your first two acts. You could tackle Act I today and Act II tomorrow.

Questions to Help You Chart Act I

Act I events occurred before your eighteenth birthday. The following questions should help ignite your memories.

Family traditions:

- Were there favorite holiday traditions that made you very happy?
- Did you have a fun Sunday family meal every week that made you laugh out loud because of your crazy uncle's jokes?
- Were birthday celebrations important?

Times with those you loved most:

- Did your dad or mom take you out a lot for long walks to talk?
- Did you go for bike rides with your siblings and stop by your friends' homes frequently because you liked your friends' parents?
- Did you go on vacations around the country or the world? Was traveling valued?
- Did you love cooking with your grandmother or grandfather?

Life lessons and values:

- Did your grandparents or parents talk about important life lessons or values?
- Were church, synagogue, or other faith-based experiences important to your family?

Multiple homes:

- Did you move to different cities or countries often?
- Are you seeing other places that you lived in?

The importance of conversations and relationships:

- Do you remember rich conversations at the dinner table?
- Did you feel valued? Were you asked to share what you thought, believed, and felt?
- Or were you sent to another table with children and told that kids should be quiet until spoken to?

Awards and recognitions of others and yourself:

- Was someone you respected a great deal honored for their contributions to society?
- Was your mom or dad promoted at work, then suddenly they were often away from home?
- Were you celebrated for earning a significant award?

Difficult times:

- Are you seeing darker scenes unfold in your head?
- Do you remember someone hurting you emotionally, physically, or sexually?
- Was there a divorce?
- Did someone you love die? Like a sibling, a friend, or even a pet?
- Did you lose friends, or did a significant other break up with you?

These questions should spur your memories. However, if your memories are hazy or you have trouble recalling your highs and lows from decades ago, find some old photos. Maybe I'll be dating myself if I mention black-and-white images on torn or faded paper, slides, or Polaroids. So if most of your photos are digitized, pull out your phone and scroll through your archives to see what memories get stirred up. Look through them until a memory strikes. What are some of your favorite or special moments that come to mind from your childhood and teen years?

Above all, ask yourself: What are the most vivid scenes I can recall of my younger years? And how does each one make me feel?

If you're having trouble describing your feelings, use the head, heart, and hands check-in. That will help you gauge where you are right now and what matters to you as you think about events in your Emotional Timeline. Do this often.

- **Head:** What memories are coming up for you?
- **Heart:** How do those events make you feel? For example, are you

anxious because you want to avoid them or curious because you want to learn more? Do you feel more joyful emotions or fear or anger?
- **Hands:** Do you need a break, or are you so curious that you're focusing in more? Are you hyper-focused?

Maybe you feel angry or scared every time you see your dad's name or think about him. If so, this is an essential piece of information. If you admire a family member because of how they stood up for others, this tells you something about that person's character and values. You may want to emulate them. You might feel pride. Name that feeling. Give it as much detail as you can.

Now let's look at your early adult life and chart some important emotional milestones.

Questions to Help You Chart Act II

Act II events occurred after your eighteenth birthday.

- Did you meet the love of your life in school or at work?
- Did you end up getting married?
- Or did the relationship lead to a breakup before or while you were engaged?
- Were there multiple breakups?
- Did you experience a divorce?
- Did you have children?
- Did you have miscarriages?
- Did you go on trips around the world that opened your eyes to different cultures?
- Did you go to college and graduate school, or did you go straight to work?
- Did your parents or grandparents get sick or pass away?
- What significant jobs have you had?
- What jobs have you lost?
- What awards have you won?

What events reveal themselves? Ask yourself why you've chosen to include each one.

Emotional Presentation as Data

Notice how you present your information. The distribution of your events matters greatly (i.e., how far above or how far below the ETL each event sits). For instance, when I've asked some of my clients to create their ETL, they don't hand me a timeline. They hand me a list. They refuse to assign an emotional value to their influential events. That tells me nearly just as much about them as if they'd created their ETL the way they should. When I receive a list devoid of highs and lows, I can tell that the client is uncomfortable discussing their emotions, or they can't differentiate their feelings, or they're inherently rebellious and want to assert their authority by doing things their own way. (You can tell a lot about a person by the rules they *don't* follow.)

I've also seen clients list all of their events closely around the line, with a few above and a few below, with very little range. They may not even fill the entire paper. For example, see Jordan's example below. She may be more content with her feelings, or she may be stifling them and not allowing herself to feel too much of a good thing or a bad thing. So even the shape of her ETL would make me ask her why her range is so limited.

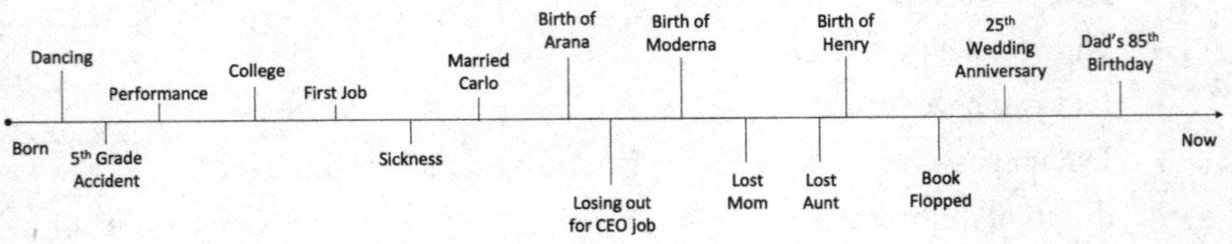

I've also seen all-positive-event ETLs, which leads me to wonder: Is the person optimistic? Naïve? Or are they afraid to tune in to negativity? Maybe they're just lucky? Similarly, if someone's ETL contains mostly negative events, I wonder: Have they had a string of bad luck? Are they depressed? Or are they mired in a state of learned helplessness where they believe that anything they do won't improve things?

I also consider whether the leader is between the ages of thirty-five and fifty-five, because that's often the best time for this kind of reflection. The biggest changes in your leadership tend to happen between those ages—if you confront your blind spots. Because you've experienced enough success and failure, and you've begun to consider how you want to be remembered, or to address challenging development areas, this time frame is often your best opportunity for growth. Yes, you can still see and understand your implications before that time frame (and many clients wish they had done this work a decade or two earlier), but you may not be as motivated to do so. Why is that? Because you may be thinking about personal achievement and being recognized as valuable rather than focusing on becoming a better leader. You're working on your technical skills rather than your leadership skills. In other words, you may not have enough hindsight to clearly see the connections.

Remember: Tune in to what you are thinking and feeling, as well as in to your visceral reactions. When you recall a certain memory, does your stomach tense? Do your shoulders pull up to your ears? Do your arms tighten? That's a sure signal you may have a higher emotional response to that event than your mind is telling you. Assume that both your highest and lowest events will result in your strongest visceral reactions. This means you'll need to pay close attention to these events while you review your Act II. As you do this work, register these significant milestones in a notebook. They matter most.

I'm sure you've discovered that your story is filled with many vivid moments or events you haven't thought about or emotionally felt. Like popcorn, memories are popping in your head! Do they make you smile? Or scare you? Either way, I hope you recognize what an interesting life you've lived. It's your story, and it matters. Whether you have siblings, parents, or grandparents who are still alive, you will only remember it and experience it emotionally in the way it emerges in your head and heart.

Run toward these memories and not away from them, no matter how frightening they may be. Be insatiably curious about what you are discovering. When you do that, you're starting to build your self-awareness using emotions. You're using your emotions as data to discover yourself.

What Your Emotional Timeline Reveals About You

When you place the highs and lows of your life on a single sheet of paper, you're gifted three benefits:

1. You're reminded of your mortality and that the best day to change yourself is today.
2. You see connections you may have never seen before.
3. You feel empathy for yourself or others.

And maybe, just maybe, you allow yourself to feel emotions you haven't let yourself feel in a long, long time.

Now that you have your life on a page, try to take an objective look. Like I said in the introduction, pretend you're an audience member watching a play, except you're also the play's main character. Imagine that this main character has reenacted all the experiences on your ETL, that you've watched the story of your life unfold before your eyes in just a few short hours.

What do you realize about the person whose life story you've just seen?

How does the story make you feel?

To go deeper, assume the role of an investigative reporter trying to get to the bottom of why this person is the way they are. You want to dig deeply into the data so you can uncover the real story of your life. Become insatiably curious about who you are and what made you the individual you are. Ask yourself question after question.

Such a mindset gives meaning to all this work. What data do you have? To whom can you talk in order to get more information about yourself and others? As you gather the data, keep piecing the elements together and look for patterns. Be desperate to know. Write your thoughts down too. Get a special journal and keep notes.

After you've completed Acts I and II and have let a few days pass, reflect on the events across your full timeline. What patterns emerge between your events and your emotions? Eventually, we'll look at those patterns and how the events and people in Act I impacted the events and relationships in Act II.

Before doing that, we need to discuss something that's held an even larger sway on the story of your life: the people who shared the stage with you in Act I.

[2]

Meet Your Childhood Cast

Please take a seat in the front row of your childhood.

As the curtain parts on the stage before you, you see your childhood home. You see its refined wood-grain paneling (or its peeling paint). At center stage, you see the comfy couch (or the one you were never allowed to sit on). You feel the living room's warm coziness (or its cold sterility). You hear the music that always seemed to be playing in the background, maybe rock or jazz or classical or religious (or you hear a cacophony of voices, or a dearth of silence). And you breathe in deep the aroma that reminds you of home.

Now the main cast enters the stage.

Who's there?

More importantly, when each person walks on stage and into your childhood home, how does that make you feel?

Whether you want to acknowledge it or not, your childhood cast holds immense influence on who you are today. Who you were influenced by as a child may define much of who you've become. Your characters shape your character.

The reason you need to bring up this sometimes long-forgotten history is that the solutions to your problems, both in your leadership and in your life, depend on your *why*. In other words: *Why* are you flying off the handle at a paper jam? *Why* are you unable to engage in healthy conflict? *Why* do others see your leadership as passive?

There's a quick answer to these questions, but those are Band-Aids. When you search through your past for the true origins of these issues, it's my hope you'll find a cure. However, you'll have to conduct some challenging self-diagnosis first.

In the coming pages, you're going to dive deeper into recalling your childhood cast. I'm going to ask you questions to spark your memories—and your feelings—about the people who may have most influenced you during your first eighteen years of life. Remember: The cast of your childhood isn't composed of actors written by a playwright. They are real people who are all too human. As you review your cast, I encourage you neither to idealize them nor to villainize them. Give yourself the time, space, and mental and emotional energy to remember these people *as they were*—the good, the bad, and the in-between—when you were young.

As you read, keep their faces before you and your emotions alongside you.

Who Was Your Mom?

The throughline between childhood and adulthood is rarely straightforward, but you don't have to look very deeply into Martha Stewart's life to see how she became *Martha Stewart®*.

In the Netflix documentary *Martha*, Stewart calls her schoolteacher mom "such a good cook." With six kids, "Big Martha" had to whip up sixteen meals a day. More often than not, young Martha was at her mother's side in the kitchen, absorbing every cooking lesson step by meticulous step. Martha, who some considered the first *influencer*, became one of the best cooking instructors out there.

However, Big Martha influenced her daughter in another way that was less noticeable yet still powerful. As Martha said in the documentary, "I wasn't educated about how to be a great mother from my mother." Big Martha agreed, saying, "I didn't hug her enough." This withholding of love and affection eventually resulted in history repeating itself when Martha, at just age nineteen, gave birth to her daughter Lexi. Martha admitted that she was "a little chilly" toward her daughter and didn't dote on her. When she was older, Lexi was blunt in her assessment: "I grew up in a very uncomfortable house, and we suppressed our emotions." Big Martha gave much to her daughter, but she also withheld what Martha may have needed most.

When clients and I begin reviewing their childhood cast, I always start with their parents, and I always start with their mom. Why? Because attachment theory suggests that, during the first three years of their lives, the most secure children experience psychological attachment to their mothers (who are usually the primary caregivers). Consequently, I want to understand how close your relationship was with your mom and am trying to figure out what characteristics you, as a child, absorbed from her. I start by asking about your mom's personality. I am trying to get a picture of her characteristics, style, warmth quotient, mental state, and energy. I want to know what kinds of things you talked about. Eventually, I will ask you how you are like your mom—that is, what you take from her.

As you see your mom walk onto the stage of your childhood, ask yourself these questions:

What was her personality like? Was your mom beautiful, fun-loving, and energetic? Was she a jokester or more serious?

Or was she cold and aloof and distant? Did it seem like you always bothered her? Was she an angry or bitter person? Did she get irritated or fly off the handle? Or was she depressed? Did she hide in her bedroom most of the time? Did she drink? Was her behavior unpredictable?

Did your mom work inside or outside the home? Did she quit work to take care of you when you were a baby because she always dreamed of being a mom? Or did she have to work to bring in money for the family? Were you the center of her universe, regardless? Did she dote on you? Or did she not even shift her gaze from what she was working on when you got home from school?

Was she ambitious and driven to achieve goals? Or was she so self-focused that her needs usurped your own? Did her work create joy for herself, and did that inspire you to achieve great things? Or were you jealous of her time being focused elsewhere?

How did she show her love to you? It's helpful to think through that question with Dr. Gary Chapman's five love languages: Was she physically affectionate through hugs and kisses? Did she share words of affirmation? Do things for you? Spend quality time? Buy you gifts?

Once you see her as fully as you can, ask yourself: How am I most like my mom? The goal is to understand what your mother modeled for you that you wanted to emulate—or to act differently from her. In other words, what did you take from her?

As you think through these questions, more salient and relevant characteristics may come to mind. Write those down so you can look at them later. The goal is to recall and describe your mother during your childhood as best as you can, to see her as a full person with both strengths and flaws.

Now let's turn to who may have been the next most influential figure in your childhood.

Who Was Your Dad?

When Martha Stewart is asked about her perfectionism in the documentary, she flatly replies, "It runs in the family." She explains that her father "was a dissatisfied, unhappy human being who started each morning with a large red wine and coffee." She pauses and asks herself, "Was he an alcoholic? Maybe . . . But he wasn't a sloppy one who couldn't function." She then says he "could have done anything" and that he was "the most handsome father," noting that his turquoise tie matched his blue eyes. (You can see where her sense of color came from!)

According to Martha, her father taught her and her five siblings how to garden. She said, "I was the ideal daughter, his favorite. He liked to teach, and I listened. He loved me. He trusted only me to iron his white linen shirts and Harris tweed jacket."

Off-screen, someone asks, "Why?"

"It was obvious. I was most like him. He was a perfectionist, and so was I. He got the job done, and so did I." Even in her doting, she recalls his drill sergeant nature, even in their garden. Her siblings remember the whippings. He'd always say things like "You're not doing it right." And so Martha summarizes her father in one word twice over: "He was mean . . . *mean!*" Without her father's influence—the good, the bad, and the in-between—Martha would never have become Martha Stewart.

Now see your father take center stage. (Or is he standing off to the side?) As you begin to see his face and smell his aftershave, shift your focus to him. Just like mom, describe your dad's personality. Try to capture his personality style, level of warmth, and mental state and energy. I want to know what you talked about and the types of play you experienced with him (if you did!). Think through these questions:

What was your dad's personality like? Did he play with you?
Did he talk with you and if he did, what did you discuss?
Was he a fun-loving person who coached you in whatever activity you wanted to do?
Did he play with you at the end of each day and have dinner at the kitchen table with you each night?
Was he talkative and lively? Or quieter and more subdued?
Did he work endless hours and come home tired at the end of the day? Or was he lazy and unmotivated?
Was he gone most of the time?
Did he have to entertain clients and meet them for dinner or at bars?
Was he cold and uncaring? Angry? Or mean?

None of these characteristics may speak to you about your dad. That's fine. Write down what you remember about him. You'll need this later.

Once you see him as fully as you can, ask yourself: How am I most like my dad?

Now let's consider how both of your parents influenced you.

Who Were Your Parents?

See your mom and dad both on stage. They were the first relationship you likely ever observed or learned about. For instance, did they respect each other, or ignore each other? How did their relationship model for you what a healthy relationship could, or should not, look like? Did they love telling you about what they adored about each other? Or were they always focused on the negatives? All of this modeled what you should pay attention to when it comes to your relationships.

One way to investigate what you know about your parents is to ask yourself, "Do I know the story of how they met?" Many of my clients have rarely asked their parents this question. Recalling the story can help you connect with memories of your parents. How much you know about your parents' origin story also tells you how comfortable you felt asking them about themselves or other private matters in your home—i.e., how inquiring you were, which is an important part of having high-quality conversations (our main topic in Act III).

My mom and dad were quite attractive people: Dad was tall, dark, and handsome. Mom was thin, with blue eyes and, at that time, blond hair. They met at a christening. He was quite drawn to her, yet there was a problem. She'd come to the party with someone else. Dad, the gentleman he was, asked the guy if he could take my mom to her home. That night, he started teaching her how to drive a car. To this day, they teach and take care of and look out for one another. It started that night. My dad's behavior taught me about doing the right thing, chivalry, and caring about someone.

After reflecting on how your parents met, think about how affectionate they were with one another in front of you. How did they react to each other? A warm embrace? A little too much PDA? Did they even make eye contact? Did they ignore one another, or even hurt each other physically?

What beliefs and values did they model for you? Did they believe you could accomplish anything if you worked hard? Or did they see the world filled with threats, so they were doomed to fail no matter what they did?

Were there important values that they wanted you to keep front and center in your life? The importance of family? High integrity? Respect for others?

Was religion important in your home? Did you pray together? Or were your parents atheists and dismissive of religious beliefs and traditions?

Did they verbally share these beliefs and principles with you or show them through their actions? Did you agree with them? Or disagree?

What was your parents' ethnic background? How did that play out in your home? Were there traditions or customs that mattered?

Now ask yourself: What traits, values, and principles did I take from them? What did I take from them about how they operated as a couple?

These are some of the most important questions you need to ask yourself and examine because you were most likely around your parents the most out of all the characters in your life. Daily, you witnessed their behaviors toward you, to each other, and to others. After seeing how they show up, you made choices about which behaviors you wanted to emulate and which ones you wanted to rebuff.

Which ones mattered most to you?

After you've given both your mother and your father ample stage time, let's invite on stage the broader cast that influenced you.

Who Were Your Grandparents?

When I think of my grandmother, I hear sizzling burgers. I smell grilled onions. I see her hands messy with spice after baking the cakes my grandfather loved and devoured. In that image, I remember how much I cherished her and how much she adored my brother and me. Before many women her age did, she lived and worked in New York City. She never learned how to drive a car, so, after working long days, she'd take trains and buses to come out to Long Island and care for us when our mom and dad were working or going to school. Considering her commute could take two hours, I wondered if she secretly called it Long *Drive* Island. Then again, she wasn't the one driving. I remember running outside of my house to see her coming. She always brought treats and cans of chocolate drinks. I often stayed at my grandparents' home too, where she always cooked me thin steaks and small hamburgers because she knew I loved them. By her life, she modeled for me that women could work hard, love their families wholeheartedly, and prioritize them thoroughly despite also having their husbands to care for and several houses to tend to.

I hope my recollection has begun to jog your own.

Now see both sets of your grandparents enter the stage. If your grandparents passed away many years ago, this may be an emotionally difficult scene to witness. Still, as you ruminate on the following questions, try your best to remember them as you saw them when you were young.

How far away did they live from your home? Were they down the street or hours away? Maybe even across the country? How often did you see them or stay with them?

What nationality were they? What values and beliefs did they hold dear as a result?

Did you have a special relationship with one of your grandparents or either or both pairs of grandparents? Or with either or both sides of your family?

What attributes did you take from your grandparents? (If you don't know, consider asking your parents or other close family members for their perspective.)

Parents and grandparents have the most significant behavioral impact of anyone on children. Has that held true for you? In my decades of experience in bringing clients through this process, they routinely come back to the influence, whether through their presence or their absence, of their parents and grandparents.

Who Were Your Siblings?

While parents and grandparents probably adored and focused on you more than anyone, don't count your brothers and sisters out, whether full biological ones, stepsiblings, adopted ones, etc. Positively or negatively, their presence completes the immediate environment you grew up in.

When my client Peter was a teenager, his house was chaotic—especially when his older brother was at home. Kevin was tall and muscular, even at an early age, and he knew how to use his size to intimidate Peter. Kevin also had an explosive personality, often taunting and yelling at his brother. Once, when Peter won a game of horseshoes, Kevin threw one at Peter's head. He missed, but he broke a glass window in the family's garage. Another time, when Peter was taking a shower, Kevin hammered his fists on the bathroom door with such force it shattered the mirror hanging on it. Anytime he saw his brother around, Peter would sweat and try to hide. Peter's relationship with his brother certainly created some low points on his ETL, and it represents the kinds of negative sibling relationships that can occur. (Fortunately for Peter, he had a father and grandfather who counterbalanced the bullying he received from his brother.)

If you have siblings, I sincerely hope your recollections are more positive than Peter's. Yet even if you had a difficult relationship with your brother or sister, it's still important to recall what that relationship was like when you were younger. This eventually informed how you interacted with your peers or colleagues at work.

Did you have many siblings? Or were you an only child? Was one sibling a troublemaker or a confidant? Do you have a twin sister or brother with whom you have an unbreakable bond? You looked at one another, and each knew what the other was thinking about.

Did you play endlessly with your siblings, joke around, or maybe study together? Or did you fight with them? Did they quietly (or not so quietly) physically or emotionally hurt you or embarrass you in front of others?

What attributes did you take away from your siblings?

Who Were Your Secondary Characters?

Though the roles of your parents, grandparents, and siblings may have loomed large in the story of your childhood, you had an even larger secondary cast surrounding you. That could be aunts, uncles, cousins, teachers, or anyone else you can recall who had a definitive impact on your formation.

Unfortunately, just as with your primary cast, your secondary cast can be notable for its "bad actors"—i.e., the people who negatively influenced you. I think every one of us has at least a few stories from childhood that, when we hear a certain word or phrase, we're instantly transported to that embarrassing, shocking, or tragic moment that's forever seared into our memories.

For instance, my client Stephanie couldn't ascend any higher in her company because she wasn't a confident public speaker. Even though she was a warm and capable communicator with her team and colleagues, she'd long turned down any opportunities for public speaking—including the ones she knew could help her achieve a promotion she greatly desired. In meeting and talking with Stephanie, I couldn't believe that she had such a deep fear of public speaking. She's a public servant who leads a team of twenty. She's bright and personable. I could easily see her on any stage. I wondered why she couldn't see herself there.

So we began searching for the origins of her reluctance. Eventually, we wound up in her fourth-grade classroom. On a fateful day she'd never forget, every student had to give a short speech on a topic of their choosing. When it was her turn, she nervously walked to the front of the class. With hunched shoulders and her eyes down, she began her story about a lost dog.

Her teacher immediately cut in. "You've already told us this story. Go sit down."

The class erupted in jeers. Stephanie ducked her head to avoid looking at her classmates.

Like a reel of film on an endless loop, the moment stayed with her for decades. She turned down every request to speak in public. Just the thought of being laughed off the stage again paralyzed her. Yet once she discovered the source of her anxiety, she worked on overcoming it. She recruited a group of trusted friends and colleagues to be a safe place for her to practice giving presentations. Their attentive feedback gave her the confidence to pursue her first public speaking engagement since that fateful day in the classroom. Even though her hands shook as she spoke, she saw the friendly eyes and nodding heads of a few of her colleagues in the audience. Once she finished, many people complimented her on the talk, which only fueled her bourgeoning sense that she could accomplish anything. Thankfully, this story has a happy ending: Stephanie got that promotion she'd wanted for so long.

By far, our teachers and instructors are some of the most influential and encouraging (or discouraging) cast members of our childhoods.

The best teachers are those who see our promise before we do. That's how I remember Jack Romano, the creative artistic director at the famous Stagedoor Manor theater camp, where stars like Robert Downey Jr. and Mandy Moore started out. In the mid-1970s, I attended the camp and later studied with him in New York City. During one lesson, he told me, "Pam, imagine you are in a box, and you have to get out of that box. Get on the floor and crouch into it."

I thought, *He's a legend. Just go with it.*

I sat on the floor and curled up tightly, my knees against my chest. I started scratching at the edges of my invisible box, piercing each corner and crevice to figure out how I could escape.

Jack liked it but wanted more. "Brilliant, Pam! Now dig deeper! Think about *why* you want to get out of that box. What *emotions* are you feeling? *Why* are you feeling them?"

I desperately wanted Jack to see and recognize my talent, so I dug deep within so I could dig myself out. *Why am I here? Why am I not scared? When I need to show emotion, where does it come from?*

I didn't realize it at the time, but I was learning a lifelong lesson that I still apply to myself and my clients today: Pay attention to the *why*. Jack's reinforcement validated my drive to slow down, be insatiably curious, and to keep asking why. The solutions to your problems, both in your leadership and in your life, depend on *why* you're showing up the way you are. Put another way: To discover your best possible solution, you need to understand the origins of your emotions, your choices, and your reactions. And the people who surrounded you and influenced you as a child still hold an outsized influence on you today.

Now see your secondary characters come onto the stage. Who walks in? Think about your cousins, aunts, uncles, or other family members and teachers.

Of these secondary characters, was anyone a hero to you? A villain?

Did you feel unconditionally loved and safe to speak your truth with all these characters? Or none of them?

Did you respect an idol in your home? Or were you frightened to be around certain family members because they responded in a dysfunctional way?

Whom did you turn to most? Whom did you confide in and why? Whom were you closest to? Did you feel close to anyone?

How Does Your Full Cast List Make You Feel?

Now that your cast is assembled on stage, what thoughts are popping up for you and what emotions are you feeling? It's a lot to pull up memories about people from our lives. Let's do a head, heart, and hands check-in:

- **Head:** Who are you thinking about most? Those who were there, or those who were missing?
- **Heart:** What feelings are you experiencing as you think about them? Angry, lonely, devalued, or happy and content? Or just empty?
- **Hands:** What is this making you want to do? Call someone? Slam the book down? Go for a run or walk? (Coaching advice: getting outside in nature helps all of us. I encourage you to do that frequently as you do this work.)

Remember, the goal is to faithfully answer these questions: What are you feeling now and why?

Do your memories of these people make you joyful because you feel secure and loved? Or do your memories make you scared or angry because of something an individual did to you?

Were guests welcome? Were they cherished? Did your family pull out food and ask guests to stay? Was there a constant fun energy in your home from the visitors and the conversation? Or were family members quieter and more insular, keeping to themselves and limiting visitors for various reasons? Maybe your parents even got annoyed when others showed up. What did you take away from how visitors were treated?

When you bring together all of the memories of these characters in your childhood home, what does the energy in the house feel like? Is there a fun buzz? Laughter? Or a quieter, more serious tone?

Here's another way to look at the house you grew up in and the people who most influenced you as a child: If you had to describe the scene and cast on stage before you to a complete stranger in just a few sentences, what would you say? What people, themes, or feelings take the leading role in their continued influence on you?

In taking the time to answer these questions about the people who shaped you as a child, you are unearthing the origin of your leadership capabilities and motivations. By addressing how your cast made you feel, you're using your emotions as data to tell you what—or whom—to pay attention to. You are discovering both the strengths and development areas that were modeled for you when you were young, which you are likely still carrying with you into every meeting and every relationship. When you seek to remember specific moments and people from your childhood, you're ultimately pursuing the answer to a central question of life: Why do I do what I do?

Within those answers lies such great potential for your future growth.

Charting Act I of your Emotional Timeline may have been challenging. Bringing back the central cast of your childhood may have been difficult. I promise you, the work is worth the result. In our next step, you're going to discover so much more about who you were and how that's still affecting you today.

[3]

Envision Your Childhood Setting

First, bravo to you for choosing to revisit your past. So many of us—and particularly high-level leaders—get so caught up in present concerns that looking back seems like a waste of time. Yet, as my executive-leader clients can tell you, their decision to do the work of retrospection and introspection has resulted in a brighter future they could have only imagined, both in their jobs and in their homes. I promise you: The work before you is worth the effort. You've come this far, and the following chapters may be the reason this book found its way to you.

Let's turn from remembering the people who shaped you to revealing the environments that formed you. Your childhood setting—i.e., the home or homes in which you grew up—have deeply influenced you, both in apparent ways and in ways that may still be invisible to you. Why does this matter? Broadly speaking, as adults we either emulate a positive childhood environment or actively work against a painful childhood environment. Those from challenging environments can get stuck repeating certain behaviors simply because it's become an innate survival mechanism, or they can purposely choose to act differently. These habits can later appear in your leadership, and you may have little to no understanding as to why.

That's not to say that all childhood environments are bad—far from it. Even those from stable homes can grow in their leadership by understanding the origins of their behaviors and inclinations. And regardless of the type of home you come from, once you gain a better understanding of your formative environment, you will experience growth in your leadership. Even better, you'll grow in self-empathy.

Over many years of reviewing thousands of Emotional Timelines, I've discovered that highly successful leaders share nine common childhood environments. Some only have a primary environment. Some come from both a primary and a secondary environment. Each environment fits into three broad categories:

- **Homes of Stability** are positive, idyllic, or predictable. I categorize them as *The Nest*, *The Model Home*, and *The Matriarchy*.
- **Homes of Complexity** make someone question themselves, their worth or their value. I categorize them as *In the Shadows*, *The Nomad*, and *The Phantom Limb*.
- **Homes of Trauma** offer little to no security. I categorize them as *The Maze*, *Slings and Arrows*, and *The Sounds of Silence*.

Another way to think about the main differences between these three types of home environments is to consider how loud your thoughts are.

- **In a Home of Stability,** children feel free to share their thoughts, so their beliefs are mostly in the outside world to share. On the whole, their minds are relaxed or calm.
- **In a Home of Complexity,** children have lots of swirling thoughts. *Am I worthy? Did I cause them to leave? Do people like me?* There is a lot of noise inside.
- **In a Home of Trauma,** children don't have a voice to share, or they have to fight courageously to stand up for themselves. There's a lot of noise but little belief they'll be heard.

In the following chapters, you'll discover which type of home you grew up in. Before you dive in, let's set some ground rules:

1. **Start with yourself.** As you read, you'll recognize others you care about, as well as your family, friends, and coworkers. Resist focusing on them. Start with you.
2. **Review your ETL.** Pull out your Emotional Timeline and think about the events and characters in your early life. Recall how they shaped your patterns of behavior. As you remember, pay attention to your emotions.
3. **To identify your primary and secondary environments, ask yourself:** Which environments resonate more than others? Does one primary environment fully and authentically represent you? Do you see yourself in pieces of different environments? Does a combination better fit your life? Do none of them represent you? (If you don't see yourself in any one environment, consider your life's patterns and data points to see what other connections reveal themselves.)

Each specific environment description also includes questions to help you determine what your development areas might look like, and whether you've leveraged the strengths that are common in that environment. If a question doesn't apply, feel free to skip it. Every environment ends with improvement suggestions for leaders coming out of that environment.

A few caveats: Our lives are complex. I came up with these nine environments to make it simple for you. They are also what I have witnessed most in my work. These nine environments are not all-inclusive. They're offered to stimulate your thinking. Your goal is to identify your primary environment, since it will inform you about the potential strengths of your leadership style or development areas you haven't yet addressed.

While you may be tempted to only read the chapter or chapters that align most closely with your childhood environment, I encourage you to read about every home type. This will help you better understand others and the kinds of home environments that have helped shape them into who they are today.

No matter which environment you grew up in, you still have room to grow.

[4]

Were You Raised in a Home of Stability?

In a Home of Stability, children largely experience a safe and secure relationship with their caregivers. What differs is what the home revolves around, resulting in these three categories:

- In **The Nest**, nothing is more influential than parents' unconditional love for their child.
- In **The Model Home**, nothing is more influential than the values of the parents and grandparents or primary caregiver.
- In **The Matriarchy**, nothing is more influential than a strong mom.

In the following pages, you'll learn more about each of these home settings. However, you may already identify with one. If you were raised in a Home of Stability, you may not be facing a significant block to your full leadership capability. Still, fine-tuning will help you learn what specific strengths you can harness to increase your impact, or see what development areas you need to overcome or avoid.

Were You Raised in The Nest?

My client Krisi is a child of The Nest. "My environment had constant support," she once told me. "Mom and dad would want to hear about my day. My house was also all about family. The house was full of people most of the time, and even when they weren't around, we were surrounded by the importance of family. No matter who was over, we would talk about everything and nothing, and we would laugh a lot. I remember liking to be a part of the dialogue as a kid—listening when I was little and participating when I was a teenager."

Krisi's mom was the ultimate believer in the American dream. Consequently, she was strict and set incredibly high aspirations for Krisi and her brother. Hard work at school and completing chores were essential.

Krisi's dad offset his wife's drive. He didn't push as hard as her mom did. He was a soft-spoken, gentle, and supportive man, the peacemaker of the family. Her friends described him as a big teddy bear. Together, Krisi's parents taught her to believe in herself and to know that what she achieved was merit-based, yet their love for her never was.

She knew she was loved unconditionally.

Was The Nest Your Primary Childhood Environment?

Here's what to look for. As you read this section across the childhood environments, notice how they feel emotionally. This is data!

- **You remember a *happy* home with parents who focused on you.** Psychologically speaking, children who grow up in The Nest form a close bond with their caregivers. This "attachment process" is especially important in the first three years of life since it allows children to regulate their emotions and form secure ties with others. Because of this secure attachment, you grew up understanding what love is and what it feels like. Today, you may be described as empathetic and compassionate. Many of my clients who grew up in The Nest describe their childhood as *joyful*.
- **You were challenged to work hard, confident you could achieve, and felt supported during struggles.** Your parents may have set high expectations about work, family, respecting others, and contributing to the community. They conveyed their belief that you can achieve anything with hard work and good choices. They taught you to believe in yourself. You developed confidence because your parents supported you and reinforced the belief that your efforts would be

successful no matter what you tackled. Your parents helped you when you failed or struggled—and they kept you humble when you succeeded.

- **You never forgot that family comes first and that safety comes from them.** From an early age, you were taught to look after family members, in both good and difficult times. Extended family members were often around. Relatives were interested in your life and asked about your school and hobbies. Often, there was a lot of laughter and rich conversations. You learned the benefit of feeling happy and psychologically safe. You also learned what it felt like to have conversations about things that matter and the fulfillment of achieving your goals. People wanted to know what you thought, believed, and sometimes what you felt. Your voice mattered. Your parents expressed pride in you for your achievements, which further reinforced your internal drive, self-confidence, and satisfaction with your accomplishments.

What Do Children of The Nest Look Like as Leaders, and What Leadership Strength Often Emerges?

At their best, they become *Nurturing Achievers*.

Children of The Nest become leaders who aspire to recreate their childhood environment for their employees and teams. They *nurture* others as their parents nurtured them. These leaders feel incredibly responsible to their employees, shareholders, board of directors, leadership teams, and customers. They strive to achieve results beyond expectations.

Today, Krisi is the chair and CEO of a large international advertising agency with thousands of employees around the world. Even as she's laser-focused on her organization's performance and can be tough when necessary, she genuinely cares about her leadership team—undeniable echoes of her mother's influence. Extremely empathetic, Krisi is interested in her team members as people and always welcomes hearing about their spouses, parents, and children, as if her father were perched on her shoulders.

Imagine being a member of her team. During your first interview, she tells you what you need to achieve while also stressing the importance of vulnerability. She talks about her emotions and why sharing them matters. When you join her team, she shares her personal story, the home she grew up in, her values, and what she's meant to do with her life—her leadership purpose. She then asks you to prepare your life story, including your childhood, your greatest joy, and your most profound sorrow. She urges you to be authentic. She tells you not to share your work history or where you went to school, because that only demonstrates competence. She wants you to get personal because people connect as human beings.

This may sound scary to you. You may not be used to opening up like this at work. In my experience, most people feel that way. Krisi has learned that this intense sharing expedites the kind of team trust and relationship building required for teams to have real and honest conversations about their work, company mission, and strategic goals. The good, the bad, and the ugly are all fair game. Krisi's nurturing ensures that her team can be vulnerable in a safe environment.

Like both of her parents, Krisi believes that anyone can achieve anything they want with hard work and determination, and that they deserve support. Since her younger days, she has also striven to make others happy. Her mother had high expectations, and because Krisi loved her, she wanted to please her. Krisi's combination of drive, high expectations for herself and others, strong ethics, support, and care is why I think she goes beyond the *Nurturing Achiever* label. When her company suffered a controversy, I witnessed her *steely* nurturing firsthand. She was steadfast in doing the right thing for the customer and the company. I witnessed her integrity in action, and I know her parents would have been proud of her.

Strengths emerge easily in stable homes, although no environment is perfect. Children from a home of stability may still need to overcome developmental areas to achieve the full benefit of their strengths. Here's what to look for.

How Can Children of The Nest Become Better Leaders?

Like Krisi, if you grew up in The Nest, push yourself to do the following.

1. **Realize that performance and caring for others are not mutually exclusive.** You can achieve both, which are necessary for creating followership and loyalty. Some leaders focus on one, performance or caring, at the exclusion of the other. Leaders who focus on just performance can be seen as too "hard." Those who prioritize caring for their people at the expense of delivery can be seen as too "soft." The best leaders realize that nurturing or supporting employees during stressful times, while providing recognition for achievements and focusing on their development and family challenges, will significantly improve performance outcomes.
2. **Refuse to people-please for others to like you.** If you courageously lean in to giving feedback to make others better and engage in debate to get the best possible outcomes on difficult issues, other employees will feel grateful for your honesty and inspired by your courage. (We'll discuss this more in depth in Act III.)
3. **Reframe your beliefs about the inspirational nature of your childhood.** Many who grew up in The Nest take their childhood environment for granted, not realizing its rarity. You may think that your safe, happy, comfortable childhood has no impact on you as a leader and that the story would bore others. That's far from the truth. Sharing positive stories inspires others and makes joy an aspiration, especially for those from homes of trauma.

Some people raised in The Nest feel guilty for having a "perfect childhood." They may feel shy about sharing their stories or may even be embarrassed by them. However, there's power in that near-perfect past. Because Nesters tend to replicate the same kind of supportive environment in their organizations, their people tend to be highly loyal. For instance, Krisi's team is incredibly devoted to her. She may be tough, yet her team knows that her efforts are focused on the good of the company, her customers, and her employees.

By learning and practicing vulnerability, Nurturing Achievers can use their life story to inspire others, teach them what their parents did to develop a close bond and create unconditional love within the entire family, and challenge others to achieve their dreams and to believe in themselves.

Having a happy childhood doesn't mean a problem-free career or life. Leaders from The Nest may need to reframe self-limiting beliefs to develop into Nurturing Achievers and inspire others to follow them. A self-limiting belief is negative self-talk that can keep you from leading. If you're a Nester and you think, *My life story is boring. I haven't experienced trauma so people won't be interested and will tune out*, it's important to reframe that thought and turn it into a positive: *By sharing my story of joy, I will show others that a happy life is possible. I am going to go for it.* Or, like Krisi, you may have been a people-pleaser when you were younger and must learn to lean in to complex conversations. For people-pleasers, it's often scary to tell someone that their behavior isn't helping a difficult situation or that they have a very different point of view about a political or social issue. Consequently, Krisi was traditionally focused on giving constructive positive feedback. After our work together, she had built muscles in giving constructive negative feedback to make others better—something we'll discuss in more depth in Act III of this book.

Often, Nesters don't need to make large-scale changes to how they lead. In most cases, they grow by fine-tuning their behaviors.

The Nest Reflection Questions

Most leaders from The Nest are aware of the impact of their childhood environment on them. If you aren't sure, consider these questions:

Are You from The Nest?

- Were you deeply attached to your mom or primary caregiver when you were young?
- Were there high expectations of you in your home or for school?
- Were you often told something like "You can do anything you set

your mind to do," which suggested that the people saying it believed in you and your capability?

- Do you feel safe to speak your truth, particularly during conflict?
- Are you a happy and positive person? Do you feel a lot of joy?

Are These Development Areas for You?

- Do you often contemplate and feel conflicted about being kind and nurturing versus pushing others?
- Do you ever get feedback from people that you are less vulnerable than others?
- Are you a people-pleaser?
- Do you hold back from talking about your story because you think your life is unremarkable? Or do you not want others to feel jealous that your life had no trauma?

Are You a Nurturing Achiever?

- Are you a leader who pushes for higher performance levels and nurtures your team? Do you believe you do them both simultaneously?
- Are you ever asked to give constructive negative feedback to employees because you do it in a direct and caring way?
- Do you feel accountable for getting higher-level results and impatient if results aren't achieved quickly enough?

If you answered yes to most of the first set of questions, you are from The Nest. If you answered yes to one or more of the questions in the second set, you have opportunities to grow as a leader. If you answered yes to two or more of the questions in the third set, you have acquired the strength of a Nurturing Achiever.

Were you Raised in The Model Home?

When I met Jill, she was the VP and chief human resources officer at Cummins Inc., a position she ultimately held for twenty-two years.

All told, she'd invested her professional life at that company for thirty-six years, a lasting and impactful tenure by anyone's standards. One formative story she shared with me from her high school years reveals what so many of her employees know to be true about her: She fights for the rights of the underdog.

In the summer when she was sixteen, she tried out for the varsity cheerleading squad. She thought her tryouts had gone "fantastically well"—until the coach called. "You did everything first-rate, but you're too athletic, and when you cheer, you're too focused on the game's success rather than inspiring the fans. I'm sorry. I didn't put you on the varsity cheerleading squad, but you can be the first alternate."

Jill later discovered that others had been cut for the same reason. However, no one else was chosen as an alternate. Rather than feeling relieved that at least she still had a chance to make the team, she was furious. She wondered, *How could one person determine the fate of so many individuals? And why were talented girls rejected?* She believed that the coach's decisions were unfair and that the rejected cheerleaders had performed better than those who'd made the squad. The idea that they hadn't been selected because they *cared about the game* struck Jill as entirely ludicrous.

A few weeks later, the coach unexpectedly called her again. "You're on the team, Jill. One of the girls isn't passing her classes. I need my first alternate."

"Thanks for letting me know, Coach." She paused. "But I found out that other girls got cut for the same reason as me. So I've decided to start my own cheerleading team of athletic, sports-minded women."

"You can't do that!"

"Yes, I can. Watch me."

The next day, Jill went to the superintendent's office and got his approval. She called all the girls who'd been cut, and they started their own cheerleading team. The newly minted Varsity Pep Squad cheered for all the men's and women's sports teams that didn't have their own squads. Jill's mom even made uniforms for both the home and away games.

For Jill and the other women on the squad, it was an amazing experience. They learned not to let someone else's decisions control their destiny. And they became role models at the school because they had stood up for what was right. This wasn't surprising given the role models Jill had as parents. Her mother was a natural caregiver and a nurse. Her father was very kind and generous. They had also long shown care for people they hardly knew. Throughout Jill's childhood, teenagers who'd been thrown out of their homes were welcomed into hers by her parents, to help them get their lives straightened out. Jill often shared her bedroom with these teens, which taught her about helping anyone who needed it—especially if they were an underdog.

Even more significant were Jill's summers, starting when she was about ten years old, at the church camp where her mother volunteered as the camp nurse. This is where Jill discovered Jesus, not necessarily as a religious figure, but as the person he was during his thirty-three years on earth. His selfless service particularly moved her to take care of others, and his insistence on advocating for what was right constantly inspired her to do the same.

In The Model Home, values are central. While these families are often religious, faith is not a requirement. Instead, their values can often be found in principles such as anti-racism, social justice, or the importance of character—as Jill's story readily revealed.

Was The Model Home Your Primary Childhood Environment?

Here's what to look for:

- **You remember the importance placed on values or character.** Being a good person or doing the right thing took precedence over everything else in your home growing up. Your parents or grandparents may have insisted or encouraged you to prioritize values over everything else. Many such children feel proud of their parents' focus on values, while others get irritated by the constant reminder about it.
- **You developed a strong sense of right and wrong based on your family's shared values.** You had a sense of clarity. You saw a clear dividing line between what was acceptable and nonacceptable

behavior as defined by the values your family espoused, whether those were religiously or culturally influenced. Phrases like these were shared: "You will not steal. You will not lie. Good people tell the truth and respect other people's property."

- **You admired, loved, and wanted to emulate a significant adult in your life whose positive behavior you profoundly respected.** You may even refer to that special adult as "my idol" or "my role model." You sought to form a close relationship with them because you wanted to learn from them and be like them. If the person was deceased, you may have searched for photos or stories about them.

What Do Children of The Model Home Look Like as Leaders, and What Leadership Strength Often Emerges?

They are Values Champions, and some become Values Crusaders.

Values Champions are self-aware about which values are most important to them and actively communicate this. They act by following their values and making decisions based on them regardless of the stress they are under or social pressures wanting them to do otherwise. Through their words and actions, they inspire others to follow their essential principles.

The greatest strength of Values Champions is that they know what is important to them because their values and principles are crystal clear. Leaders often refer to this as their moral compass. They will not allow themselves to be bullied, pressured, or forced to do things that conflict with their values. People who unfailingly lead in ways aligned with their values are said to have great integrity because their actions and decisions match their words—they walk their talk—and because they stand up for what they believe in. When they make mistakes or are tempted to go off-course, their values help them get back on track.

Leaders articulate and share their values with their employees because it helps their people understand how they can succeed. Many Values Champions consider social justice, integrity, transparency, inclusion, and respect to be mandatory values. Values are translated into standards of behaviors that they hold themselves up to and expect others to demonstrate.

For Jill, creating the Varsity Pep Squad was one of the most significant events on her Emotional Timeline. She learned she was unwilling to stand aside when people were mistreated. Successfully defending those young women fueled her internal fire to advocate and fight for underdogs. For instance, Jill thought that Cummins's hourly employees had the most difficult jobs. To ease their work and get the best producers, she wanted them to have the best leaders, and so she poured herself into developing their managers. When her board sought to increase executive salaries, Jill studied the salaries of their hourly employees and fought to move them toward a living wage across all countries. In other words, she saw inequality that others had overlooked, whether willfully or not, and she desired to balance the scales.

As a result, she became not just a Values Champion in her leadership role, but what I call a *Values Crusader*. As the name implies, Values Crusaders are particularly attuned to the inconsistencies they see between stated values and actual behavior, whether those values stem from them as a person or a company. Consequently, a Values Crusader may have a personal mission to drive certain behaviors in their companies or other areas of influence. When others act hypocritically, a Values Crusader courageously calls out the gap between their actions and their values. They will passionately fight for an important cause, even taking drastic measures like quitting their job, if they cannot persuade their organization or leader to change behavior that opposes their values. There are examples of Values Crusaders throughout history, like Joan of Arc and Nelson Mandela, who died or went to prison for their cause. Jill had the same fire in her belly.

In partnership with the CEO, myself, and many leaders in the firm, Jill co-built an inspiring leadership culture at Cummins. In fact, she *crusaded* for it. While her CEO had an aspirational goal to develop exceptional leadership among the top three hundred, Jill pushed her own vision to educate all ten thousand leaders (i.e., anyone who managed at least one person) globally within five years. Jill the crusader, in partnership with many internal facilitators, achieved that dream.

How Can Children of The Model Home Become Better Leaders?

Like Jill, if you grew up in The Model Home, challenge yourself to do the following:

- **Be more interested in someone else's values rather than your own.** Real dialogue about what matters to you will result more often if you begin with a genuine interest in another person's values. Switch your focus to them. Asking questions about what is important to them, assuming goodness on their behalf, and deeply listening with compassion to understand their values will create deeper learning for you and help them feel accepted. If they feel heard, they will listen to your perspective more.
- **Stop being self-righteous and overzealous about your values.** Constantly espousing your own principles can exhaust others around you and make them tune out. Ask yourself, "Why am I fighting so hard? What am I afraid, fearful, or worried about? Will something happen to my reputation if they don't follow my lead? Will something go wrong?" Tune in to why you are responding the way you are. You need to figure out what is causing this reaction in you and develop a plan to show up differently the next time it happens. Focus instead on your long-term goal for the person, team, or company.
- **Develop and use your referent power to convince others to change their behaviors.** Do you remember our discussion about power? Informal power, and more specifically referent power, is most influential. When others see you as a good human being with sound character, plus your other forms of expert, informational, and relational power, they will listen because you inspire them. You may need to take a look at the informal powers you use and build your self-awareness.

Gena Gwen, a manufacturing company leader in France, grew up in a religious household. Her father was a Christian minister who preached about the importance of faith and family every Sunday. Outside the home, her parents were highly affectionate and revered as a wonderful couple. But inside the home, Gena's father was emotionally abusive to her mother. Monday through Saturday, he was often absent, and even when he was home, he was invisible to the family. The reality was that he didn't practice what he preached. This was disingenuous, and it was hard for Gena to respect, or like, her father.

Does her father's hypocrisy mean that Gena *isn't* from The Model Home? On the contrary, juxtaposing her father's hypocrisy and her mother's extreme unconditional love and devotion exposed differences in faith and family values, even when others misbehaved. All this confused and angered Gena, which made her question the institution of marriage and whether she could trust men. It also made her withdraw and keep her emotions and thoughts to herself. Because of her different experiences with her mother and father, Gena doubled down on three essential values: faith, authenticity, and responsibility.

As a result of her father's negative influence, Gena established clear ethical boundaries regarding unsuitable standards of behavior. Her father's actions taught her what not to do. The problem was that she was consumed with anger. She promoted the importance of authentically caring about friends and family. Yet the shadow of her father's hypocrisy clouded how she behaved in the workplace. She would shut down and not share her feelings with anyone. Her team couldn't figure out what was important to her. Others found her cold and intimidating. She ended up not being promoted to more senior positions. No matter what all of us tried, she couldn't shed this protective armor.

Leaders from *The Model Home*—in fact, all leaders—benefit from articulating their values for their own self-awareness and in order to reveal those values to others. Values shape whom we want to work for—the organizations and the types of managers—plus the friends and community groups we want to be a part of. Leaders should specify what their prized values mean to them and what they look like in action when lived well. They should also describe the antithesis: what others should not do or it will anger them or make them retreat. This is the leader effectively setting their ethical boundaries. Leaders also need to know that when those ethical boundaries get triggered, they have a plan to handle it maturely. This can bring you comfort. You don't have to scream or run away. You can handle the situation productively—e.g., take a walk, give feedback about it, or explain why a response is difficult for you.

It's also important to determine where the value stems from. For instance, consider which character during Act I of your life lived the value (or did the opposite, which caused you to want to be different). Or, what key events showed that certain behaviors were essential? When you share the origin of a value, others will understand why that value is a big darn deal to you.

The Model Home Reflection Questions

Most leaders from The Model Home are aware of the impact of their childhood environment on them. If you aren't sure, consider these questions:

Are You from The Model Home?

- Do you proudly talk about someone from Act I of your life who had a significant impact on you because they emulated values you admire?
- Do you feel proud and confident about your values? Are you defiant if people ask you to act in ways that are dissonant with them?
- Can you easily articulate what behaviors are right or wrong to you?
- Do you feel focused and purposeful in ensuring your behaviors match your desired values? If they don't match, do you change your behaviors?

Are These Development Areas for You?

- Are you seen at times as arrogant or overly righteous about what is right or wrong?
- Have you ever been told that you are singularly focused, overly passionate about your point of view, or inflexible?

- Do you stop listening to people who do not share your values?
- Do you get emotionally triggered by their response?

Are You a Values Champion?

- Are you a person who pays attention to whether people are demonstrating behaviors consistent with values that are important to you or your organization?
- Do you teach people about the importance of behaviorally demonstrating specific values?
- Do you point out when people do not act per your values and applaud them if they do?
- Have you ever been asked to speak to a group of people about your values because others find you to be a person of good character?

Are You a Values Crusader?

- Do you advocate forcefully for values that are important to you or the good of all when no one else does?
- Do you feel focused and purposeful in ensuring other people's behaviors match these values? So much so that you call out inconsistencies?
- Do you often feel an intense visceral response when someone behaves inconsistently with values that are important to you or the good of the organization? As a result, do you call out hypocrisies?
- Do you feel compelled to implement large-scale initiatives to transform behaviors throughout your company or community—and do so?

If you answered yes to most of the first set of questions, you are from The Model Home. If you answered yes to one or more of the questions in the second set, you have opportunities to grow as a leader. If you answered yes to two or more of the questions in one or both of the third and fourth sets, you have acquired the strengths of either a Values Champion, a Values Crusader, or both. Not all Values Champions are

Values Crusaders, but all Values Crusaders are Values Champions. Values Crusaders forcefully drive behavioral transformations at large.

Were You Raised in The Matriarchy?

My client Tom Linebarger, whom you may recall from the prologue, grew up in The Matriarchy.

When Tom was six, his father left them. Child support payments were inconsistent at best. Consequently, Tom's mother had to raise and provide for her two boys by herself. Their family lived on government assistance, surviving on food stamps and childcare programs. For a few years, they even lived with another family to share expenses. Even at that early age, Tom knew how difficult his mother's life was. Still, she focused on improving her future. She earned certifications and found internships in her chosen field of occupational therapy. Eventually, she finished her degree and began working full-time at a job she found meaningful. Through it all, she modeled to her sons what can be achieved through sheer determination and a conviction that, no matter your circumstances, better is always possible.

Because of his upbringing in The Matriarchy, Tom often talks about bootstrapping. It's a term that reflects how his mother shouldered her many responsibilities in juggling work, her own schooling, the care of her children, and their financial challenges. Yet she never wavered. (Interestingly, Tom admits that his daughters are proud of his achievements, but he doesn't think they'd say he faced such big obstacles to obtain them.) Through seeing his mother's resiliency every day, Tom learned that women can handle not only the "soft stuff" but also a business filled with solving problems. And he saw how well she multitasked, which showed him how to become a highly effective manager.

As a child of The Matriarchy, Tom witnessed his mother doing everything she could to ensure their flourishing, and he believes that's partly why he became CEO at Cummins. Ultimately, he learned that, if they choose to, women can move mountains.

Was The Matriarchy Your Primary Childhood Environment?

Here's what to look for:

- **Your home was ruled by a powerful woman or multiple powerful women.** In these homes, mothers, or sometimes grandmothers or aunts, are forced to take over the multilayered responsibilities of the family, often after the death or divorce of a spouse. They selflessly devote themselves to their children's well-being. A woman's physical, mental, and emotional strength grows as she conquers each new task.
- **Your mother (or maternal figure) got things done.** She overcame obstacle after obstacle in order to provide for you and nurture you. Working tirelessly, or ignoring her fatigue, she moved through task after task: fixing things, overseeing homework, studying herself, and managing her kids' emotional highs and lows.
- **You might define your mother as one with an overriding sense of confidence and determination.** Your house was filled with emotions of focus, determination, and self-assurance. Your mother had no other option, so she leaned in and did it. There was no time for doubt. Some women quietly enjoyed their independence and drive. They were proud of what they were achieving.

What Do Children of The Matriarchy Look Like as Leaders, and What Leadership Strength Often Emerges?

For young boys who grow up in The Matriarchy, the most common and best result is that they become leaders and men who feel completely comfortable working with female peers and bosses. It's easy for them to imagine strong women leading companies. These men become *Champions of Women,* who protect and advocate for women and promote them to high-level positions—just as Tom did.

Today, he actively promotes women into senior roles and advocates for females to become officers. He helped develop and promote Jennifer Rumsey as his successor to chairman and CEO of Cummins Inc. Not only is she the first female in the history of Cummins to be chosen as one of the company's top leaders, but she's also one of a shockingly small number of such women in the US and around the globe. Tom's goal was to have 50 percent of the organization's leadership team members and board positions filled by women as soon as possible, an increase from the 33 percent of these positions that females previously held.

The Matriarchy also profoundly impacts young girls. The daughters of strong mothers become confident, focused, and determined leaders who want to get results and transform the world. Because they witness strong female figures early in their lives, they emulate them. This environment instills in young women the belief that they can achieve anything—their confidence and passion make them what I call *Drivers*. Whether married, widowed, single, or divorced, a household with a strong woman at its center breeds a successful, confident female leader in her own right.

My client Sara Levinson is a great example. As the glue of the family, Sara's feminist mother had bigger dreams than jobs typical for women in the 1960s. She wanted to be a doctor. While studying at George Washington University, she was one of three women accepted into medical school after her junior year. However, she had to drop out for financial reasons. Sara remembers her mother saying, "You can be whatever you want" and "You don't have to do something that is a typical female occupation." Sara's father also reinforced that belief, as he shared in household duties that weren't gender-specific.

Sara told me, "My mom wanted me to see the possibilities. She also had a wanderlust that I definitely inherited." Sara witnessed this in her mother's pursuit of higher education. Her father was a chemist, yet her mom was the family's intellectual. After having her fifth child, she returned to college at William and Mary, switched her major to history, and earned her master's degree. In her fifties, she earned a Fulbright Fellowship to study in India for ten weeks—all of which was quite radical for a woman in the 1970s. Sara's mom then rented an apartment in London to pursue a doctoral degree (which she regrettably never finished). As Sara told me, "Living in London was really a cover for her to have a room of her own finally."

One small experience left a lasting impression. Sara came home from school one day with a report card full of top marks, yet nobody seemed to notice. When her younger brother showed off his far less impressive report card, their mother said how proud she was. That irked Sara. She pulled her mom aside and asked, "Why don't you ever make a fuss about my grades?"

Sara's mother looked at her sternly and said, "Don't make good grades for me. Make them for yourself."

That memorable moment instilled in Sara the belief that she needed to do things for herself and that she didn't have to follow everyone else's example. Such lessons played a significant role later as Sara blazed a trail in high-profile, game-changing roles with MTV, the NFL, and Harley-Davidson. Like other women from The Matriarchy, Sara uses her power to influence behavioral change in others and accomplish much. She traveled the world to bring MTV to the global youth. As a daughter of The Matriarchy, she knew her power. She became a marketing genius who empathized, saw possibilities, used humor wisely, and focused on everyone else's power. People loved working for her. She can see an opportunity. She's incredibly optimistic and goes for it.

Both Sara's and Tom's examples show that daughters and sons of The Matriarchy saw that their mothers (or other maternal figures) had huge capabilities as individual leaders and managers. They had dreams and ambition. Yet they had to deal with constant challenges and some limitations set by society and family structures. For Sara's mom, money was an issue, and society didn't acknowledge the same opportunities for women as for men. Seeing her mom's determination to return to school reinforced Sara's need to overcome obstacles to achieve aspirations.

Women from The Matriarchy can also be perceived as overly aggressive, which forces them to negotiate the complex interplay between drive and aggression. Women with drive believe they can figure anything out and push forward with passion. Women who operate from a place of fear attack, dismiss, or undermine others who get in their way. Their fear is born out of insecurity, whether that's from imposter syndrome or shame. Sara is a driver. She knew nothing about football—one of the most macho and aggressive of sports—before taking the job with the NFL. She told me, "I made dramatic changes there going in, not knowing what I was really doing." Still, she enjoyed a groundbreaking and successful career at the NFL. When she lectured at Baruch College, she titled her speech: "A Fish Out of Water Who Learned to Swim with the Sharks." When Paul Tagliabue, the NFL commissioner, wrote his memoir, he mentioned Sara by that same title.

Growing up in a home with a strong female figure at its heart usually leads men and women to respect women's unique strengths and see their value to families, communities, and organizations. Leaders of both genders tend to share their opinions and thoughts quite actively, as matriarchal households often encourage everyone to speak up. Men prioritize *Protecting and Championing Women* and surrounding themselves with highly capable females who are equally committed to making men successful. Women will help women as well as men succeed; however, their main strength is being *a driver.* Both are forms of boosterism, or promoting the powers of women in all aspects of life.

How Can Children of The Matriarchy Become Better Leaders?

As a woman, if you grew up in *The Matriarchy*, push yourself to do the following:

- **Define your balance.** It means different things to different people. You need to figure out what it means to you beyond "work vs. home life." Women seeking balance (and men as well) could learn a lesson from Amy Schumacher, president and CEO of the Heritage Group, which manages fifty-plus companies specializing in environmentally sustainable construction. When envisioning her life as CEO, Amy wanted to ensure that if she took the role, she would be able to live her life in a truly balanced way, because her daughters were in middle school. We ended up defining balance for her along five dimensions: spiritual, physical, mental, relational, and emotional. At any one time, she had to have three of these dimensions operating simultaneously. Working on a challenging mental project with a team, she would be intellectually stimulated and have enriched relationships that emotionally fulfilled her. If she wanted to challenge her body, she would do it with other professional women by whom she was mentally stimulated and emotionally fulfilled. Balance is not just work versus home. It's multidimensional, and women from The Matriarchy need to think about that.

- **Manage stress proactively to avoid being overwhelmed.** Learning to recognize how you show up when you take on too many responsibilities, and how you deal with being overwhelmed is key. Jennifer Rumsey, CEO of Cummins Inc. today, wrote a newsletter about recharging her life, not just the energy of the world. She includes hobbies like biking, which is her moving meditation; having a centering music playlist; spending quality time with family; and leading with care. Consider developing a well-being plan of activities that bring you joy—e.g., mindfulness, exercise, breathing, hobbies, etc.
- **Become less aggressive or assertive during conflict, especially when stressed.** Personality theory work, especially around the Myers-Briggs Type Indicator (MBTI), can show you how you perform at your best, under stress, and at your worst. All of these come with tips for being your best self. Consider using personality assessments to help you understand yourself. Leaders can also participate in receiving a 360 feedback assessment to determine how others experience them under stress and get tips for overcoming their shortcomings.

As a man, if you grew up in The Matriarchy, push yourself to do the following:

- **Identify and share your emotions.** Men may find it difficult to address or talk about their emotions. This sometimes stems from the fact that their mothers primarily worked on "getting everything done" with little room to spare for sharing emotions in a healthy manner. As a result, these leaders may need to learn how to tune in to their feelings and address them. They can also become overly aggressive during conflict, especially if stressed. So many of the tips in this book are about building your emotional muscles as a strength and dealing with real conversations.
- **Like women, deal with work-life balance issues.** See Amy Schumacher's example above.
- **Stop focusing on boosterism alone.** You need to hear what is important to other people. You're obviously a good person because you care about promoting women. Bravo! If this strength is keeping you from tuning in to other people's needs, please pay attention to the chapter on empathetic listening in Act III. Men can also keenly define their purpose to include how they want to use their championing of women for good.

The Matriarchy Reflection Questions

Most leaders from The Matriarchy are aware of the impact of their childhood environment on them. If you aren't sure, consider these questions:

As a Woman, Are You from The Matriarchy?

- Do you usually feel confident and powerful? Do you believe that if you focus on the work in front of you and are determined, you can make anything happen?
- Occasionally, do you question your competence?
- But when you are vulnerable and ask for help, do you regain your power and belief in yourself?

Are These Development Areas for You?

- When you struggle, is it because you are trying to do it all? Do you

commit to too many things? Do you get irritated if others tell you that you cannot do it all simultaneously?
- Do you become overly aggressive or annoyed and impatient when stressed?
- Do you lose your ability to listen?

Are You a Driver?

- Do you have a long list of accomplishments that you are quietly proud of? Maybe you keep them to yourself and tout the successes of others?
- Do you tend to be a collaborator, wanting to involve others in the journey?
- Do you promote the efforts of other women?

As a Man, Are You from The Matriarchy?

- Do you feel self-secure and proud of the women in your life? Are you not threatened by them?
- Are you excited to promote women and actively do so?
- Do you surround yourself with accomplished women who enable you to achieve your goals?
- Do you feel delight that your mom would be moved emotionally or be proud because you actively promote women?

Are These Development Areas for You?

- Are you over-reliant on women (or others) to make results happen?
- Do you struggle with self-awareness or sharing your feelings?
- Do you become overly arrogant or lose your ability to listen when people resist your recommendations?

Are You a Champion of Women?

- Do you look for opportunities to showcase women's talents in your organization?
- Do you proactively promote women into more senior roles?

- Do you lean in and sponsor them when they have difficult moments in meetings or presentations?

If you answered yes to most of the questions in the first set for either gender, you are from The Matriarchy. If you answered yes to one or more of the questions in the second set, you have opportunities to grow as a leader. If you answered yes to two or more of the questions in the third set, you have acquired the strength of a Driver as a woman and a Champion of Women as a man.

In Conclusion: Lucky You!

If you were blessed to come from one of these stable home environments, you largely experienced a safe and secure relationship with your caregivers. Whether you experienced unconditional love from your parents, learned the importance of values, or saw your maternal role model being a strong and determined woman, you knew you mattered.

But even if you came from such an exemplary home, you might be experiencing problems in your life and leadership today. Problems that may very well have had their origin in your idyllic home.

Remind yourself of the takeaways from the last three stable environments we have discussed.

- In **The Nest**, nothing is more influential than parents' unconditional love for their child.
- In **The Model Home**, nothing is more influential than the values of the parents and grandparents or primary caregiver.
- In **The Matriarchy**, nothing is more influential than a strong mom.

Now let's look at the next three home environments. Unlike homes of stability, these environments are filled with obstacles and challenges that may still thwart you today.

Childhood Environment	Common Leadership Deficits That Result	Areas of Work to Address Deficits	Potential Emergent Strengths
The Nest	Lack of vulnerability; Elevating performance over people—or people over performance; Frustration with others for not performing; Due to people-pleasing, may not be direct	Self-awareness; Public storytelling about authentic self, blocks, fears, development areas, strengths, etc.; Practice giving feedback	Nurturing Achievers: Strive to achieve results beyond expectations and provide the supportive environment they had
The Model Home	Self-righteousness, overzealousness, rigidity; Hypercritical of others; Inability to influence	Articulate values—where they stem from and what they look like when done well; Examine ethical boundaries and how you show up if triggered; Develop a plan to modify your behavior; Build referent power to influence others—start with enhancing listening and assuming goodness	Values Champions / Values Crusaders: Serve as moral compass for organization; Fight for important causes concerning values

Childhood Environment	Common Leadership Deficits That Result	Areas of Work to Address Deficits	Potential Emergent Strengths
The Matriarchy	Women: Overdo their strengths of confidence, focus, and determination; Become aggressive or sarcastic during conflict under stress; Struggle with balance issues (both genders can experience this). Men: Over-reliant on women to do it all; May not be in tune with emotions; May stop listening when focused on promoting women	Both: Define dimensions of balance (not just work/family)—e.g., spiritual, physical, connection, etc.—need to have 2–3 of those at the same time; Use accountability partners to help; Get a 360 of behavior from peers and other stakeholders, develop a plan for how to handle negative behavioral responses in stressful moments (a 360 can be helpful in all environments to understand the impact of a leader's behavior on others, *after* leaders have examined the impact of their childhood on their leadership). Men: Develop *advocating for women's* goals, determining what is important for them to achieve (purpose)	Women: A Driver; Self-confident, focused, determined, using their power well. Men: Champions of women (proactively promote and advocate for women)

[5]

Were You Raised in a Home of Complexity?

In a Home of Complexity, children must deal with significant changes in their lives, like loss, physical moves, or comparisons with others, which make them question their identity and value. They experience persistent internal dialogue or self-talk abounding with questions like "Why did my parents divorce and leave me?" or "Why don't other people like me?" or "How am I special?" What differs is how the complexity presents itself, resulting in these three categories:

- In **In the Shadows**, a child's well-known family member outshines them.
- In **The Nomad**, a child's family constantly moves or travels.
- In **The Phantom Limb**, a child suffers significant, unexpected loss, either through death or divorce.

Growing up in any of these environments may result in issues that block a leader from achieving their full potential. Children from homes of complexity almost always have work to do to overcome their block and to free what is in their minds and hearts. They also benefit largely from working on their identity as a leader. When they accomplish both, their emergent strengths are mighty because they've been forged in the fires of a challenging childhood.

Were you raised in In the Shadows?

My client Jim Schacht succinctly summarized what it means to have grown up In the Shadows: "People knew my dad before they knew me."

In Columbus, Indiana, everyone knew Henry Schacht. After all, he was the CEO of the small Midwestern town's largest employer, Cummins Inc. For Jim's entire childhood, he was always "Oh that's Henry's son." Although Jim is the first to say that he had a wonderful childhood, with loving parents, living in the shadow of such a looming figure led to an unusual upbringing. "I was born with a blue blazer on," Jim recalled. "I was always dressed up, not out of arrogance, but out of respect. My parents were young, and they were very visible in our community. They felt we were representing Cummins, and how we dressed (and behaved) was part of it."

This became problematic for Jim on the school bus. Since all the kids knew who his dad was—some of their parents very likely worked for him—Jim worried about what his appearance said about him. He remembers "climbing onto the big yellow school bus, which by then was already filled with kids from more rural parts of our town, and being self-conscious of my nice clothes. I wasn't embarrassed, but I was aware of the contrast, and I felt anxious that my nice clothes might make some kids feel uncomfortable because of their clothes. Or, worse, that kids might perceive me as thinking I was better in some way . . . At this very early age, I began to develop an awareness of how others perceive me and . . . to downplay or hide any differences so people would see me for who I am and not misperceive me as someone I'm not."

Jim also keenly remembers the expectations he felt to live up to the Schacht name and, by extension, the Cummins way. His parents frequently had guests over for dinner. Before their arrival, Jim was given index cards with the names of every guest. He was to memorize every name so he could properly introduce himself out of respect and to make a good first impression. As he recalled, "I had expectations of myself because of my dad, which always were higher than I could ever achieve. This has been my biggest challenge, personally and professionally my entire life, trying always to manage other people's expectations of me while also managing my own expectations of myself."

Jim's father may have been loving and caring and a man Jim deeply admired, but he still cast a long shadow over Jim's identity.

Was In the Shadows Your Primary Childhood Environment?

Here's what to look for:

- **You were constantly aware of the presence of your notorious, larger-than-life parent or parental figure.** Maybe your mom or dad was an athletic coach at school, your grandparent was a well-known actor, or your older sibling always had leadership roles, like student council president. Regardless of their level of fame, your mind was always consumed with thoughts of the person and you constantly compared yourself to them.
- **You were self-conscious of how others perceived you and had very high expectations of yourself that were impossible to meet.** You constantly wondered how you should adjust your behavior or style to make yourself less conspicuous. Like Jim, you assumed that some people had really high expectations of you ("You're really smart. You deserve to be here.") while others expected less ("You're only here because of your father."). In fact, no one was harder on you than you.
- **You seldom spoke up for yourself.** As a child of a famous person, you tended to listen well and observe how the revered one spoke and interacted with others. However, you held back your views about issues or behavioral feedback unless you were asked. Even then, you may not have spoken your truth.
- **You had trouble differentiating your identity from the person you admired or compared yourself to.** You might have felt that "doing your own thing" wasn't allowed because of how it would reflect on your famous relative. Or your expected priority was supporting the famous person in any way they required.

What Do Children from In the Shadows Look Like as Leaders, and What Leadership Strength Often Emerges?

They are *Illuminators*.

They honor the light of others without feeling they must either outshine them or remain in their shadows. The long-term impact of growing up In the Shadows requires them to become deeply self-aware so that they differentiate themselves as leaders and human beings. In other words, they learn self-confidence.

A famous person isn't always revered, which is difficult for a child in this environment. If your famous relative does something ignominious or is blamed for something they didn't do, how your parent handles the situation (or others around you do) matters. Plus, you are now affiliated with the negative event in your mind. Sometimes, a famous parent gets fired or is publicly shamed. Suppose your parent handles the loss with grace. In that case, you will accept the loss as a way of life and develop resilience. While you will hurt for your parent's loss, you can understand it as a fact of life. On the other hand, if your parent becomes angry or bitter, says they were wronged, and wants to fight back, many other negative emotional states can emerge for you. You may assume that the world isn't safe or fair, that you cannot trust people, or that only certain people can get ahead. So, you shut down even more.

Understandably, Jim struggled with the shadow of his father's vaunted career. When he was hired at Cummins, he was asked, "Are you okay with the fact that your dad was CEO?" Jim said yes, yet his later actions would reveal the truth. Even though he was proud to work there, he didn't introduce himself to others. He didn't want anyone to think he was there only because of his father's influence. However, that left his coworkers believing he was unfriendly and aloof, which is far from the case with his natural extroversion. Early on, he'd devise products alone at his desk. Not only was this completely inefficient, but it also went against Jim's strengths, which blossom when he works with others. In essence, Jim was trying to hide his past, the same way he wanted to play down his difference on the school bus. He was still living in his father's shadow.

So how did that change?

Over a few years in working with my team, Jim claimed his life In the Shadows. He came to terms with his heritage and celebrated his father's legacy while differentiating his own. He reflected on his life and the values he'd learned, as well as how to own them and feel proud of them. He wrote endless iterations of his purpose statement, which I define as what you believe you are here on this earth to do, which gives your life meaning, regardless of who you are with. Such a statement can be used to help inspire others to follow you as a leader, either because they share similar passions or are impressed by your level of candor and vulnerability. Jim's purpose statement finally became "to live a life of character . . . and to spend time with people of like values." After his long journey, he became comfortable with himself and no longer felt the need to live up to anyone else's expectations. Far less worried about how people perceive him, he is an Illuminator, as well as vice president at the company his father previously led. To those who listen, he proudly says, "The entire experience has been life-changing. I am a better person. I know it was instrumental in my career and I am deeply grateful."

Now, wearing a blue blazer, he steps into the light with confidence—and he uses the same size index cards to remind him of the key points he needs to say in his speeches!

How Can Children In the Shadows Become Better Leaders?

As Jim did, if you grew up In the Shadows, challenge yourself to do the following:

- **Deepen your self-awareness and decipher and differentiate what is important to you as a human being.** It doesn't matter what others think now. It matters what you know about yourself. Creating your Emotional Timeline is the perfect place to start. Enhance your insights by getting a picture of your strengths through personality inventories like the Myers-Briggs Type Indicator personality test or Gallup's CliftonStrengths assessment (formerly known as StrengthsFinder).
- **Clarify and define your leadership purpose and your values.** Your purpose explains what you are here to do on this earth, regardless of who you are with. Your values are about the how. How should people behave? What kind of culture should I be a part of? What type of manager would I work best with?

- **Translate your values into expectations of others and yourself.** If people are to be successful with you, not your parent, you have to tell them how to do that.

In the Shadows Reflection Questions

Most leaders from In the Shadows aren't always aware of the impact of their childhood environment on them. If you aren't sure, consider these questions:

Are You from In the Shadows?

- Did you grow up in a home with a famous person?
- Were you told that you had to act a certain way because of that person's reputation?
- If this person was wronged in some way, like being fired from their job or being blamed for something that seemed unfair, did you hurt deeply?
- Were you embarrassed or angry or confused about it? Did you shut down and not share your feelings about it?

Are These Development Areas for You?

- Did you struggle with your own identity?
- Did you ponder if you would/could be as "special" as this person was? Or if you would be seen as being as special as this person in your lifetime?
- Are you overly self-conscious of what others think of you?
- Have you constantly spent time in your own head doing negative self-talk? "I'll never be good enough. I have to do so much more to be recognized. I will never get ahead."
- Have your own efforts hindered your career path at times?

Are You an Illuminator?

- Can you easily explain to others what's important to you (i.e., your values)?

- Can you easily tell people how to be successful with you (i.e., your expectations)?
- Do you know what work you are here to do on this earth (i.e., your purpose)?
- Can you explain what was special about the famous person in your early life versus what's special about you?
- Do you strive to help other people see what is unique and special about them?

If you answered yes to most of the first set of questions, you are from In the Shadows. If you answered yes to one or more questions in the second set, you are facing some of the common development challenges of those In the Shadows. If you answered yes to two or more of the items in the third section, you have acquired the strength of an Illuminator.

Were you raised in The Nomad?

My client Earl can't remember where he was at any childhood age because of how often he moved. "Other people have historical stories where they remember playing baseball in a vacant lot when they were five," he told me. "I have none of those." When you've been moved at least twenty-six times in the span of your early years, that's understandable.

With each transition in those years, Earl tried to combat the loneliness of being in a new place with no friends by resorting to his room. He'd take his electronics out of the moving boxes and build robots. Then, to stave off boredom, he'd transform the moving boxes themselves into other creations. His mom would come in, see what her nerdy son had built, and show him love through pride. That was how they connected and supported each other. Earl would build and his mom would marvel, no matter how silly his construction was. Over all the moves, that became how he began every transition, by looking to build something. That's where he found love and acceptance, and that's how he found his place in the world.

As you discovered in The Nest, when there is a secure attachment between the caregiver and a child, there is a healthy balance of closeness and independence, which leads to a lifetime of autonomy and trust. Instead, when I met Earl, I found him to be self-reliant and emotionally guarded. This indicated a form of early attachment called *avoidant*. Adults who experienced avoidant attachment tend to distance themselves from others, assuming others will disappoint them. Nomads believe they can affect their own relationships, working others to their own benefit. When we were to start his Emotional Timeline, Earl instead handed me a 149-page book he'd compiled of photos and words that he called *The Newsomes & Moores: A Family History*. He told me: "This is me. This is all you need to know." I felt his walls go up. I wasn't sure if he wanted to keep me at a distance or, for efficiency, tell the same story he always told. But it wasn't surprising to me that he would later have a hard time checking in on his emotions. For a long time, I couldn't get him past just saying, "I feel good." Eventually, we got to a breakthrough when he said, "I was often alone, but never lonely." This was different from what he later told me. In fact, he *was* lonely. I didn't care that his point about loneliness differed over time. His first mention of having been alone was a real beginning.

Over time, I learned that Earl had grown up in a single-parent home. His birth father had left when Earl was very young. His father wasn't talked about; consequently, Earl spent all his early years with his grandfather, who served in the military, was a civil rights activist, and played the part of his dad. Later in his life, Earl would have multiple marriages, always seeking the incredible marriage of love that had been modeled to him by his grandparents. And since his grandfather had been his primary father figure in childhood, he esteemed their marriage even more highly. Earl was also disappointed in himself because he didn't have close relationships with his children, though he is striving today to make them better.

As a leader, Earl created a training course to teach his team to develop six-word stories about their lives. You can say a powerful message in a few words that invoke emotion, encourage questions, and more. Earl's favorite is "You're the Story You Tell Yourself," which refers to your personal narrative and how it can limit or unleash your potential. What struck me most was that Earl's stories focused on facts, never emotions. He couldn't, or wouldn't, tell me how he felt. I once asked him "Why are stories so important?"

"FCT, Pam," he told me. "Familiarity, Comfort, and Trust."

When he couldn't rely on others, he could at least rely on the familiarity, comfort, and trust of what would never leave him: the facts.

Was The Nomad Your Primary Childhood Environment?

Here's what to look for:

- **You moved around far more than your peers.** You were always the new kid, and just about the time you got comfortable, you moved again. You moved frequently because your parents were either in the military, in governmental or diplomatic roles, or were corporate executives. You make friends easily, but you do not always feel a sense of attachment to those outside of your family. Frequently, you find it easy to move around without commitment.
- **You had superficial friendships.** Because you felt friendships would likely never last, you never allowed yourself to be deeply known. You charmed people and were warm and friendly in order to get along. You would try to enjoy yourself for as long as you were there, but you knew it was short-term so you wouldn't invest.
- **You were a self-reliant lone wolf and distanced yourself emotionally.** Because so much felt out of your control, even if subconsciously, you relied on yourself. In secure attachment situations, even when people leave, you know they will return. They may text you during the day or call to see how you are doing. When you're from the avoidant attachment world, you assume people will disappoint you, so you don't engage.

What Do Children of The Nomad Look Like as Leaders, and What Leadership Strength Often Emerges?

They are *Chameleons.*

A Nomad could be the life of the party or the lone soul—or both, as

Earl appeared to be. His many physical moves led to his ability to get along with everyone, from the nerds to the jocks. He developed "the gift of the gab," which he says came from his mom. He has a huge personality and wears colorful, vibrant clothes that stand out, yet he can modify his behavior and become reflective and quiet if necessary.

As *Chameleons*, Nomads take on lots of different roles in order to feel valued, depending on the situation they are in. You'll often see Earl being the master of ceremonies, the DJ creating playlists for his team, the soldier or protector of his peers, or the one who helps people to think about the "art of the possible." He will show up as needed. As a Nomad, he learned to pay attention to what his friends needed so they would like him. As a result, he became a good listener and could meet their needs emotionally.

Tuning into his own emotions was another story.

How Can Children of The Nomad Become Better Leaders?

Like Earl, if you grew up in The Nomad, push yourself to do the following:

- **Deal with attachment issues.** Nomads typically experience avoidant attachment. Investigating more about the differences between avoidant, anxious, and disorganized attachment issues, to determine which one you have and how to address them, is key. See the table at the end of this chapter.
- **Actively observe your own emotions and consider how and why you pull away.** Learning how to name your emotions, to describe how you feel, and to allow others to love or like you and not pull away from them will take a lot of work and effort. Be patient with yourself. This is hard. Start by doing a head, heart, and hands check-in with discipline and ask someone you trust to push you to name your emotions.
- **Define what makes a strong relationship, what would make you feel loved, and what commitment means to you.** And if a block is preventing you from committing to a relationship, that's where you should dig in! Pay attention to Act II of this book.

When Earl is around you, he brings so much joy. He has a heart of gold and wants you to respond in kind. Yet I had to work hard to let him love and connect with us, his tablemates, and his coaches. Today, instead of building robots out of cardboard, he is learning more about his biological dad and forming relationships with lost siblings, as well as strengthening those with his children.

The Nomad Reflection Questions

Most Nomad leaders are aware of the impact of their childhood environment on them. If you aren't sure, consider these questions:

Are you from The Nomad?

- Did you live in many different locations before age eighteen?
- Were you always making, and then physically leaving, friends?
- Do you distance yourself from others because you assume they will disappoint you from a relationship point of view?
- Are you happiest when socializing with people for an evening out?

Are These Development Areas for You?

- Do you struggle with loneliness or emptiness at times?
- Is there a string of people you've met throughout your life whom you are not connected to?
- Do you avoid observing what you are feeling?
- Are you guarded with sharing your own emotions?
- Do you struggle with commitment issues?

Are You a Chameleon?

- Can you blend in to any situation or fit in with any group by taking on various roles that are needed or varying your personality for the situation?
- Are you emotionally intelligent, with a particular strength in being *socially aware* of what is happening for others? Can you tune in to the needs of others and adjust your behavior to bring out the best in them?

If you answered yes to most of the first set of questions, you are from The Nomad. If you answered yes to one or more questions in the second set, these may be development opportunities for you. If you answered yes to two or more questions in the third set, you have acquired the strength of a Chameleon.

Were you raised in The Phantom Limb?

Matt Levatich was a C-suite executive at Harley-Davidson, whom I was asked to work with as he was being considered for CEO. (You'll read much more about his story in Act II.) As we began working together, I learned that Matt was twelve years old when his parents divorced. As he later told me, "I didn't see it coming, because why would I?" I've heard this sentiment often echoed by those who grew up in The Phantom Limb. Their otherwise happy childhood is suddenly disrupted, and their notions of family are forever altered.

Scottish physician William Porterfield coined the phrase *phantom limb* in the seventeenth century after suffering a leg amputation. He frequently experienced the sensation that his leg was still a part of him. Researchers later found that even after a limb is gone, nearby nerves can still send pain signals from the missing limb. The brain, clinging to its old body map, feels the pain. Children who grow up in The Phantom Limb suffer this same kind of lingering emotional pain when they lose a parent or sibling through death or divorce. Psychologically, a child who loses the daily presence of a significant person in their life will experience emotional pain—as if the missing person were still there.

Divorce is even more difficult for children who are younger, especially when they are five or six years old. They are old enough to realize and feel the pain of the loss while watching their remaining parent separate. Yet they're too young to be thrust into the absent parent's adult role in the house. These young children suffer by wondering if they are the cause of the divorce, affair, or other separation. Little boys often become the little man of the house if their father leaves. They try to ease the pain by providing tissues for their mother's tears, or talking to their mom as if they were the spouse. Little girls can become the woman of the house quickly if the mother is the one who left. They fill the gap of cooking, cleaning. and comforting.

For Matt, the divorce offended his definition of *family*. He never forgave his father for leaving them. Making matters worse for himself and his emotional health, he never voiced his anger about the divorce to his father. In many ways, because he was a child trying to keep the peace, he pretended his life were relatively normal—as if his "limb" were still where it was supposed to be.

On the other hand, Matt was more fortunate than other children who suffer the pain of their parents' divorce. His parents handled their divorce masterfully. While Matt had many siblings he was close to, he also had an older sister who deeply loved and cared for him, and particularly during those trying years in the immediate aftermath. This relationship was one reason why Matt resiliently got through that time.

Still, growing up in The Phantom Limb haunted Matt for decades.

Was The Phantom Limb Your Primary Childhood Environment?

Here's what to look for:

- **At an early age, one of your parents passed away, or your parents divorced.** It is even more complicated if your parents separated because of an affair.
- **You blamed yourself for the loss.** Children of divorced parents often wonder if they "did something wrong" to cause their parents' separation. Those who've lost a parent or close family member to death think about what they could have done differently to prevent that loss. This goes on for years.
- **You often felt sad, depressed, or anxious.** You deeply missed your parent. If your parent who left was having an affair and you didn't know it, life felt even more tenuous. You experienced guilt and shame and wondered if life was as you believed it to be. You may have even turned to substance abuse or other addictions to self-medicate.

- **You felt abandoned, alone, or unloved.** Because a primary caregiver was no longer in the picture, you may have felt like you lived on an island, remote from everyone else. You may carry anger toward the parent who left, especially if the reason for the divorce was an affair. This is confounded with deeply missing your parent, and it can become even more complicated if your parent leaves to be with a partner who has other children. A child may never feel like they matter again, especially when the divorce or death occurs during early childhood.

What Do Children of The Phantom Limb Look Like as Leaders, and What Leadership Strength Often Emerges?

They are *Resilient Committed Partners.*

You'll get to know Matt in more detail in a few chapters when we discuss the implications of your childhood on who you are now. For the moment, you should know that one of Matt's guiding principles is loyalty. During his tenure as CEO of Harley-Davidson, Matt was committed and deeply invested in the work and personal lives of his team members and employees. He is very close to his wife, Brenda, and his boys, Max and Sam. He didn't define success by what he accomplished during working hours but by whether he was available and present for his team and his family. I've often witnessed a higher level of commitment to family and colleagues, through quality time spent and acts of service, in those who grew up in The Phantom Limb.

Because of what they've endured through loss, many children of The Phantom Limb also tend to display a lifelong strength of resilience. Linda Hoopes, PhD, the founder of Resilience Alliance, has studied resilience for over thirty years and has found that resilient people cultivate seven "prosilience muscles"—i.e., characteristics they can employ to develop resilience: positivity, confidence, priorities, creativity, connection, structure, and experimenting.

The biggest contributing factors to Matt's resilience were his *confidence* and *creativity*. He believed in himself. He is certainly humble; however, he knew that whatever you threw at him, he could handle. He also loved being creative. Like his father and mother, he could generate lots of ideas. If one solution didn't work, he would try another. He knew he could get through any moment of difficulty. He trusted that.

What also helped him when the divorce occurred was his sister's practical and emotional support. Human connections, says Hoopes, not only provide hugs and a listening ear when someone is feeling down but can also provide good ideas, logistics, and advice. Because of his confidence, Matt internalized the advice his sister gave him.

Not everything is sunny though. Phantom Limb children tend to get lower scores on positivity, which is about believing in finding possibilities in a challenging world. Heck, they lost the parents they felt most secure with, so I have found that these Phantom Limb children can become cynical, or sometimes skeptical, about the world.

In fact, no matter how loyal or resilient these leaders are, I have noticed a quiet sadness to them, which breaks my heart. They don't want to take a chance being jubilant because they don't want to be disappointed by another loss.

How Can Children of The Phantom Limb Become Better Leaders?

Like Matt, if you grew up in The Phantom Limb, with grace, challenge yourself to do the following:

- **Deal with your grief, loss, and feelings of abandonment.** I want you to confront the sources of pain and loss that you experienced. I am always saddened when I hear that children of The Phantom Limb didn't go through counseling. It is truly never too late. Please prioritize yourself and your emotional health. There are different resources available to process loss and they vary by focus—e.g., death, divorce, etc.
- **Work through your block.** Harboring the anger you have toward the parent who is no longer around is unhealthy. You may need to have a

conversation with the person who hurt you or with others who were around at that time. Tune in to Act II to learn how.

- **Process the cynicism that results at work or home.** As you learned, the world seems unsafe or unpredictable, and so you may be skeptical about people's motives. You may see more threats in the world. By reframing the way you look at each situation (switching negative thoughts to positive ones), you can build your resiliency muscles in positivity and optimism about the world.

The Phantom Limb Reflection Questions

Most leaders from The Phantom Limb are somewhat aware of the impact of their childhood environment on them. If you aren't sure, consider these questions:

Are You from The Phantom Limb?

- Did your parents divorce during Act I of your life? Or did one of your parents die?
- Did you feel abandoned, unloved, and deeply wounded when the person left your immediate world?
- Did you experience grief, sadness, and depression after the parental figure was gone?

Are These Development Areas for You?

- Are you still experiencing grief and sadness?
- Are you afraid of losing people close to you?
- As a leader, do you take it personally when your team or organization members leave?
- Are you sensitive if those closest to you do not include you?
- Do you attempt to make others feel guilty for not prioritizing you?
- What about your voice? Do you keep your thoughts and opinions to yourself? Do leaders tell you that you should speak up more?
- Or are you sarcastic and prickly to keep people at a distance?

Are You a Resilient Committed Partner?

- Do your teams love working for you because you care about them and they see you as a good manager?
- Will you drop everything to take care of your family and team members because you feel accountable to them?
- Are you emotionally empathetic to the loneliness of others?
- Do you want to take care of human beings in pain?

If you answered yes to most of the first set of questions, you are from The Phantom Limb. If you answered yes to one or more of the questions in the second set, you have opportunities to grow as a leader. If you answered yes to two or more questions in the third set, you have acquired the strength of a Resilient Committed Partner.

In Conclusion: You Matter! You Are Valuable!

If you came from one of these homes of complexity, you probably spent a lot of time in your own thoughts. You were probably deeply loved but, because of other circumstances—having a famous parent, moving continuously, or your family having to deal with loss through death or divorce of parents—you wondered how much you mattered.

Listen to me: You are valuable.

My overall hope is that you give any negative internal self-talk in the quiet of your mind a microphone. Release the emotion and give voice to it so others can empathize and help you.

Before we turn to the last group of environments, Homes of Trauma, remind yourself of the takeaways from the last three environments, of complexity, that we discussed.

- In **In The Shadows**, a child's well-known family outshines them.
- In **The Nomad**, a child's family constantly moves or travels.
- In **The Phantom Limb**, a child suffers significant, unexpected loss, either through death or divorce.

Childhood Environment	Common Leadership Deficits That Result	Areas of Work to Address Deficits	Potential Emergent Strengths
In the Shadows	An Identity crisis: cannot differentiate their own identity from others that they admire	Authentic Leadership work is ideal; Deepen self-awareness to determine what is unique about you; Start with ETL and define your purpose and values; Translate values into expectations; Use personality inventories to confirm strengths	Illuminators; Step into the light; Shine the light on yourself while honoring the light of others; Long-term: help others identify their light
The Nomad	Superficial friendships; Disengaged; Distances themselves from others; Emotionally guarded; Lone wolf; Attachment issues	Deal with three types of attachment issues vs. *secure*—characterized by a healthy balance of closeness and independence (leads to a life of trust and autonomy): 1. *Avoidant*—involves a reluctance to depend on others and preference for emotional distance; 2. *Anxious*—super-concerned or preoccupied about relationships and a fear of abandonment; 3. *Disorganized*—a mix of anxious and avoidant behaviors, often stemming from trauma or inconsistent caregiving; Address commitment issues; Build emotional muscles	Chameleons; Befriend others easily; Charming; Can fit into any situation; Tune in to the emotional needs of others and adjust

The Phantom Limb	Quiet sadness, depression, feelings of abandonment, not being loved, grief	Deal with grief and feelings of abandonment, confront sources of pain and loss; How you deal with the grief depends on the loss (death vs. leaving); Release anger via removing blocks; Build resiliency by reframing skepticism about people's motives	Resilient Committed Partners; Step into the vacuum—e.g., become man of the house with divorce or death of father, take care of siblings with death of mother, etc.

[6]

Were You Raised in a Home of Trauma?

In a home of trauma, children endure pain and suffering. These home environments have problems so overwhelming that the adults are often incapable of providing their children with any reliable sense of safety and security. The trauma can take many forms: addiction, mental illness, emotional abuse, physical abuse, sexual abuse, criminal behavior, or dark, unspoken secrets. Consequently, a word of warning applies to this chapter and the next. We'll be discussing issues that may trigger some, such as abuse and rape.

I've witnessed the following three heartbreaking environments in the backgrounds of too many clients in my work:

- In **The Maze**, a child must navigate the disorienting chaos of an alcohol-addicted parent or parents.
- In **Slings and Arrows**, a child must dodge a parent's verbal, emotional, or physical onslaughts.
- In **Sounds of Silence**, a child suffers the shame of sexual abuse.

Leaders who survived a home of trauma almost always have major interior work to accomplish in order to process and move past their trauma. This is of the utmost importance because, as my clinical psychologist colleagues have told me, the age at which the trauma occurs is the age to which the traumatized person will always return—unless they seek and experience healing from that formative event. For example, if someone was raped at sixteen and hasn't healed from the event, their mind may always return to those most painful moments. Their mind remembers being sixteen and emotionally they feel that age and they act as if they still are. (Additionally, if they feel shame, the person must address their shame—and not just the memories of the event—in order to fully heal.)

In Act II of this book, we're going to look at how to discover and overcome what I call a "block." This is a significant negative event in Act I of your Emotional Timeline, often associated with a specific person from your past, that you will need to identify and deal with before making the kind of progress you hope to see in your adult life. Understandably, children from homes of trauma often have the most significant blocks to overcome. Sometimes they can accomplish this deep interior work on their own. More often, the help of a trusted therapist with specific experience in their block is necessary.

These situations can be incredibly painful and complicated. If you grew up in any of these types of homes, I need you to take care of you and get support to help you navigate this. Please reach out to a professional counselor to help you. I promise you: You can feel better and trauma can be overcome. Take baby steps for me. If you know of a counselor, call and interview them. If you don't, yet you know someone who has suffered similarly, ask who they worked with. Or search online for professionals in your area. The key is to just start your journey toward healing.

In the meantime, I hope that the following information will reveal the dynamics that may have been at play during your childhood *and* how you can overcome your trauma to reach your fullest potential as a leader.

Were You Raised in The Maze?

When I asked my client Jenna, a developmentally stunted strategy executive at an accounting firm, to give me a glimpse of her childhood, she immediately recalled this story. After a long, hard day at high school, she walked into her house, being sure to shut the door gently. She never knew what was going to set her mom off, so she was careful about *everything*. She dropped her bag in the hallway and went to grab a snack from the kitchen. As soon as she entered the kitchen, her mom lit into her. "Why'd you slam the door? I bet you put your book bag in the hallway again, didn't you? And did you even think to bring in the empty garbage pail?"

Jenna didn't have an immediate answer. She just stared at her mom, sitting at their kitchen table, holding an empty bottle and a half-full glass of whiskey.

Annoyed, her mom asked, "What are you staring at?"

Appeasingly, Jenna replied, "Mom, I'm sorry. I'll do whatever you need me to. Just tell me."

"I already told you."

Jenna grabbed a snack, moved her bag, and brought the trash in. Then she went to her room and hoped that her mother would sober up before her father came home. Dinnertime was often tense because her father also had an alcohol use disorder. But on this day, once he arrived, they had a surprisingly uneventful dinner, despite the fact that Jenna's mother was still inebriated. Still, Jenna was on edge the entire time, alert for the slightest sign that her mother's anger would explode again. As she excused herself from the table, Jenna and her dad exchanged a knowing glance. *Yes, she's you know what. Watch out.*

A few hours later, just as she was about to fall asleep, Jenna heard them arguing, followed by the unmistakable sound of breaking glass. She ran down the hall to separate them so they wouldn't hurt one another.

She shouted, to no avail, "Mom! Dad! Stop!"

For Jenna, it was just another night in The Maze.

Addiction is a disease that affects not only the substance abuser but the entire family. When a child lives under the same roof as someone dependent on alcohol, they have to navigate and endure the chaotic world of addiction. They often feel trapped in this emotional, unpredictable roller coaster of a home. Believing there is no way out, they run around and around, trying to control anything they can to survive. One of my clients even said it felt more like a "hot mess!"

Was The Maze Your Primary Childhood Environment?

Here's what to look for:

- **You were raised by someone with alcoholic use disorder.** One or both of your parents (or primary caregivers) was dependent on alcohol and drank throughout the day. They may have hid it. They may not have.
- **You were often on edge.** Because your parents demonstrated erratic behavior, often dominated by anger or rage, you never knew what to expect. You were always on the lookout for danger. As a result, you did not feel psychologically safe to speak your mind or share your feelings. You just wanted to keep the peace, yet internally, you may have viscerally felt unsafe, uneasy, tense, and scared. Eventually, fear became "normal."
- **You frequently shouldered parental responsibilities.** For example, you strove to maintain the peace and set expectations for appropriate behavior. You kept up appearances and maintained family secrets, protecting the image of the family and making it appear normal. You may have explained away or made excuses for inappropriate behavior. If a parent was in an accident, you were the one to speak to police officers, doctors, etc. You may have even handled the finances for the family and set boundaries for what could be spent on alcohol versus rent, etc.

Children who grew up in The Maze also often feel embarrassed by their parents' behavior. Jenna remembers being utterly mortified when her drunk mother went up to her high school friends at a party and kissed one guy directly on the lips. Jenna was even more embarrassed when her friend told her how hot her mom was. Jenna just apologized, shook her head, and walked away.

Because they strive to keep the world out of their homes, children of alcoholics have friends but don't share as much about their challenges with them. Due to the trust issues and shame they feel about their families, their friendships can be distant and superficial. Sometimes, they have one close friend whom they have shared it all with.

This is especially difficult between the ages of ten and twelve. That's when children begin to realize the fuller extent of their parents' issues, and that's accompanied by their increasingly greater need for peer approval. At the age of ten, children also start to notice how different their home life is versus what their friends experience. Maybe their friends experience a home filled with giggling and jokes and joyous conversations, and they become envious or sad that it's not their home. Boundaries between parent and child become blurry at this age for children in The Maze, leading to them taking on parental responsibilities, which can result in children believing this is normal, until they notice that their friends do not have to do it.

In an ideal world, the family will get psychological help to deal with the addiction and its causes. This is often difficult because many self-identified alcoholics—and sometimes their families—are in denial about the existence of the problem. Frequently, it doesn't feel safe to have honest conversations about the issues and negative feelings that usually go along with alcohol dependence.

With all of these problems, it's easy to see how a child can lose themselves in The Maze.

What Do Children of The Maze Look Like as Leaders, and What Leadership Strength Often Emerges?

They are *Consistent Stabilizers.*

Because they experienced so much shifting ground in their childhood, they want to create environments of consistency and stability for themselves and others.

They are often keen observers of others' emotions. They excel at caring for and protecting others, always attempting to smooth things over and avoid interpersonal conflict when possible.

They are self-reliant. On the job, if they are asked to do something or say they will do something, they deliver. Most set very clear expectations and do not fear telling their employees whether they have met them. Many are good at giving feedback if they feel safe, because they have spent so much time observing and making judgments about their parents' behavior. Now that they are adults with agency, they want to communicate directly.

One crucial differentiator among the leaders from The Maze I've coached is whether the parent stopped drinking while my clients were still children. If the parent gave up drinking, the child takes more risks as a leader, feels more of a sense of agency, and believes that even in the worst circumstances, things can change. Adults whose parent continued drinking may have more learned helplessness, pessimism, and cynicism about people changing.

Children of The Maze also tend to be the Hero, as categorized by Sharon Wegscheider-Cruse, an expert in addiction and codependency. Licensed clinical social worker Sharon Martin paraphrases Wegscheider-Cruse, and her words perfectively describe what I see in my executives from The Maze: "The hero is an overachiever, perfectionist, and extremely responsible. This child looks like he has it all together. He tries to bring esteem to the family through achieving and external validation. He's hard working, serious and wants to feel in control. Heroes put a lot of pressure on themselves, they are highly stressed, often workaholics and exhibit Type A behavior." As a child, they tried to bring the family together to create a sense of normalcy, wanting to save their parent and cover up the bad behavior. Often, this role is taken on by the eldest child, who desires to provide hope to the family.

This both benefits and detracts from who they become as leaders.

How Can Children of The Maze Become Better Leaders?

Like Jenna, if you grew up in The Maze, with kindness, push yourself to do the following:

- **Address blocks that are stopping you.** You may be holding anger toward your parent, sibling, or other relative who created the unsafe space in your home. You may be angry toward other members of the house who didn't stand up and protect you, or because they put the burden on you to deal with the issues on their behalf. You may be stuck and need to lean in to how to identify and overcome your blocks in Act II in order to fix this.
- **Strengthen your ability to have intimate, real conversations and build relationships.** As Wegscheider-Cruse says: "Heroes struggle

with intimacy and trust in relationships. They have difficulty expressing their feelings and loving themselves." In Act III, you will learn the importance of bringing intimacy and safety to your conversations, and how to do it. And in Act II, you will learn about loving and forgiving yourself. A leader needs to build relationships and have real conversations. Consider the possibility that you can!

- **Build up your *own* identity (rather than trying to be the Hero) for your family.** You may be struggling with avoidant attachment, like our friends from The Nomad. Spending time on your patterns of attachment, the role you play in the house of addiction (are you the Hero?), how you want to shift that role, and defining who you are as a leader via your leadership purpose, values, and expectations, will increase your own confidence and power.

In my work with Jenna, I helped her identify her life purpose beyond managing her parents' addictions, taught her to communicate directly with her boss and colleagues about interpersonal concerns, and encouraged her to risk telling her children about their grandparents' addictions. Jenna needed several years to accomplish all of this, and there are still scary topics for her to address, yet she was promoted to president of her business because of her willingness to be vulnerable with others and grow.

The Maze Reflection Questions

Most leaders from *The Maze* are unaware of the impact of their childhood environment. If you aren't sure, consider these questions:

Are You from The Maze?

- Did one or both of your parents drink multiple times a week in your home?
- Were you unsure how they would respond each time you were home—e.g., angrily, emotionally, happily, or calmly?
- Was their behavior unpredictable?
- Did you feel unsafe? Were you constantly on edge or scared as a result?

- Did you feel you had to keep everyone safe and protect the reputation of the family?

Are These Development Areas for You?

- Are you afraid to speak your truth?
- Do you have difficulty articulating your feelings?
- Do you feel rage, shame, or have low self-esteem because of how your parents made you feel in the home? Or because others failed to protect you?
- Do you distance yourself from everyone around you? Do you struggle with intimacy and trust in relationships?
- Are you afraid to speak your truth rather than represent the truth of others?

Are You a Consistent Stabilizer?

- Do you see different patterns of destructive behaviors and know what you have to do to calm things down?
- Do you feel highly responsible for the welfare of your team and leader?
- Do you go out of your way to protect everyone?
- Are you willing to step in and handle tense moments?

If you answered yes to most of the first set of questions, you are from The Maze. If you answered yes to one or more of the questions in the second set, you have work to do as a leader. If you answered yes to two or more of the questions in the third set, you have acquired the strength of a Consistent Stabilizer.

Were You Raised in Slings and Arrows?

My client Jason, a sales executive in a liquor-based company, dodged as many arrows as he could during his childhood, but he couldn't escape them all. His father was a trifecta of abuse, an all-too-capable man who slung verbal, emotional, and physical pain at everyone near him.

Jason's father also frequently used the N-word, working it into racist jokes, yelling at the TV, and calling Jason by that derogatory term. Yet his father had invited persons of color over for dinner, had talked with them at the gas station, and had them as clients at his dental practice. Jason couldn't understand the incongruity of it.

His dad called Jason's sister, his daughter, stupid. He would even tell his wife, "She's *your* stupid kid." Every time Jason heard these sexist remarks, he hurt for his sister and his mom. He'd try to stand up for them, only to suffer more wrath from his father.

And he could never appease his father. Jason felt that for every good thing he accomplished, his father would tell him ten bad things about his behavior. When he once bought the wrong kind of rake, his father hit him in the head with it.

Jason's dad was a bully.

A Slings and Arrows home is filled with aggressive disrespect. Typically, one parent demeans their partner and children with racist or sexist comments, demands that they meet the parent's needs, and bullies them physically or emotionally or both. (In my experience with clients who grew up in a Slings and Arrows environment, that parent is often the father. But both mothers and fathers can, unfortunately, inflict such damage.) The children duck, sway, and avoid as much as they can the verbal and physical ammunition directed at them or those they care about.

Without a doubt, this is a difficult home environment.

Was Slings and Arrows Your Primary Childhood Environment?

Here's what to look for:

- **You, or those you love, were verbally, emotionally, or physically abused.** Your parent may have insulted your siblings using sexist or other demeaning labels. Or you watched one parent abuse the other. Adults from these homes have sadly said that they got used to being called names, having their feelings made fun of, and being physically kicked, punched, or pushed. They felt more distress when they saw the caring parent or sibling hurt. As a result, they felt even more protective.

- **You heard racial slurs or observed racial tensions.** You would end up with stomach pains if racial slurs occurred. Because you are a child of this parent, you may feel guilt or shame by association.
- **You never felt like you could please the abusive parent and had low self-esteem.** You may have also developed learned helplessness, the belief that change isn't worth trying because it feels impossible. No matter what you did, it didn't work. As a result, your self-esteem plummeted.
- **You had few friends and/or were often isolated and lonely.** You were humiliated if your friends saw your abusive parent in a tirade, or worse, if your parent mocked your friends. So you distanced yourself even further.
- **You may have also been a bully as a child.** Without healthy role models, those who've been bullied as children may become bullies themselves.

The long-term impact on a child who grows up in this kind of environment is often catastrophic emotionally and socially, unless they choose to stand up and fight back and decide that the abuser will not dictate how they are treated.

What Do Children of Slings and Arrows Look Like as Leaders, and What Leadership Strength Often Emerges?

They are *Assertive Diplomats.*

Children born in Slings and Arrows environments will not tolerate injustices. They do not want anyone to endure the pain that they have. So they will stand up on behalf of others. Some, though not all, speak up for themselves, but that happens after they've pushed just so many times to do it. They are sick and tired of being the receiver of the tirades, so like steam coming out of a volcano that needs to be released, they fight back. And I am proud that they do!

Some leaders emerge from Slings and Arrows with a keen eye for reading people. Like those from Sounds of Silence (next up), they become so observant because they are used to watching for the danger. They have had to protect themselves. As a result, they also like to protect others from the danger.

Now some of these leaders refuse to act the same way their parents did, so they speak up in a diplomatic way. They choose to role model how forceful influence and advocating should be done. Don't get me wrong: Others may be people-pleasers or hold back their thoughts. That's until they are tired of that too.

How Can Children of Slings and Arrows Become Better Leaders?

Like Jason, if you grew up in Slings and Arrows, lovingly push yourself to do the following:

- **Overcome the significant block that your abusive parent created in your childhood.** That's the focus of Act II of this book. You may also have to work through your emotions toward your non-bullying parent. Are you angry at that person because they didn't protect you, grateful that they did protect you, or sad that they were also hurt? Have you ever spoken to your non-bullying parent about any of this? What needs to be resolved?
- **Learn to speak up for yourself.** This can happen as you discover how to have real conversations, the focus of Act III.
- **Ensure you haven't become a bully yourself.** If you are demonstrating the same negative behaviors that your abusive parent did, you need to get help. And you need to get feedback from those who will be honest with you. The question is whether you are ready to listen to them and become more self-aware. A sign that this applies to you is that you are consumed by rage and it comes out in unhealthy ways.

Slings and Arrows Reflection Questions

Most leaders from Slings and Arrows are not fully aware of the impact of their childhood environment. Consider these questions:

Are You from Slings and Arrows?

- Did one or both of your parents, your siblings, or your grandparents physically or emotionally abuse you?
- Do you experience a confluence of different emotions, including anger, rage, empathy, shame, and sadness, often simultaneously, when you think about the abusive person in your early life?
- As you read through the childhood environments, can you see yourself described in multiple homes of trauma, where negative behaviors in one feed others? For example, your parent's excessive drinking causes her to lose control and physically abuse you, making you experience The Maze and Slings and Arrows.
- Did you ever bully others as a result of the world you lived in?

Are These Development Areas for You?

- Do you ever get feedback that you fight too hard or too often on behalf of others—e.g., women—or have bias in reverse?
- How often do you feel paralyzed, not knowing what your next move should be? You want to stand up and fight for others or yourself but do not know how to give feedback and lean in to conflict?
- Are you ready to fight? Are you a bully at work?
- Or do you keep your thoughts to yourself because you don't know how others will respond?

Are You an Assertive Diplomat?

- Do you advocate for the underdog and doing what is right?
- Will you not tolerate an injustice?
- Do you speak your mind on behalf of others and do it constructively and with compassion?

If you answered yes to most of the first set of questions, you are from Slings and Arrows. If you answered yes to one or more of the questions in the second set, you have opportunities to grow as a leader. If you answered yes to two or more of the questions in the third set, you have acquired the strength of an Assertive Diplomat.

Were You Raised in Sounds of Silence?

I once walked into a local restaurant and immediately noticed a waitress working there who seemed preoccupied, even sullen. She knew me from previous visits and knew I worked in psychology. When I asked her "How are you doing today?" she felt safe to tell me the truth.

Jodi was being sexually harassed by her ex-boyfriend, and it reminded her of a scary moment when she was younger.

When they were in junior high and high school, her mom and aunt's families lived together. On the days when she and her cousin Sam both arrived home to an empty house, Jodi would run inside and down a hallway to her room. With her adrenaline pumping, she'd slam her door shut. But she knew it was a futile gesture to keep her cousin out. Her door had no lock.

And so her cousin would barge in and touch her where she didn't want to be touched. Frightened, ashamed, and powerless to stop him, Jodi would pray for his abuse to end quickly. After staring at the dark red walls around her for what seemed like an hour, she'd close her eyes, her only avenue for escape. She'd never forget her cousin Sam's perverse words: "It feels good, doesn't it?"

When Jodi stopped talking in the restaurant, she took a breath and then said, "I'm sorry. I said more than I thought I would. I haven't shared that with anyone for a long time."

Like so many who grew up in the Sounds of Silence environment, she had remained quiet because she felt deep shame, and she may have even believed she'd somehow allowed the abuse.

But it is *never* the victim's fault. Sexual abuse or molestation occurs when an abuser uses their power to control and coerce their victim to do something sexually that they do not want to do. That can involve sexual acts ranging from inappropriate physical touching to penetration. Additionally, sexual coercion is not always the result of force; some abusers groom their victims over time and prepare them psychologically. For instance, sexually abusive mothers connect closely with their young children and tell them they touch them because they love them. As a result, children get confused about where intimacy and love begin and end. Molestation, however, is not only sexual abuse but a crime.

Abuse doesn't always have to be physical either. "Sexual boundary crossings" is a broader term coined by my colleague Eva Margot Kant, LCSW-R, to cover the many ways this abuse can take place, and because victims find it easier to say. Crossing a boundary may be:

- **Verbal:** Someone says something about your body that feels wrong.
- **Auditory:** You hear noises that one or both parents make during sex, or one of your parents makes you their confidant and tells you about their sexual history.
- **Visual:** Your cousin or a neighbor makes you watch pornography or an R-rated movie when you are much too young.
- **Physical:** Physical molestation ranging from touching to rape.

So as you consider whether you were raised in a Sounds of Silence home, remember that sexual abuse sadly has many forms.

Was Sounds of Silence Your Primary Childhood Environment?

Here's what to look for:

- **Your sexual boundaries were crossed (verbal, auditory, visual, or physical) during your first eighteen years.** This could have happened once or repeatedly. The fact is that someone in power exerted sexual control over you.
- **When you tried to tell an adult, you were dismissed.** If you were "lucky," your parent believed you and stood up against the perpetrator for you. More likely, you were told "I'm sure they didn't mean it" or "You're imagining things" or "That's just how things are."
- **You never felt safe.** When you're abused *and* you're dismissed, you

never feel safe. As a result, you believe you'll never be taken seriously if you stand up for yourself. Your voice becomes even more muted.

- **You often felt deep shame, which led to low self-esteem.** You may have been a withdrawn child and always thoughtful and very cautious about what you shared with others.

Most people who were sexually abused as a child or teenager felt shame and guilt at the time that the abuse occurred, which followed them into adulthood. Note that shame and guilt are very different things. When children feel guilty, they regret an act that they participated in or how they behaved. So they feel guilty about responding with arousal to inappropriate touching and may say things like, "My body got aroused." When a child feels shame, the feeling is tied to their identity. They might insist that "I am bad or dirty or disgusting," or "There must be something wrong with me." Shame leads to lower self-esteem among victims.

These feelings can also take on different shades of pain depending on a family's religious or cultural background. An individual's response to sexual abuse can be complicated by their feelings about the person who molested them. Typically, an abuser is someone they trust, and they believe the person cares about them. On the one hand, the act felt disgusting, and they knew it was wrong. On the other hand, they didn't want to disappoint the person who cared for them. Or they didn't want to get the perpetrator in trouble, because they loved or cared about that person.

This happened in Jodi's case: She adored her cousin. Even though she hated what Sam did to her in those moments, she felt she would betray him if she told her parents about what had happened. That is where the secrets, and the silence, began for Jodi and countless others. And why I call this environment Sounds of Silence.

What Do Children of Sounds of Silence Look Like as Leaders, and What Leadership Strength Often Emerges?

They are *Vocalists*.

But they have to find their voice first. Children of Sounds of Silence are quiet. They tend to wait for others to speak. They also hide their body in any way possible, whether through wearing dark, loose clothes or covering themselves with papers in their laps. They have little confidence in their own thoughts or body.

When I coach leaders whom I later learn have been sexually abused, I often hear things like: "John doesn't share his opinions. He is quiet and shuts down when challenged. I pay him to share his views." Or: "I don't know what's wrong with Ginger. When I ask her to share her thoughts, she shrugs her shoulders or recommends that I ask someone else."

It's not surprising that leaders from Sounds of Silence act this way. Long ago, they learned that their safest place was within themselves. Alone with their thoughts, they stopped sharing their opinions and feelings with others. Over time, they allowed their voice to disappear.

But not all abuse victims stay silent. When they tell someone else about the abuse, and they see that person confront their abuser, the victim may gain the confidence to stand up for themselves. Once their self-esteem rises to a healthy level, they often become more willing to speak up for others later in life. Because they never had one to defend them as a child, they become Vocalists for others.

Like many sexually abused people, Jodi developed first-rate observation skills. As a teenager, she would sit by a door and plan her exit strategy if her abuser entered the room, or she would pin herself next to another person so she felt protected. Observing and quieting her thoughts, she tuned in to her visceral reactions, clues she had learned to read to help her understand her feelings concerning her safety. She consequently developed an exceptional ability as an adult: being extremely alert to hearing people well and "feeling" their emotions. As a leader, Jodi now "sees" what her peers are struggling with. When something is wrong, she can often figure out the issue and coach them through it.

It took Jodi time to gain confidence in her voice. Once she did, she used it to share her observations and work as a facilitator in the DEI space. Now a DEI project manager in an East Coast pharmaceutical company, Jodi encourages all leaders to live wholly and authentically.

Like her, others who grew up in a Sounds of Silence home may also be in a dark place, keeping secrets, and questioning their worth because of sexual boundary crossings. But as her story attests, they can end up in a very different place and become a highly valued leader who optimistically and actively helps others.

How Can Children of Sounds of Silence Become Better Leaders?

As Jodi did, if you grew up in Sounds of Silence, gently challenge yourself to do the following:

- **Identify your block, and confront and forgive the person who hurt you, not to mention yourself.** Adults who grew up in Sounds of Silence often have significant interior work to accomplish. Act II of this book will help you with this work. However, I can only imagine how difficult that may be for you if this was your childhood home environment. Seeking outside support, whether with a trusted therapist or a therapy group, may prove helpful. Above all, give yourself grace and ample time to work through your block.
- **Find and use the gift you probably have for listening and "seeing" what others are experiencing.** Make sure you learn or reinforce the tips in Act III to increase the power and impact of your voice.
- **Know that you are beautiful or handsome.** Sometimes, it helps to work with an image consultant to help you see how gorgeous you are. If you have deeper body image concerns or think you have an eating disorder (which can result from this environment), there are many great resources available across the country to help you.

Sounds of Silence Reflection Questions

Most leaders from Sounds of Silence are not fully aware of the impact of their childhood environment on them. If you aren't sure, consider these questions:

Are You from Sounds of Silence?

- Did someone you love or trust cross your sexual boundaries?
- Growing up, was your mind often consumed with thoughts about what happened or the person who harmed you, or is your mind consumed with these thoughts to this day? Did you (or do you still) feel guilty for the role you might have played (as ridiculous as that is)?
- Did you feel ashamed of the situation? And did you therefore struggle with telling anyone?
- Did you wonder if you should tell anyone? And if you did tell someone, did you question if they would stand up for you?
- Did you watch out for the person who abused you so that you could survive their abuse?

Are These Development Areas for You?

- As a leader today, are you hiding your voice, waiting for others to ask for your opinion?
- Do you have body image concerns or an eating disorder?
- Do you have negative beliefs in your head about yourself?
- Do you cover your body in dark clothes or garments that are too big for you so that your executive presence is diminished?

Are You a Vocalist?

- Do you feel responsible to stand up on behalf of others?
- Do you protect the marginalized?
- Do you feel deep empathy for people in emotional pain?
- Do you point out when others aren't being listened to or heard?
- Are you a strong facilitator, ensuring that all voices are heard?

If you answered yes to most of the first set of questions, you are from *Sounds of Silence.* If you answered yes to one or more of the questions in the second set, you have opportunities to grow as a leader. If you answered yes to two or more of the questions in the third set, you have acquired the strength of a Vocalist.

Childhood Environment	Common Leadership Deficits That Result	Areas of Work to Address Deficits	Potential Emergent Strengths
The Maze	Anger toward the person with alcohol use disorder or another person who enabled their addiction; Reactions vary—e.g., cautious, learned helplessness, deferential, pessimistic, angry, cynical, negative, or overly responsive; Struggle with intimacy and trust; Difficulty expressing your feelings and loving yourself	Examine the role you played in your childhood home and your identity today; Deal with the block; Process anger, criticism, or difficulty in chaos; Build your ability to have intimate, trusting relationships (Act III) and forgive yourself (Act II); Personality work and a 360 can point out patterns of behavior if you need it proven to you; Clarify your identity	Consistent Stabilizers; Navigate the unpredictable; Responsible; Protective of those on your team; Clear communicators
Slings and Arrows	Low self-esteem; Can become a bully themselves	Deal with the trauma: Confront the bully in your home or people who knew them (block); Do a 360 to see who you really are.	Assertive Diplomats; Demand respect; Protect others from bullying
Sounds of Silence	Quiet—doesn't share opinions in the room / withdrawn, low self-esteem, dressing modestly and in dark colors to remain hidden	Address the block and confront the person who hurt or disappointed you; Find your voice and speak your truth by having direct conversations with the abuser or those who didn't protect you or know; Build executive presence through image consulting	Vocalists; Stand up on behalf of others; Use voice productively; Highly observant because you were always on the lookout for your abuser

In Conclusion: What Happened to You Is NOT Okay!

If you came from a Home of Trauma, you endured terrible things. What your perpetrator did to you is wrong, and I am so sorry that you had to experience that. Whether you dealt with someone who had an alcoholic use disorder; endured physical, mental, or emotional abuse; or your sexual boundaries were crossed, you need help to process this. Anyone would.

Hear me: I *hear you.* I *believe you.* You are a good person and don't deserve what happened. My overall hope is that you get counseling and use your lessons for the good of others—those who have sadly suffered similar events. Be a leader for yourself and others!

Before we examine the so-what of all this, remind yourself of the takeaways from the last three environments of trauma that we discussed.

- In **The Maze**, a child must navigate the disorienting chaos of an alcohol-addicted parent or parents.
- In **Slings and Arrows**, a child must dodge a parent's verbal, emotional, or physical onslaughts.
- In **Sounds of Silence**, a child suffers the shame of sexual abuse.

Now that you've surveyed the nine typical home environments I encounter with my clients, there's one more question to investigate: What if you resonated with more than one home environment?

[7]

Were You Raised in Multiple Home Environments?

In reading through the nine childhood home environments, you may have identified with more than one. Maybe your parents were divorced and you felt you were in The Nest at your mom's house and The Phantom Limb at your dad's. Or if you grew up with both parents in the same house, maybe you experienced The Maze and Slings and Arrows at the same time, two homes of trauma that often commingle. The fact that you originated from multiple home environments may have marked you in ways you're not fully aware of, so it's important to pause and consider just how the combination affected you.

For instance, what's particularly disorienting for a child who experiences multiple home environments within the same household is the lack of balance. Effectively, there is no status quo. Or if there's a semblance of a status quo, it can be suddenly eradicated. For example, a child from a home of trauma may still experience a relatively loving environment six days every week. But if one parent routinely gets drunk every Saturday, that seeming calm devolves into walking on eggshells so as not to upset the inebriated parent. It's as if the child is prized one minute and despised the next. As they become acclimated to such disparate familial climates, they never know what to expect.

For some, this can be awful. Others learn to cope. None have it easy. And while each child's situation is unique, they all suffer from unsure footing, never able to truly rest, always wondering what will tip the balance of their day due to the vacillations of their all-too-human parents.

This constant switching from joy and love to abuse and neglect results in a child experiencing deep internal conflict. Because the child can't understand what's going on—this is their home, the air they breathe, it's all they know—that warring conflict within them is rarely resolved in their childhood. Rather, the unseen, fomenting ramifications of their multiple home environments continue to affect how they relate to everyone (and not just their parents) until they realize just how deeply such an unsure environment impacted them.

That may be you right now.

And can I just say how sorry I am that you had to endure that?

Yet while you may not have been given the tools and opportunities of a stable home environment, you still have untapped power and strength to overcome what's been holding you back. I've witnessed it with my "multiple home" clients many, many times before.

So if you grew up in multiple types of home environments, what does that reveal about you?

Let's look at Georgia Nelson's upbringing, a mix of The Maze, Slings and Arrows, and Sounds of Silence. As a word of warning, her story involves childhood sexual abuse. When she was growing up in the South, her dad loomed large, both physically and mentally. He was six-foot-four and 220 pounds, and he worked in construction. He was a hard worker who also embraced a strong set of ethics. Georgia thought of him as a big teddy bear and a protector—when he was sober. But when he drank, he often became angry, violent, and frightening. Georgia told me, "We had a thing in the family that when my dad drank bourbon, he was predictable. But when he drank vodka, he was crazy. I don't know why. He was harsh in a lot of ways." He was also a racist and frequently made derogatory comments about nonwhite people.

According to Georgia, her mother was "quite complicated" and also often angry. "She was always a strict disciplinarian, but she mellowed over time. She always wanted to be an actress and would loved to have been Ava Gardner. But she also loved to laugh and tell jokes. She liked martinis until she was eighty-seven—a real character."

Georgia's parents let her down at critical points in her childhood. The most severe time occurred when her parents discovered she'd been raped at six years old by her older brother, in a tent in the backyard. Georgia recalls being in the tent at other times but cannot remember how many times the abuse occurred before she was six. Georgia knew it was wrong. She was also terrified and believed her parents would blame her for doing something bad. When Georgia's father discovered them inside the tent, he flew into a rage and began beating her brother. Georgia remembered crying and saying, "I am so sorry. I am so sorry." She felt bad for her brother. As children in this environment often do, she took the shame and blame of it all. To make matters worse, Georgia's mother said, "We will never speak of this again."

"And we didn't for many years," Georgia told me.

As much as Georgia loved her mother and father, she couldn't trust that her home was safe. At times she thought everything was fine, and then her father would do something absurd like demanding to give her a pelvic exam. He wanted to check if she was still a virgin after going on a date.

What an inferno. Three environments in one. How could that little girl possibly emerge mentally healthy from such a complicated world? And with such a mixture of emotions and confusion to process: empathy for her brother and abuser, appreciation and fear for her father holding her brother accountable, the terror of being blamed, the deep shame? Like others who have endured one or more of these environments, she could have given up. Or she could grow through the challenge and learn to fight for herself.

Her choice became apparent just a few years later. When Georgia was in the second grade, people labeled her a "tomboy," partly because she'd beat all the boys in gym class. She especially loved playing baseball. However, the summer Little League teams only allowed boys. So Georgia complained to their city's parks and recreation director. She told him the city should create a girls' league if they wouldn't let her play on a boys' team. "He patted me on the head and told me to go away. And then he called my parents. Of course, my dad was furious, and my mother was so embarrassed that I was that obnoxious to try to do that."

However, that was a big first step in Georgia learning to stand up for herself, a muscle she was forced to use repeatedly growing up and even as she began her adult life. While finishing high school, she had to confront an obstacle preventing her from pursuing her chosen future: her dad. She dreamed of becoming the first person in her family to attend college. When a thick packet arrived from the University of Southern California detailing how she'd received a full scholarship, she couldn't wait to tell her father. When she filled him in on her big news—the school was also paying for her room and books!—Georgia's father brushed her off with a grunt. She was crushed. "I couldn't have been more upset and disappointed because he knew that was my dream. He just stomped on it. It was devastating." Yet she chose to fight back. "I got angry. I felt such rage. I cried and then said: I'm going. I'm going."

Her father rebutted: "This really should have gone to a boy. It would be best to return it because you won't use it. You're going to go there to meet a husband. You're going to go there and get pregnant. You need to give it back."

"I don't care," she said. "I'll figure it out. I'm going."

And she did. Going to college over her father's objections was a monumental step in her building a sense of self-efficacy, which proved to her that she could change outcomes.

Years later, after Georgia's dad died, her mom told her, "You know. I would have left your father years ago, but he never allowed me to work, so I was financially dependent and couldn't leave." This impacted Georgia. She never wanted to feel like she couldn't exercise her own free will just because she couldn't support herself financially. To this day, she continues to prioritize her financial independence while also sticking up for people who have been discriminated against.

Georgia had dodged enough Slings and Arrows to eventually find her way out of The Maze.

Did any, or even all, of Georgia's story resonate with you?

If so, consider the types of home environments you grew up in, the hand you were dealt.

How were your multiple environments similar? How did they differ?

Were you strengthened by one and discouraged by the other? Or did both bring you down?

Did you actually experience a mix of more than two environments? Looking back, what do you feel for the child who had to navigate those multiple settings?

In other words, as you see the story of your childhood play out on the stage of your life, and you see scene change after scene change, what do you think that kid is thinking and feeling?

And how has that led to the person you are today?

The curtain has closed on Act I.

Now let's see how all that's happened to you in your childhood reveals itself in Act II.

ACT II

The Roles You're In

Who you are today, both at work and at home, is a direct result of your childhood. This may seem like an obvious statement, yet we don't give it as much credence as it truly deserves. Remember that statistic I shared at the start of this book, that 80 percent of the way you show up as a leader and a human being is due to the way you were raised? In my work with some of the world's most successful leaders, I've seen time and again how often they go from disbelieving that their childhood could have so much sway over them today to revelatory aha moments that deeply transform them from within, with ripple effects throughout their companies and their lives.

I hope that you have begun to see a few connections between your childhood and your life today. If not, fear not. Act II is all about connecting the dots between who you were and who you are. After doing the hard interior work of revisiting your childhood, this is your next step.

You can discover the implications of your childhood in three ways:

1. By the strengths (and development areas) that advanced within you as a result of your home environment (Act I)
2. Through seven dimensions of your identity today (Act II, and the focus of this chapter)

3. By how you engage in conversations and build relationships today (Act III)

In Act I, you learned that you developed strengths and blind spots due to the home environment in which you grew up. Each environment identifies a strength that emerges if you address development areas and overcome your blocks. Maybe you are an Illuminator from In the Shadows, who is not only clear about who you are versus your famous parent, but also loves to shine a light on other people so they are confident in their own self as well. No matter what type of home environment you come from, I want you to be proud of your great strengths. Most people believe it's better to be humble than to be cocky. However, if you put your strengths to good use, consider the impact you could have on this world.

You can also discover how your childhood still affects you by looking at how you engage in conversations and build relationships today. More specifically, how your childhood cast treated you is often indicative of how you appear and treat others as a leader in organizations, in your community, or in your family. After all, your childhood is where you learned and practiced how to converse and build relationships. We'll discuss this more in Act III, where you will learn how to harness your relationship-building and communications strengths from your childhood, and overcome challenges based on your early home, to increase your referent power through improving your ability to have real conversations.

What's also critical to recognize is that you experienced both positive and negative outcomes from what you learned to practice in childhood. This is especially important if the events were particularly negative or if you grew up in one of the more challenging environments, like Slings and Arrows or The Maze. When I'm working with clients who have suffered in their early years, I ask them to reflect on these questions:

- How have your experiences changed your motivation to be a better leader, spouse, or parent?
- How have your experiences improved your relationships with your colleagues or your friends?
- How have your early experiences changed what you share out loud?
- Have your experiences given you new opportunities in business or the community?
- Have your childhood experiences made you deal with conflict more directly, or avoid it?

Highly successful people respond to adverse events by focusing even more on excelling. They use their negative experiences to push themselves forward positively. This choice is only sometimes conscious.

My goal is to help you understand the connection between what you learned in childhood and how you act and interact with others as an adult. The more time you spend unpacking those links—including the behaviors you learned from the characters in your life—the better you can identify moments in your professional and personal lives where your conduct or performance is altered because of your experience. You can leverage deep insights using your emotions as data to become a better leader. You can identify what you need to unlearn. You can overcome the challenges of your childhood. And you can harness the strengths that emerged from living in a specific environment.

Now let's look at your identity today.

[8]

The Implications of Your Childhood

When you know your *why*, you can change your *how*. Put another way, when you understand the influential factors of your life, you can choose how they affect you. For instance, your childhood informs so much about you—e.g., your source of motivation, like your purpose or your values, and the positive or negative beliefs in your head, like "I am a good person" or "I am of no value." When you come to understand why you're motivated toward certain goals or why you have specific beliefs, you can change your target.

In my work with clients like Matt Levatich (whom you met in the Phantom Limb section of Chapter 5), I help them bring light to seven foundational areas that undergird everything they do:

- **Childhood:** Easy enough to explain, this is who you were as a child. It includes your supporting cast and the home environment in which you grew up—everything we've so far discussed in this book.
- **Constitution:** This is how you grew to think and how you developed your personality and your physical condition—a mix of genetics and environment. This includes your intelligence, critical thinking, numerical fluency, and vocabulary, plus your personality preferences, needs, and physical dexterity.
- **Motivation:** This is your passion and your purpose. This is what is important to you and where you have devoted your time. It also includes the values you hold most dear.

- **Skills:** This includes your education and any skills—whether technical, managerial, leadership, etc.—that you acquired in Act I of your life.
- **Experience:** This is what you learned outside of a classroom, through jobs, good and bad bosses, and culture—i.e., what your job and life have taught you.
- **Beliefs:** This is what you believe about yourself and the world around you.
- **Situation:** These are core memory events that deeply affected you.

Imagine these characteristics like concentric circles, as if you just threw a rock into a lake. In the center lies your childhood, and from there ripples out every other characteristic: your constitution, motivation, etc. When the ripple hits the shore, that's what others see—e.g., that's how you're performing today. So each of these seven characteristics factors into your actions. They build upon each other. And they all begin with where you began: your childhood.

Now think about your own story in your Emotional Timeline. Maybe you wrote down an experience involving a mean and arrogant boss you hated working for, forcing you to quit a job you loved. Is it possible that your former boss reminded you of someone from your childhood who acted and treated you in a similar way, which triggered negative feelings and therefore you responded badly to your boss? Or maybe you're always drawn to work for female bosses and have gained a reputation as a champion of women in the workplace. I'd wager that you grew up in a Matriarchy, with a strong mother figure. Or if you're the kind of leader who believes that anything is possible with enough hard work, demonstrating good character, and focusing on people, you might have grown up in The Nest.

With this framework in mind, let's return to Matt's story to bring it to life. As you read, remember: The goal is to understand the connection between what you learned in childhood and how you act and interact with others today as an adult.

Implications in Action

When I met Matt Levatich, he was being considered by the Board of Directors for president and CEO of Harley-Davidson. He was the chief operating officer at the time, reporting to CEO Keith Wandell. As I do with all of my clients, I met with several of the company's board members, Keith, Matt's direct reports, and his wife to discuss his strengths and areas of development and what he would need to do to become CEO. The praise came quickly: Matt was smart, kind, compassionate, strategic, and funny. He was a good listener, had high integrity, and cared about people. He also had a strong desire for progress. He wanted to get things done. He was a creative, innovative engineer who loved Harley's motorcycles!

Who wouldn't want someone like that to be their CEO?

However, as I kept digging, some warning signs appeared.

One colleague best summarized their worries: "I love the guy. I'm just very worried about him. I will follow him off the cliff, but I do not see where he is going." Matt was a highly organized leader who was clear about his goals. But he could be more effective at inspiring his team to accomplish tasks in an aligned and coordinated way. Another said, "Where's the Matt we used to know and love? I miss him." She meant that even though he was highly self-confident, he was over-functioning to please others. He was more serious and guarded than usual and held back his sense of humor, which had been a pivotal strength. He was also overly deferential to his boss. He had always been quite charming and a gentleman, but also someone who spoke truth to power in a respectful way.

I thought, *There's a disconnect. So let's find the Matt they know and love.*

As I worked with Matt, we homed in on the aforementioned seven dimensions of his identity so we could discover why he wasn't quite ready to be CEO.

Childhood

"Matthew is still running headlong into everything he does and often hurts himself physically."

No, that wasn't from a board member.

Rather, that was written by Matt's mother to his aunt when Matt was in the sixth grade. When he discovered that gem of a letter during our work together, he laughed. "Wow, that's me today." His mother had also noted that Matt was a curious child who was adept with his hands, and he remembered how he "could fix anything, including my sister's tape recorder."

As we expanded on the cast that surrounded him during his childhood, Matt fondly recalled his special bond with his sister Sue. Though he'd had a good relationship with each of his four siblings, Sue had taken him under her wing. She helped shape who he'd become, especially after the defining moment of his childhood.

As you learned in the Phantom Limb section of Chapter 5, Matt's parents divorced when he was twelve, and his dad left their house and their family. Fortunately, Matt's parents handled the divorce masterfully, despite how painful it was for his mom. That's not to say that Matt was "fine" about the divorce. Rather, the divorce had offended his definition of family. He never forgave his father for that injustice. Yet Matt still took after him in many ways.

His father was an architect, an artist, and a mechanic. A native of Bratislava, he immigrated to the US after World War II and as an eighteen-year-old got a job working for the US Army fixing radios in postwar Germany. "My father could fix anything," Matt told me. "Everything from electronics to equipment. He was also a designer. Growing up, we were exposed to a lot of beautiful things. We had a beautiful house that Dad designed in a mix of mid-century classics and early American pieces from his mom's family. He valued straightforward, pure designs."

The shared interests with his father helped explain why Matt was so drawn to work for Harley-Davidson. Matt loved beautiful objects and solutions. Harley motorcycles were beautiful and clever designs. He was always at his happiest when he saw somebody come up with the best, most innovative, cleverest answer to a difficult problem. That's when Matt would smile.

While the weighty stone of his parents' divorce started the ripples of his life, he didn't become defined by that moment. Listening to his story over the years, I was struck by how unique his situation was. Most children from divorced homes witness their parents bad-mouthing one another. Most end up feeling the repercussions of a lack of full commitment in good times and bad. They often feel abandoned and betrayed, and lose trust.

In Matt's case, I was struck by how professional and diplomatic his parents had been with each other in front of him or around him. As much as the divorce had deeply wounded his mother, his father saw a certain sense of duty in supporting her. In fact, this often happened with Matt as a conduit. For example, if something went awry in the house, his father would fix it with Matt's assistance. As Matt recalls, his father was neither happy nor resentful to provide such help. It was simply his duty. This taught Matt multiple lessons, both practical and relational. Through demonstration, he learned how to install a dishwasher and also how to serve from a deep sense of duty. Plus, as his parents' go-between, he became a compassionate, genuine listener—an essential trait for when he later became the conduit between his employees and his boss at Harley-Davidson.

For each of the seven dimensions of identity, I'm going to provide you with questions for further reflection, a way to help you process the connections between your childhood and adulthood. The questions are separated into those about your past (aka your *why*) and those about your present (aka your *how*). You could also think of this separation as questions about the cause versus the result—i.e., what others observe you doing.

What Was Your Childhood Like?

- Did any of the nine childhood environments resonate for you?
- If not, what was missing? What patterns or issues came to mind that you need to think about from that time?
- What emotions did you experience as you read through the environmental descriptions?
- What strengths emerged from your childhood environment?
- What development areas came to the surface?
- Is there anyone or an event that makes you really uncomfortable?

How Does Your Childhood Still Affect You Today?

- What development areas surfaced in your childhood that are getting in the way of you achieving success—e.g., communication, relationship-building, emotional intelligence?
- Is there a secret you are holding about someone who hurt or disappointed you (a block) that you need to confront to move forward?

Constitution

Your genetics, plus the influence of your childhood environment, have resulted in constitution—i.e., how you think, even how you move, and, most relevant to this book, how your personality presents itself. Executives love scientific data to influence their thinking. So, when people are skeptical about the importance of childhood influences, I lean on personality data to reinforce or validate the points I am trying to impress on them. The two sources complement each other well.

Dr. Allen Hammer, my colleague, advisor over the years, and friend, is one of the most world-renowned experts in personality assessment. I love the way he explains what personality inventories are: At the most basic level, they're just samples of behaviors that make up your constitution. Because we cannot follow these leaders around all the time and cannot get into their heads to figure out what they are thinking, why they are behaving in such a way, or what they're feeling and why, we have to rely on them to describe themselves. Through these inventories, they're saying, *This is what I want you to know about me*. Consequently, when they complete a personality inventory, we can use that sample of behavior to generalize how they might likely act or react in a given situation. We can predict their behavior whenever they face a choice at home or work.

Each inventory has its own focus. If it's how to deal with chaos, we look at the Prosilience Questionnaire to check the subject's resiliency levels. The CPI 260 will show us their leadership or management behaviors. FIRO-B reveals their interpersonal needs for inclusion, control, and affection. And the MBTI Step III captures their preferences and level of executive functioning on decision-making, etc. Some instruments mirror childhood (like FIRO-B), some mirror the subject's innate predispositions (MBTI), and others show behavioral skills the subject has honed, like TKI (which describes how they show up in conflict).

We can do this because an effective inventory has a lot of validation and reliability research backing it up. For reliability, we employ test-retest, a statistical technique that measures consistency of the measurement tool when administered to the same subject at two different points in time under similar conditions. We also check internal consistency of the items to see if the person completing the instrument will get the same answers over time across situations and if the items are really getting at the same thing. The validation studies correlate the participant's answers to other variables to see if we're really measuring what we want to. The same set of questions is asked over and over of different people. Because the instruments are standardized in this way, we can compare the responses of one person to another person, one group to another group, or one country to another country.

This information is invaluable for executives, managers, employees, or volunteers because they must make daily decisions using the information available. They must resolve conflicts. They have to work on teams with other people. How people will react to these situations is what these inventories attempt to measure. Using that data, we might predict how someone's boss will react to them based on whether they are introverts or extroverts. And because the information is standardized, we can monitor progress over time and see the growth in people over time.

With Matt, I noticed there were two distinct patterns I wanted to check, so I had him take a personal inventory called the Myers-Briggs Type Indicator and also fill out a resiliency questionnaire. The MBTI measures the sixteen types described by Isabel Myers, based on the work of Carl Jung. Maybe you've taken the inventory yourself (and I recommend that you do). It identifies your preferences for living in the inner world (introversion) versus the outer world (extroversion), whether you take in information based on reality or rely more on your intuition, and how you approach decision-making, handle differences, and structure your life in relation to the outside world.

Harley-Davidson was facing real financial challenges. Baby boomers, who loved riding motorcycles, were getting older, so use was going down and sales were declining. A new vision was essential. The leader, Matt, would need to establish the new vision. I wanted to check his strategic thinking capability, which I assumed was strong because of a story he told me about his dad:

> Pam, there's a process I go through to sort of step back, create space for myself. This takes time. It takes a commitment that the fast-paced world tends to rob, but to create that time for reflection and then say, "Okay, now what? How does that apply going forward?" There's something that my father taught me when I was learning how to drive that I always remember, and I think about it in this way as you kind of look forward. He said, "When you're driving at night, your focus should be at the farthest reach of your headlights. And when your focus is there, your eyes and your mind will see everything that's going on between that end of your vision and the windshield. If you're focused on the hood ornament, all you'll see is what's going on between the hood ornament and the windshield. And when that deer jumps out, you will hit it." So the lesson he taught me was, as you think about looking forward, what are the farthest reaches of your vision? How can you challenge yourself to push as far out as you can? And that will set a direction for you that the winds and the turbulence and everything else that goes on in our world today, you'll have that vision in mind, and you will stick to that direction.

Based on what I'd heard about Matt and this endearing story, I assumed that Matt was quite strategic. His MBTI personality results validated that for me. He is an ENTJ (Extroverted Intuitive Thinking Judging)—the same as his father. ENTJs love solving problems, thinking strategically about the solution, rationally approaching how to make decisions, and building plans to address the issues. Learning this about himself helped Matt understand how his personality reinforces his skills and passions. This inventory also revealed his blind spots, such as failing to tune in to people's emotional needs or celebrate successes. ENTJs don't dwell on what's already happened; they enjoy moving on to the next issue to address and solve.

The second pattern I wanted to check concerned his resiliency—i.e., how resilient he was while in a very ambiguous, chaotic, or unknown situation. Resilience questionnaires ask, in times of uncertainty, what do you fall back on? Matt's questionnaire results showed that he was highly resilient. He believed in his own capability. He was confident and believed that any problem thrown at him could be handled. He loved solving problems and generating lots of potential solutions. He took risks and moved to action quickly and enjoyed solving the problems with others. He loved creating problems for himself to solve.

As he told me, "I remember a boss getting angry at me once when I was doing something that was off topic from work. Basically, I was doing something I shouldn't have been doing. So, I create problems in my personal life that I can solve. I have a saying and this came out of my mouth when I was probably thirty, to a boss who caught me doing something I wasn't supposed to be doing off job, off task, and I just blurted out, 'Sometimes I need a problem I can solve.' And I really do. It's like a Scooby snack for me. It makes me think: 'Okay, I am re-grounded, I can do this.'"

The resiliency profile also measures how optimistic you are about the world. The difference between how Matt felt about himself, his own self-confidence, and what he believed about the world was revealing. When I met Matt, he saw threats that made him uncertain and angry. He saw hypocrisy in action and was skeptical about the actions people around him at work were taking.

That's why colleagues who loved him wondered what was wrong with him.

His parents' divorce had shaped his view that the world is unsafe.

What Was Your Constitution Like as a Child?

- Have you examined yourself through personality and physical assessments?
- Do any confirm or challenge what you learned in your childhood?
- What is your IQ?
- Have you been tested for specific aptitudes like critical thinking, numerical fluency, and vocabulary/ability to read?
- Personality preferences
  - What are your preferences? Do you prefer extroversion or introversion? Sensing or intuition? Feeling or thinking? Judging versus perceiving? (e.g., MBTI)
  - How do you handle chaos and manage change? How resilient are you? (e.g., prosilience questionnaire)
  - What are your interpersonal needs to be your best self? Do you need to be included? In charge or told what to do? Do you need people to be warm and open with you or not at all? (e.g., FIRO-B)
- What is your managerial and leadership style? (e.g., CPI 260)
- What are your levels of physical strength, endurance, and dexterity?
- Which personality attributes of yours confirm or contradict one another?

How Does Your Constitution Still Affect You Today?

- What missing cognitive, personality, or physical abilities may make it difficult for you to excel right now?
- Are there ways to develop these missing abilities or not?

Motivation

Motivation is fueled by what is most important to a person and informed by their passions, purpose, and values. My main questions in exploring this foundational area are always: "Are you motivated to do your best work and live your best life?" and "If not, why not?" Or "Are you motivated to change?" Ideally, your work and organizational culture fulfills your purpose, passion, and values. Matt found motivation through his niece, who has Down syndrome. She brings him incredible joy. Through her, he's seen how "we are all equal, we are all God's children, and we all have value and something to contribute." So it is no surprise that Matt's mandatory values are related to honoring the value in each person. To be more specific, they are equality, truth, justice/fairness, integrity, respect, and responsibility, as well as learning/growth, creativity, achievement, and courage.

"I won't tolerate hypocrisy, which stems from integrity and truth," Matt told me. "To me, hypocrisy is the disconnect between saying one thing and doing the other. Personal integrity is of utmost importance. It's a personal imperative, and I want it in everyone. If you respect others as God's children, integrity is a nonnegotiable." Again, he learned respect of the human being from his father, who ensured that he and his mother were taken care of after the divorce.

Matt struggled when we spoke because he felt a lack of integrity and regard for the truth in both domestic and corporate politics. He is curious and relentlessly interested in getting to the root of a problem, that bedrock truth. Matt shared a quote from Dean Julio Ottino of the McCormick School of Engineering and Applied Sciences at Northwestern: "There is no credit given for solving in the right way the wrong problem." As he told me, "When someone isn't interested in finding out the truth, it's a trigger for me."

Another of Matt's very important values, which he got from his mother, is dedication to family. She never remarried. She loved his father, cherished her kids, and was devoted to them. Matt has tried to live his own life similarly. As a father to Max and Sam and a husband to Brenda, he is a devoted father and husband. Nothing matters more. "As a dad to my kids, I don't want them to think of me in any other capacity," he told me. "If I am successful, it's about whether I was there for them, whether I helped them grow, not that I had some job or anything else." I have seen this in other children of divorce in *Phantom Limb* environments. They are incredibly loyal and committed to their families, no matter what.

Matt's motivations were formed through the modeling of so many people in his life. Today, you can often see his motivations in how he pursues his passions and his purpose in life.

What Was Your Motivation Like as a Child?

- What did your childhood teach you about your purpose and passions?
- What did you want to spend your time on that fulfilled you?
- Regarding your values, what was most important to you in your life?
- What did you learn about your ethical boundaries from your childhood?

How Does Your Motivation Still Affect You Today?

- Do your work, manager, and culture enable you to fulfill your purpose, passions, and values? (Ideally you need to match your purpose, passion, and values to work you love and a culture that matches it.)
- Are you doing work you love? If not, why not?
- Regarding your ethical boundaries, what gets in your way or gets you in trouble? (If ethical boundaries are triggered in a relationship, there will be tension. You may need to address interpersonal issues that result.)

Skills

You've heard me talk about all the skills Matt learned from his father and how, as a result, Matt developed a love of design and building things, both at work and at home. When he told me about a bathroom he was designing and building, he took the time to describe the beauty of the wood he used for a counter. Matt also enjoyed fixing things—even going so far as to find problems around the house that he could solve, like noticing the lawn was browning in a certain area, or mushrooms were rising in the garden.

From both of his parents, Matt developed skills in listening, in learning, and in engineering—all of which would serve him well as an adult and as a future CEO.

What Were Your Skills as a Child?

- What fun activities did you enjoy with your caregivers when you were young that led to real skills later—e.g., working on cars, cooking, designing, drawing, etc.?
- Which technical, managerial, and leadership skills were you encouraged to develop when you were young?
- What educational degrees were you encouraged to get? Or were you encouraged to find your own passion and get the degree for that? Or were educational degrees put down?

How Do Your Skills Still Affect You Today?

- Do you have all the skills you need to do what is being asked of you? What is missing?
- Do you have the specific educational background to do the job?
- What degrees do you have?
- What leadership strengths do you have?
- What are your leadership development areas?
- Are you lacking technical training?
- Does your job require a specialty (and/or certification) that you do not have—e.g., engineering degree, psychology degree?

Experience

You are a product of your experience to date, and you need to determine if there is other knowledge or know-how you need to acquire to handle your current challenges. Types of experience can be working in teams, in functional or management roles, working in different-size companies, or in an expatriate assignment like Matt's. He always chose roles and jobs that challenged him and put him outside his comfort zone. Why? Because it created the highest level of learning for Matt. One of his favorite experiences was working in Varese, Italy, and living in Lugano, Switzerland, for several years with his family on an expat assignment. Because none of his family members spoke the local languages, they all sat for hours over dinner to talk about their days in English! The family got tighter as a unit.

You are a product of your experience, and you need to determine if you have the experience you need for the situation at hand. If not, you need to acquire it.

What Were Your Experiences Like as a Child?

- What experiences were you exposed to as a child—e.g., watching your dad work in his office—that either led you to pursue certain work (like being a manager, working in an office) or not?
- What experiences have had the biggest impact on you?
- What experiences did you long to have that you didn't (like going backstage at the Opera House to meet the singers, or going to Spring Training in Florida to see professional ballplayers)?

How Do Your Experiences Still Affect You Today?

- Do you long for and enjoy new experiences or being put into a job assignment that will stretch you—e.g., working in teams, in different sizes of companies, in functional or general management roles, switching from Marketing to Sales?
- Do you get bored if your job doesn't change every two years?
- Do you enjoy working for all types of managers? Are you better in one culture or another?
- Do you like to work outside of your country?

Beliefs

Matt's beliefs also emerged from his childhood environment. He has always believed that if something isn't difficult, it isn't worth doing. "I have that perspective about most things," Matt told me. "That's leaning into stuff that I have no experience in, just rolling up my sleeves and trying to figure it out. And there is a tremendous amount of learning that comes with that. A lot of value comes from hard, difficult work."

This includes having the courage to look back at how your childhood impacts how you show up as a leader.

What Were Your Beliefs as a Child?

- What assumptions and principles were you taught when you were young—e.g., if you work hard, you will excel; opportunities only come to "other" people; white people are privileged?
- What beliefs do you have about yourself and the world?
- What did your parents tell you about your capability?

How Do Your Beliefs Still Affect You Today?

- Are you confident? Do you believe in yourself?
- Or do you have self-limiting beliefs (*I am no good; I am not valued*)?
- What do you believe about your capability?

Situation

The business situation at Harley-Davidson was challenging from 2012 to 2020, when I saw and worked with Matt off and on, first with him and then with the board. Not only was the business situation challenging, so too was the political world, and there were many social issues that Matt cared about helping to solve.

Disingenuous behavior or a lack of transparency was difficult and would have triggered anyone in Matt's situation. Matt did in fact become president and CEO and then worked hard to establish a new vision. It was a very challenging time. Matt retired in 2020. And of course, he did it with grace, like his father did.

What Was Your Situation Like as a Child?

- What did you learn from your childhood environment about the type of work and family world you needed to be your best?

- What dimensions of psychological safety were most important to you?
- What did you learn about the kind of environment that empowers you or keeps you from doing well at work?

How Does Your Situation Still Affect You Today?

- Is the leader you're working for good? Do they motivate and inspire you? Do they help you grow in your job? Do you like working for good versus bad bosses? You learn more from bad bosses!
- Are expectations of you clear?
- Are you learning new roles that are fun for you? Exhaust you? Or make you miserable?
- Do you get feedback? Have you been told what you are doing well and what you are not doing well?
- Are there interpersonal dynamics or tensions that are getting in your way? Are you in a stretch assignment?
- What is the culture like?

Taken together, you can see the connections between these seven foundational areas and how they play such a critical role in how you show up as a leader—and how you can use those insights to become a better leader.

In Matt's case, as we worked together to understand the implications of his childhood, he eventually moved into the CEO role. That's when he coined a concept he called his "decoder ring." He shared the key insights we had uncovered by exploring these seven areas with his team. As he told me, "I used the output of our work to describe to them who I am and why I am, as a starting point. I had people in the room that had worked with me for decades. And one said at the end of the meeting, 'Matt, I've worked with you for a decade, and there are things I didn't know or didn't understand. And I'm so psyched that I get it now because you're going to be so much easier to work with.'"

Matt also came to recognize that what he had begun wasn't a onetime effort. As people cycled off his team and new members joined, those new people began to wonder why he was acting the way he was. "I hadn't explained it to the new people," he told me. "I hadn't explained it in a long time to some of the other members of the team, and it gave me pause to step back and say, 'These things need to be revisited in ourselves and with the team as a way just to make sure that we're consciously working on ourselves all the time.'" Matt was setting expectations for his team, which is great—especially when so many of them had concerns about what was going on with him as their leader.

Imagine if you had your own decoder ring. You could help your team, your colleagues, and your bosses—even your family—understand why you do what you do and say what you say. They could have a deeper and better appreciation of your behaviors, beliefs, values, skills, strengths, and blind spots.

The more time you spend unpacking those links between your childhood and how you act today as an adult, the better you can identify moments in your professional or personal life where your conduct or performance has been impacted by your experience.

What if you don't see any links? What if you know something needs to change but you can't put your finger on it?

Then a significant childhood event may be preventing you from moving forward.

We're going to address that next.

Just be sure to take a deep breath before you turn the page.

[9]

What's Stopping You?

Imagine two large boulders on either side of a small river. Suddenly, a significant boulder falls between them, completely stopping the water's flow. Unless steps are taken to remove the third boulder, the river will be dammed for ages. All of its potential downstream energy has been cut off from its purpose.

Human beings experience this too.

I call it a block.

Because of one or more negative events or a person in your Act I, you're prevented from achieving your full potential in Act III. For many of my clients, the central challenge of their Act II is overcoming their block. In this chapter, we're going to consider what these obstacles look like and how to identify your significant hurdles. In the next chapter, we'll look at how to confront—and possibly forgive—any person from your past who's responsible for your block.

You may be able to immediately identify what—or who—has been holding you back. Or you may have an uneasy, undefined feeling about your block. Or you may have no idea that you have one. (It's also possible, though rare, that you have none at all!) If you do have a block, you will never exceed your current ceiling until you address and remove it.

My client Lisa was thoroughly blocked.

I was standing in my client's kitchen having a cup of coffee before beginning an intense day of high-performance team building exercises with an executive team. I noticed Lisa across the room. Everyone on the team was finishing their last-minute emails and calls while Lisa sat silently in a soft, blue chair in the far corner of the living room. I thought she looked sad.

When Lisa's eyes met mine, she got up and approached me. "Pam, I've been up tossing and turning all night," she said thoughtfully. "I am disturbed by my FIRO-B results. I am a cold bitch, and I must have the lowest scores in the company."

That's a line you don't forget. It was also untrue.

I'd just started working with Lisa, the head of supply chain for a manufacturing business. I'd asked her to complete the FIRO-B, a personality inventory that identifies your need for inclusion, control, and affection/openness. The self-assessment reveals how much a person needs those qualities and how often they'll express them to others.

When Lisa told me how upsetting her scores were, I shook my head. Even though she was a relatively new client, I knew she wasn't cold. And she certainly wasn't incapable of leading well. Still, she was devastated by her score, which was indeed low: ten out of fifty-four. She imagined that made her a terrible teammate and leader.

A particular work conflict at the time gave me further insight into Lisa's low score. She was in charge of the strategy for a new business division while her colleague Paul was responsible for executing the rollout. His team kept pushing back against her ideas. Lisa dug her heels in, firmly believing she was right and Paul was wrong. She didn't have faith that Paul would honor her plan. Simply put, she didn't trust him.

Consequently, she withdrew. She avoided Paul and only communicated with certain leadership team members. This is where her low selectivity score made themselves known. She stopped being transparent and warm with some peers, a sign of her low affection. She became increasingly selective about whom she'd work with, which was reflected in her low inclusion score. And she powered through her work independently, believing she could push her strategy through no matter the obstacles she had to overcome. This was a sure predictor of her low control score, which signals a preference to lead alone.

Lisa didn't like who she was becoming in her Act II, so we looked at her Act I to identify what could be blocking her.

Here's her full Emotional Timeline:

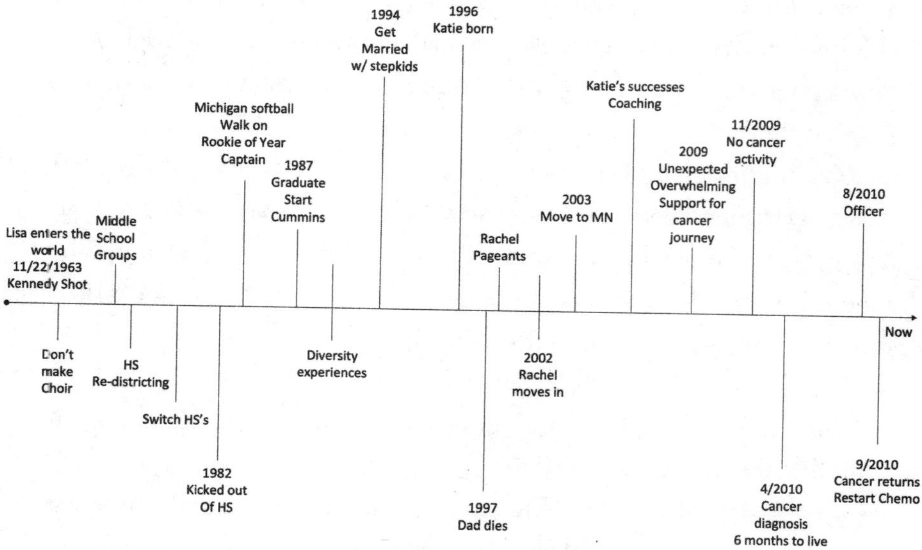

Look closely at Lisa's Act I, from 1963 to 1982. What was her block?

Now a more challenging question: How do you think that block resulted in her frustrations at her job many years later?

Here's the story behind her block, when she was kicked out of high school at eighteen years old. First, notice how it ranks almost as low as the death of her father. That's how pivotal this negative childhood experience had been to her. And yet, until we had conducted this exercise, she'd almost forgotten just how impactful that time of her life was.

Lisa was a child of The Nest. She adored her father, a devout Catholic and a deeply great man. Her parents always encouraged her that she could do anything she set her mind to. That included her decision to move away from home to attend a very well-regarded high school. Lisa, always ambitious, believed that attending the new school would offer her more classroom opportunities and better competition in field hockey than her hometown school could offer. She'd also have to live alone in an apartment, something she felt ready for.

She immediately succeeded in her new school, earning multiple academic and athletic awards. She had entered as a senior and was fulfilling her lofty goals. However, there was a catch. Other parents didn't like how an out-of-towner was stealing the spotlight and the awards from their children who had worked tirelessly in that district since they were elementary school kids. They thought it was unfair, so they banded together to fix what they perceived as a problem.

One night during Lisa's senior year, she heard a knock at the door of her apartment. Despite being alone, she answered the door to find one of the school's head administrators. He didn't waste time. The school had decided she was no longer welcome. She could not return to school the next day—or ever after.

Can you imagine what Lisa felt?

There she was, all alone and away from her family, being told by an adult that she was being kicked out of school for *being too good*. Until then, she'd been rewarded for excelling and striving to be the best. Now she was being punished for it. It was devastating—and a huge turning point. She felt she could no longer trust people, including her teachers and her friends' parents, whom she'd thought were allies.

No wonder Lisa's test scores had been so low. Because she didn't feel valued by her colleagues and didn't know whom to trust, she'd pulled away from them. Unconsciously, she was protecting herself—all because of a devastating moment with a high school administrator she hadn't thought about for a long time.

How to Identify What's Blocking You

Lisa provides a perfect example of a typical process in discovering what could be blocking you:

- **What emotions did you feel?** When Lisa received her scores, she felt upset, embarrassed, and humiliated. That night, she tossed and turned in bed, her body responding viscerally to her emotions. Those reactions were a clue that she'd hit upon a block.

- **What events happened?** Her low scores pointed her to the event that was the source of her block. With the help of her ETL, she linked her present challenges to feelings of hurt, isolation, and abandonment from her past.
- **What "aha" moments occurred?** Having made the emotional connection, Lisa then associated what had happened when she was kicked out of school for no good reason with her FIRO-B scores, which showed she didn't need other people and that she didn't express affection. Faced with a lack of support from people she had trusted, Lisa had moved forward by forging her own path—a strategy she continued for decades, and even as a highly placed executive.

Lisa used her emotions as data to discover hidden truths about herself. Now you're going to work through the same process.

1. **Review Act I of your own Emotional Timeline.** If your block is readily apparent, circle it. If not, here's how to identify what could be blocking you. There may be one negative event that stands out to you, or there might be a series of events (mostly negative with an occasional positive one) that are related to a person. Ask yourself: Is there a pattern here? Why did that person show up so much on my timeline? Why do they have such a prominent place on my timeline?

   For example, I once worked with Stacy, a high-potential young leader in an marketing agency who was a very successful and quite vivacious woman. If destiny allowed, she would be the leader of the firm someday. Her smile filled the room when she walked into it. Her intelligence, results orientation, and drive impressed. She handed me her Emotional Timeline, and I immediately noticed that her sister's name was listed five times, with many below the line. We could both see pretty easily where her block was stemming from.
2. **For each event in Act I that's below your timeline, ask yourself, "How does this make me feel?"** When seeing the event, series of

events, or name of a person listed, check in with your emotions about what you are feeling. Are you angry? Bitter? Sad? Lonely? Excluded?

When I mentioned how often her sister appeared, Stacy's smile closed. Clearly, she was annoyed. She looked right at me and said, "It's always about my sister. My parents cater to her all the time and make excuses for her behavior. I am sick of it." Stacy quickly leaned in to having conversations with her parents about her sister's narcissistic behavior (her description, not mine). She addressed this issue with the same fervor she did business—maybe not with a smile.

3. **Review Act II of your Emotional Timeline.** Compare how you showed up behaviorally and attitudinally before the event or events happened and how you show up today in Act II. Ask yourself, "What recent or current events in my life have a clear connection to my Act I?"

   For example, when she was an adult, Stacy and her family moved to Latin America so she could take an expatriate position in her company. She didn't call her parents much, and she never called her sister. Her parents' doting on her sister, and their choice not to recognize Stacy's value, had created too much emotional distance between them.

   Another way to approach this question is to look at what you're struggling with today in your work or in your life, then ask yourself questions like:

- Do I fail to speak up because I think I'm unworthy, incompetent, or not valued?
- Am I less confident than my peers?
- Do my peers seek out my help, expertise, or guidance?
- Have I closed off relationships, whether on purpose or not?
- Has the event or series of events caused me to become less achievement-oriented, less driven? Have I stopped advocating for myself to superiors?
- Am I often off in my thoughts rather than being present with my kids and spouse?

- How have events from the past impacted my relationships with my friends or colleagues?
- Have they affected how I share my views and opinions with other people in the room—either at home or at work?
- Do I typically experience sadness, depression, worry, or uncertainty?

You could also review recent comments from your boss, colleagues, or family members. Examine all of your emotional data to see what you might have overlooked or buried. Describe your current challenges, just like Lisa did when she chided herself for her low scores. Then scour your Act I timeline for an event that emotionally resonates with what you're facing today.

4. **Discover your "aha" moment by seeking what connects your present-day challenges with the events or people in your past that represent your block.** Even though Stacy was incredibly successful, she was upset because she never received the attention that her sister did. Consequently, Stacy distanced herself from her parents. Her mom missed their relationship, but, because she was angry, Stacy couldn't lean in to their relationship.
5. **Identify the person or persons involved with the event on your Emotional Timeline.** Eventually, you may need to have a conversation with the person who caused your block (which I'll help you through in the next chapter). It's wise to slow down for a moment and think about whom you are really angry at. In Stacy's case, she had to ask herself if she was truly upset with her sister, her mother, her father, or herself.

   You may need a while to recognize your block, even if you know your emotionally resonant events. Or you may know your block while not being aware of its emotionally resonant events. In either case, I urge you to put your chart away for a while and return to it another day. When you do, you may remember other events or conversations, which you can add to your visual timeline. Again, bring the individual cast members of your Act I to mind. Recall your formative scenes. Remember: You're an audience member watching the play of your life unfold before you. How is that play making you feel? What characters stand out, for good or ill? What moments seem to affect the outcome of the play the most?

What If You Still Don't Know What's Blocking You?

As you read through the following further ways to discern what could be blocking you, please keep these three guiding lights before you:

- **Be patient.** This work isn't meant to be done overnight. Familiarize yourself with the concepts, ask yourself the questions, then come back and truly reflect on how the questions apply specifically to your life. As I mentioned earlier, I often work with clients for one to two years. Be patient with your progress.
- **Continually reexamine yourself.** Don't let this become a one-and-done instance of self-reflection. Return to these questions in a week, a month, a year. You may need more information from the people in your life before you're truly prepared to answer some of these questions about yourself.
- **Lastly and most importantly, be kind to yourself.** Done with purpose, this is hard work. For some of you who revisit your childhood, it can be easy to focus on what went wrong. Yes, you want to understand what occurred and fully feel your emotions. However, make bettering yourself be your North Star. Throughout the process, be kind to the child you were and the person you are today.

Let's say you've completed the steps to identify your block through your ETL, yet you still can't pinpoint what's blocking you. Do you actually have one? Here are a few more ways to tell.

On the whole, my clients understand their blocks in four ways:

1. **They immediately identify what person and event most negatively impacted them during their childhood.** Stacy is a good example. She always knew that her jealousy of her parents' attention to her sister was impeding her progress. For many of my clients, they recognize their block quickly because of the visceral reaction they have—their stomach knots up—to recalling a certain memory. Since that's not you, keep reading.
2. **They're truly oblivious.** They have no inkling that an event from their childhood may be significantly holding them back in some way today. Often, repression and suppression are at work, both of which protect us from pain. Repression is an unconscious, involuntary psychological defense mechanism that buries the harmful event so deeply, you're not even aware of its existence. Suppression is a conscious, voluntary psychological defense mechanism that effectively gives you the shovel to cover up the hurt. You bury it under the lies of "I'm too busy," "I'll get to it someday," or "It's not really affecting me." Whether you're repressing or suppressing what negatively happened to you as a child, the fact remains: You're still in pain. Those who are oblivious often need someone to hold up a mirror to them, whether that's a coach with a practice like mine, a trusted counselor, or specific feedback from those closest to you.
3. **Their block is work-related or home-related.** In other words, it's a block that isn't related to their Act I. (A block doesn't only happen in childhood, yet the most significant ones typically do.) Smaller events throughout your career may keep you from leaning into real conversations. For example, Bill, a smart, wonderful, soft-spoken and kind manager, was often berated by his condescending manager for sharing uninteresting insights. Over time, Bill stopped speaking up and shut down. When he started working for another leader, the manager ended up firing him because Bill wouldn't share his ideas. This smaller block could have been handled quickly if Bill had spoken to the first manager and given him feedback on his own, or with the

help of Human Resources. An example of a home-related block is the all-too-typical relational difficulties between a daughter-in-law and her mother-in-law. In these instances, those closest to you can provide feedback about what they perceive as your major blocking issue.

4. **They legitimately have no block, or they've already done the challenging interior work of overcoming their block.** These clients are in the minority since a majority of us have issues in our past that we still need to face with courage and optimism. If you consider yourself in this category, I urge you to review the development areas for your home environment. Also, get real with yourself through what I call "Authentic Leadership" questions: Can you articulate who you are as a leader? Do you know your values? Do you know how other people can be successful with you? Do you tell them? Do you know what your leadership purpose is here on earth? If you live that purpose for the next five to ten years, do you know what your life could look like?

If none of these examples resonate with you, there's one more place we can turn to. Well, nine more places.

When Your Block Is Tied to Your Home Environment

While Homes of Complexity and Trauma tend to result in more blocks, even children from Homes of Stability can experience blocks they're not aware of. For each home environment listed below, I'll provide a simple example of how that home type could lead to a block. When you read about the home environments in which you grew up, pause and consider how that might have contributed to your block. Just know that not all connections clearly lead from Point A to Point B. Remember: Let your emotions guide you. Emotions are data!

Homes of Stability

- In **The Nest**, you may have seldom experienced difficulties. Today, you may be reluctant to open up to others because you feel guilty about the unconditional love, beauty, and joy you experienced as a child.

- In **The Model Home**, if someone said certain values were important but acted in the opposite way, that person's disingenuous behavior may still really bother you, especially if you never told them. When employees say what is important to them behaviorally yet act the opposite way as adults, you will probably get angry.
- In **The Matriarchy**, you may have been hurt or angry that your father (or your mother's partner) left your mother alone to handle everything. You may need to talk directly to that individual to release your grief or anger.

Homes of Complexity

- In **In the Shadows**, you may have felt angry or annoyed that you and your family had to ensure this person and their world was seen as successful. Maybe you thought the person was disingenuous or didn't deserve so much attention. You thought, *This person isn't so special.* Or maybe you felt your activities weren't as important.
- In **The Nomad**, you may have resented having been moved around so much and you missed not having long-term friends. Maybe you resent that your parent's job or other priorities required moving around for upward mobility.
- In **The Phantom Limb**, you may have been angry that your parent left you and the rest of your family for another spouse or partner if there was an affair. Maybe you wonder if you were loved. Or if you caused the person to leave, if it was your fault. Maybe you are angry for your parent dying and leaving you. Or you are angry because you didn't get to say good-bye.

Homes of Trauma

- In **The Maze**, you may have had to manage things to avoid your inebriated parent's emotional outbursts. You may be angry that you had to do it rather than another sibling or another parent, maybe because they had trouble with alcohol too. Today, you may not be able to express your emotions, love yourself, or build intimate relationships and hold real conversations with others, so you need to break through.

- In **Slings and Arrows**, you may have been physically, emotionally, or mentally abused, and you are angry about it or feel ashamed. Maybe you have never spoken to your perpetrator about it and are still holding that anger. You may be even more angry because your parent did the same thing to your sibling or your other parent.
- In **Sounds of Silence**, you may have become angry that your parent didn't protect you or, when you told them about what happened, they didn't do anything. You are probably holding anger toward your violator. Maybe you never told anyone and the secret is your block.

Do You Feel the Weight of a Secret?

Some blocks are more like a secret that weighs heavily upon you. That's partly why uncovering a block can be challenging. Your memory about the person or event may be stubborn or resistant. If you have never talked about your feelings regarding what happened to you, you might be filled with resentment toward the person who harmed you. You may feel guilt or shame for not addressing these things earlier. These feelings of anger, resentment, guilt, and shame consume your energy and focus. And because you're not sharing your feelings, they become a heavy secret you carry.

Sometimes, you might even worry that you won't be liked by people you care about if you reveal what happened to you or share your true feelings. So the content of the secret remains hidden and grows heavier emotionally over time within you. You may turn your thoughts and feelings inward and blame yourself, causing you to have a series of self-limiting beliefs like *I am not worthy of love* or *No one will believe me if I say things, so I should keep my mouth shut.*

I call these kinds of feelings "emotional loads" that can carry so much weight they become blocks. As emotional loads form, they consume your energy and detract from your focus. If the emotions tied to events are kept secret, they become even more burdensome.

Once you connect an event from your childhood to the ways in which it's still impacting you today, you can bring your leadership game to another level—just like Lisa did. Other people might have reacted to getting kicked out of school by becoming depressed or allowing the moment to defeat them. Lisa used that rejection to motivate herself and fuel her drive to become successful. She'd wanted to prove the people in her new high school wrong. They could kick her out of school, yet they couldn't take away her grade point average. She eventually played college sports and earned a degree from an elite university before becoming a rising business executive. Yet, as you know, she eventually felt stuck. Siloed. *Blocked*. How did she overcome it?

She conducted a lot of interior work to truly understand how the people and events in her first eighteen years, especially that administrator, had impacted her so deeply that it was still affecting her as an adult. When she realized just how devastating being kicked out of school had been to her younger self, she had to decide what to do with that revelation. Would she seek an apology from the administrator, even decades removed from the event? Would she speak to a group of people in the city about what had transpired so they could learn from her experience? Would she seek out the parents who wanted her kicked out?

Ultimately, Lisa chose to confront the administrator, to tell him how his words and actions had impacted her life. She didn't need an apology; she just needed to say it out loud, to express her feelings about the experience. His response didn't matter to Lisa. This was wise of her because his response proved to be disappointing. Before she spoke to him, Lisa and I had several discussions in which she unpacked and formulated her goals for the conversation. She wanted to see him in person; however, health reasons prevented her from doing so. She had to call.

When she said her name and briefly reminded the administrator of the event, he said he didn't remember that moment. Still, Lisa pressed on. She calmly and clearly said, "I don't want anything from you. I just want to tell you something. I have carried this around for twenty-five years and need to share." She proceeded to convey the positive and negative outcomes of what had happened all those years ago. Despite his denial, defensiveness, and lack of any apology, Lisa still felt good about the call. She'd unburdened herself and had finally closed that long-open chapter of her life. She felt free.

Now she could turn her attention away from her past and toward her present. She recognized that her lack of trust was holding her back from building relationships with other people. Because of what she'd endured and overcome, she had to learn how to share affection with others at work and tell them what they meant to her. She opened up emotionally, embraced vulnerability, and began to share her experiences with her team. Having grown up in The Nest, where she had long been encouraged to be brave, Lisa confronted her lack of trust and told the group how upset she was by her scores. She went even further and told her team how the events of her childhood had shaped her recent actions. When she finished, her team pulled her in for a group hug. They also began to see her in a new light. She'd become a stronger leader.

And what about her conflict with Paul? She prioritized cultivating a healthy working relationship with him. She worked to build trust with him so they could be successful together.

Lisa had toppled her blocking boulder.

Now the strong current of her leadership could run unimpeded to its full purpose.

This turned out to be an incredible gift as she died a few years later from cancer, at the age of fifty-three. Lisa forever impacted me, and I miss her so much. In my final texts to her, when she was at her weakest, I reiterated how proud I was of her for calling that administrator. She replied, "I have come a long way with your coaching and know I have many people who love me. I have learned how to accept, acknowledge, and appreciate that." I also feel joy that she finally freed herself from the block that had plagued her for so long.

If you need to likewise confront the person responsible for your block, I have a few suggestions.

[10]

How to Confront—and Maybe Even Forgive—the Ones Who've Hurt You

I walked into an executive's home and saw the comfy couch-filled living room that we would use for our high-performance teamwork event. We were about to start the two-year process by sharing life stories and learning the personality characteristics of everyone on the team. However, I'd heard there was likely going to be some normal pushback. These kinds of meetings almost always included someone who thought I was asking too much of them in a workplace setting. *Share my emotional highs and lows with the people I work with? No way. Never.*

As pre-work, I'd asked everyone to bring five or six pictures of the most important people or places in their lives. I told them, "Be ready to share your cast of characters from your childhood and what that childhood world was like, along with your greatest joy and deepest sorrow from your life overall." Their leader went first and vulnerably shared her life story. Each member of the administrative leadership team was mesmerized.

I thanked her for sharing, and I thanked everyone else for doing their homework. Then I turned to the group and said, "Now it's your turn. Each of you is going to share some of the emotional highs and lows of your life. Who wants to be first?"

I paused and scanned the room for reactions. I saw a few smirks, a few blank stares, and at least one deer in the headlights. The woman who would surprise me smiled at my question. She appeared calm, relaxed, and approachable. Since I'd led these kinds of group sessions before, I wasn't concerned. I knew that some in that room would need encouragement to open up. Everyone would need to embrace vulnerability and implicitly trust everyone else. There would be secrets they were concerned to show, or facts about their lives that they purposely kept buried because they were painful. For some workplace environments, this can be a tall order—but not here, as I would soon learn.

As each person shared from their timeline—with no pushback whatsoever—I was glad to hear how open the group was being. Maybe they hadn't all bought into what I was teaching, but still, they were going along with the process to see where it would lead.

Then we got to Frances, their Human Resources leader. When it was her turn to share, I noticed that she got choked up. When she mentioned growing up with her brother, she held back tears.

I didn't prod for more when she stopped talking. Neither did anyone else. Something told me not to. I wasn't sure if other people noticed or not, but my gut said that she had been sharing, seemingly for the first time, a deeply personal part of her story.

I moved us on to the next person. As soon as our meeting ended, I approached Frances alone in the hallway and gently asked, "Is there something there with your brother?"

I could tell I'd caught her in a vulnerable moment.

She replied, "Pam, I have never given voice to what happened to me until now."

I thought, *There's the block, and it seems immense.*

I asked her, "Will you trust me? Will you meet me in New York and share your entire Emotional Timeline with me one-on-one?"

With her tears still fresh, she nodded softly.

I knew that if she could practice sharing her story vulnerably with me, she could discover what was stopping her from becoming all she could be.

It was a start.

I met with Frances in Westchester, New York, and together we built her Emotional Timeline. Her family was very religious. Her paternal grandfather had been a charismatic preacher, so her father had found acceptance in his church. Frances's mom had even converted her faith to attend the same church as her husband, where she would teach Sunday school. As Frances recalled, "In our home, it was all about living our lives on the right path because we wanted a positive afterlife."

Her emotional highs included joining her mom in helping the community. She remembered "the intimate impact she had on others." She was a longtime Sunday school teacher who, often with Frances in tow, would go into remote areas of the community and invite children from troubled families to church. As Frances recalled, "While at church, these children received lots of love from my mom, which often included a big hug with a big smile, candy, and sometimes quarters or a dollar. She wanted them to know that despite their hardships at home, there was greatness in the world and certainly within themselves."

Frances's father struggled with the church's rules and was volatile at home. She also recalled how the church's acceptance of her sometimes temperamental father made him a more caring person, which rubbed off on her. In those memorable moments, Frances said, "I learned to love and care about people by watching my parents at their best."

However, it wasn't always possible for her to be at her parents' side. Her father was often away on business. Her mother worked two jobs. And so, starting when Frances was six years old, she was often left home alone—along with her twelve-year-old brother. Over the span of two years, he crossed her sexual boundaries three or four times, each instance a horrifying experience that she buried as deeply as she could. She told no one.

And her emotional low would silently devastate her life for decades to come.

Not only had her brother crossed her sexual boundaries, but she also recoiled every time her father made sexist and derogatory jokes about pretty women passing on the street. Consequently, Frances never wanted to draw unwanted attention like that, whether positive or negative. "I rarely wore a V-neck," she told me. "I never went sleeveless."

This tendency to hide herself showed up at her office. When she spoke, she would put something between herself and the people in the room—like a piece of paper or a chair—to protect herself. She never actively looked for a promotion, either. She didn't want to network or put herself "out there." As she told me, "I wanted to let my work speak for itself. I just wanted people to think I worked hard and earned my place."

She closed herself off in other ways too. "I didn't share my emotions. I did have empathy and compassion for people. I would defend others but not let people get to know me." Ultimately, accounting suited her because she could hide behind a computer.

Frances's childhood experiences did help her build strengths, including an observer's keen eye. She was constantly on alert for when a situation with a colleague might explode in emotion (just as she'd experienced with her father), and was often able to defuse situations. She also had a genuine fondness for other people and a desire to find ways to help them. Although she liked solving the puzzles that came with accounting, she dreamed of moving into a different role where she could help others grow and follow their life and career dreams.

She had all the ingredients to become a great leader—if she could overcome the block she had formed from growing up in an environment that included Slings and Arrows but was dominated by Sounds of Silence.

She knew that to become the kind of person she wanted to be, she'd have to confront—and maybe even forgive—the people who'd hurt her.

The Two Feelings That Will Prevent Progress

If the person who's hurt you still controls how you show up in your leadership and in your life, you won't be able to move into your full potential until you deal with that person. This doesn't mean you're required to love them or even have a relationship with them. It doesn't mean you have to reconcile with them (since reconciliation requires both parties to move toward each other). Yet it does mean asking yourself hard questions: How do I move past that deep pain? Do I forget them? Confront them? Forgive them?

Dr. Bob Enright, a psychologist specializing in forgiveness at the University of Wisconsin, pioneered a study in the early 1990s that created a model to help you forgive someone who has hurt you. During the first of Dr. Enright's phases, *uncovering*, you must find the emotional pain you feel because of what the offender did or said. You need to understand who did what to whom as objectively as you can. If the offense was significant, you may have to work through all the layers of pain and anger and recognize the effect of this act on you.

To do this, you'll have to tune in to your emotions to better understand your block and who might have caused it. This often requires coming to grips with one or both of two highly influential feelings. In my experience with my clients who've been significantly hurt by someone in their past, they are most often in denial or in a rage. Those in denial want to act like the person never hurt them or they don't want to admit to the severity of the hurt. Those in a rage want to get even.

Denial makes sense. It's often our first reaction to bad news or an unwelcome change. It's a normal psychological defense mechanism that helps us cope. Our minds will not accept the reality of a negative situation until we can summon the emotional resources to deal with the problem. Leaders who experienced trauma as children may cope by denying that it ever occurred or that it was as bad as portrayed by friends or family.

For example, Frances didn't confront her mother about what happened to her until she was in college. And the only reason she chose to confront her then was because her brother had gotten married and had had a daughter. Frances was afraid of history repeating itself. Her mother, who hated conflict, didn't take it well. She denied that anything like what Frances had described could have taken place under her roof. And so her mother's denial perpetuated Frances's denial. She never mentioned the incident to her mother again. In fact, she'd never spoken about the incident with anyone until the day she shared it with me and her colleagues in a subsequent leadership development program.

When I work with someone in denial about the hurt someone else has inflicted upon them in their childhood, I gently walk them through the facts. After hearing their story, I do my best to speak back an objective perspective on what happened to them. I want them to try to separate themselves from the deep emotional connection they rightly feel to the child they were in that terrible moment. They need to somehow become the audience member at the stage play of their life, watching their childhood self act out what could have been the most tragic moment of their life.

Understandably, this is not easy for the client or for me. So I reiterate that we're in a psychologically safe space. I consistently demonstrate my positive intent in trying to help that person see the truth of their experience. And because some clients may need more than one explanation to see past their denial, I am persistent in gently repeating the facts of their story until they can't deny their denial.

In the best instances, once the client has acknowledged how they've been hurt and who inflicted the pain, we begin developing a plan to healthily address the person at the heart of their lowest emotional low. (In the next section, I'll provide the broad steps to this sort of plan.) Yet our emotions are complex and fickle and feed off of each other. As Elisabeth Kübler-Ross wrote decades ago, in talking about grief, denial is most often followed up by anger.

Anger makes sense too. Anyone with a modicum of fairness would be upset at even the thought of a person inflicting any kind of pain on a child. When that pain happens to your childhood self, you may feel that there's no recourse for closure, and the unfairness of it all can make your blood boil. Then you will either suppress your anger or express it. On the whole, suppression happens because anger makes people feel uncomfortable. Expression happens because the anger may feel uncontrollable.

Most of the leaders I work with suppress their anger. They don't allow themselves to feel the whole emotion. They hold it in until it intensifies and then, often unexpectedly, explodes. It's teakettle anger. Freud has his "hydraulic theory" of anger, which suggests that repressing your anger only increases its intensity. If you don't let the anger out, you'll do more harm than good. Holding it in just results in stomach ulcers, high blood pressure, and the eventual blowup at the least opportune time.

Some leaders veer to the other end of the anger spectrum by expressing their anger and allowing it to run free. This can be seen in lashing out at others or throwing objects or even harming themselves. Venting anger may help in the short term. However, it can cause aggressiveness in the long run and may not solve the underlying emotion.

If you feel angry when you think about a person from your childhood, take these steps to deal with your anger and your block. It will help you emotionally and physically.

1. Feel the emotion fully and without self-judgment.
2. Notice how the anger makes you think. However, don't let the emotion become you.
3. Activate your parasympathetic nervous system by taking slow, deep breaths and trying to calm yourself down.
4. Notice any irrational beliefs that come up. Ask yourself: How can I dispute these beliefs and look at the situation more logically? Determine if there's trauma related to the event.
5. Try to understand the emotions behind your anger, either alone or by talking to someone, and decide how to proceed, considering the underlying emotions, not just the anger.

While you may not feel less angry, becoming aware of how and why you think the way you do will help you make better decisions. Unless you deal with your anger, the effects of it will likely recur. Think about how you can constructively use the energy of your anger to improve things (and not just out of vengeance).

To effectively confront the person who's hurt you, you need to have dealt with your denial and anger first. It may take days, months, or years. Just be sure that you've worked on yourself first before taking these next significant steps.

How to Confront the Person Who's Hurt You

As I tell my clients, the best way to break free of a block is to confront the person who hurt you with an honest and direct conversation about what happened. Sometimes, talking to a counselor, friend, or coach can be enough. You may just need to say the words out loud and have your feelings acknowledged. However, for many people, the conversation must be with the person who caused the block. No matter who you end up speaking with, it takes courage to lean in and have this emotionally frank exchange with people who have hurt you.

When I coach my clients on addressing their block, I rely on this process:

1. Choose whom to talk to.
2. Set your goals and plan for safety.
3. Have the conversation.
4. Forgive them.
5. Forgive yourself.

Let's discuss each step at length.

1. Choose Whom to Talk To

Most people will want to talk directly to the person who's hurt them. Yes, that will be challenging. In the following steps, I'll give you tools to overcome that challenge.

What if you can't speak to that person? What if they've passed away? What if you simply can't bring yourself to speak to them (which is perfectly legitimate)? Identify other people in your childhood cast who were tangentially involved in the issue. Seek to gather more information about the event in question. For example, maybe your father hurt you and your mother has information about his family or lifestyle that could help explain his behavior.

Frances had spoken to her mother and effectively received nothing in return. When I asked if she'd considered talking directly to her brother, her answer was sharp and immediate. "No! He chose a life of drugs and addiction. I chose a very different life. It would be like talking to a doorknob. I know he wouldn't be rational."

She paused for a moment, considering who else she should talk to. "I want to talk to my dad. I need to talk to my dad."

I asked why.

"I have questions for him. And I want him to know what happened to me, the impact he also had on me as a human being and how I show up now."

Frances knew exactly who she needed to talk to. And I was encouraged by her courage, to be so bold in choosing to bring up the most traumatic moments of her life with the person who could have prevented them.

However, it's not enough to just identify the person or people you need to talk to. You need a plan.

2. Set Your Goals and Plan for Safety

Prepare for your conversation by thinking through what you'd like to achieve. In my experience, too many people eager to have this kind of conversation run into it without thinking through their actual goals for the conversation.

First, think through what you hope to achieve. Will you ask for an apology? Will you ask just to be heard? Will you seek to learn the truth? Do you want all three? Clarity about what you want addressed is vital before confronting the other person.

If you're going to speak to the person who hurt you, ask yourself these questions beforehand:

- Do I want to say out loud that I was hurt and how the injury occurred so I can release the secret?
- Do I want to receive an apology?
- Do I want them to do something, perhaps to make amends somehow?
- Do I want to learn why they hurt me?
- If they don't give me what I'm seeking, how will I respond?

If you're talking with someone who wasn't responsible for your block yet they can shed light on it, ask yourself these questions beforehand:

- Am I seeking their explanation of my perpetrator's hurtful behavior?
- Do I want to know if other people were aware of my perpetrator's actions?
- If others were similarly affected by their actions?
- Does my memory of the blocking event correspond to those who also witnessed or heard about the event?

Whether you'll be talking to the person who hurt you or someone tangential to your blocking event, write down your goals. Make them as solidified in your mind as you can before you have what will likely be an emotionally charged conversation. Know this too: Frequently each conversation will raise more questions and more goals. When you're in a conversation, make a mental note to later make a physical note of your goals for the next conversation. Going into any conversation with a plan should help your rational mind maintain control over your emotional responses. When you feel your temperature rise, take a breath, remind yourself of your goals, and refocus the conversation.

Next, set your parameters. By that I mean thinking through:

- Where will the conversation happen?
- When will it happen?
- How will it happen?

Schedule a time when *you're* ready to have the conversation and when you won't necessarily broadside the other person. Make sure you're in an emotionally healthy place to have such a hard conversation. And find a location with as few distractions as possible.

Promise me that you will purposefully prepare for this conversation. Slow yourself down and don't rush your preparation. Having these kinds of conversations prematurely, simply because you need to air out your feelings when your anger is still bubbling, most often results in more pain and confusion for everyone involved. The goal of this confrontation is not further confrontation. Remember: It's better to understand why that person did what they did to you *so you can move on.*

To do this, you will also have to create an environment of psychological safety for the both of you. (We'll discuss how to do this in depth in Act III.) Yes, this is cosmically unfair. Shouldn't the person who hurt you be seeking to make amends *with you*? To ensure that you feel safe in sharing vulnerable details of your life? Why is the onus of psychological safety on your shoulders? Because you're the one working to better yourself. And you want this to be successful, right? You may need to do a series of conversations, texts, or letters to set this conversation up well. In our later chapter on creating psychological safety, you'll meet a role model who did this so well with his long estranged father.

One way you can do this for yourself is to role-play your discussion with a trusted family member, friend, or therapist. When you hear yourself speak words and recall memories that you may have never voiced before, you'll be able to stand more firmly behind those words when you have to speak them to the person who hurt you.

Lastly, prepare yourself by framing the conversation as part of your leadership journey. You want to better yourself at work and at home, and you believe a certain experience in your childhood may help you understand more about yourself. Plan to share what you've learned about yourself in that process—and the questions it's led you to ask, both of yourself and of your childhood.

Frances did just that when she began talking to her father about the self-reflective work she was doing with me. She had long called him every Friday night and every Sunday morning. However, their calls were often surface-level. After our discussions, she chose to start engaging her father in real conversations.

Knowing that she eventually wanted to talk to him about the traumatic experiences with her brother, she began paving the way toward that conversation. On one call, she told her father, "I'm learning a lot about myself and my life, and I want to tell you about it. There are many positives, and I've realized that you have significantly influenced my life in many positive ways."

She paused to let her father know just how deeply she felt those words. Then she said, "I also have a few questions for you that could help me."

She paused again, unsure of how he'd respond.

"I'd love to talk."

That was the last response she'd expected. Too surprised, she failed to set a date to get those answers.

Still, every Friday night, her father kept asking if she wanted to talk more about her childhood. Frances got cold feet until a weekend when her husband and son would be away.

"Dad, can you come over so we can talk?"

"I'll be right over."

3. Have the Conversation

How do you know when it's time to have what could be a potentially life-changing conversation? When you're ready to move past what's been blocking you for too long. It's also when you're past denial and anger, and when you need answers, an emotional release, or an apology.

Even with the best of preparation, having the conversation itself can prove daunting. First, you'll be discussing an emotionally intense moment in your life, and it's likely one that the other person wants to forget. Second, you cannot control how the other person responds. They may very well become consumed by emotion, from anger to sorrow to fear to denial. So, again, it's on your shoulders to create a psychologically safe space by maintaining your composure, lucidity, and transparency. Model what you want to see. When your defensive measures deploy, theirs deploy double. Remember: The goal is not mutually assured destruction. It's revelation.

Here are the steps I coach my clients to take in these all-important conversations:

1. If they become angry, acknowledge their anger and show empathy. Say, "I can see you're angry." Ask, "Why are you angry?" Listen without interrupting. If it's true for the moment, you may even say "I understand how you feel."
2. If they can't calm down, let them fully express their feelings (within reason). If they're still heated, suggest continuing the conversation at a later date.
3. If they've calmed down enough for a rational conversation, encourage them to share specifics. Anger is often irrational. When you ask them to focus on specifics, you're encouraging them to be rational.
4. When someone is in denial, specifics are also necessary. Present your evidence using data and facts. It may take more than one explanation for the person to really hear you. In my experience, three times is the magic number.
5. After they've shared their perspective, show your positive intent by stating your willingness to help. You could say, "I'd like to work with you to solve this problem."
6. If they become quiet or withdrawn, ask, "What are you feeling right now?" Don't dismiss their sadness. Instead, say, "I'm sorry that you're sad. Let's talk about it."

To seek the answers you want, you may have to run through these steps multiple times in a single conversation. You may also have to have multiple conversations. Whatever you do, don't rush the process. Keep your rational mind ahead of your emotional responses and you'll eventually discover what you need.

One of Frances's goals in her conversation with her father was to preserve his self-esteem. She wanted to create a psychologically safe environment where he wouldn't become defensive and explode on her—like he had when she was a child.

On the day her father came over expecting to talk about her childhood, she began candidly. "You have been an integral part of my life.

And I have some pain from things that happened early on that I have never shared with you." However, she couldn't bring herself to share her full story. She explained how her sexual boundaries had been crossed. Still, she didn't name the culprit. Frances was worried about what her father might do if he knew it was his son.

Her father was devastated. His first instinct was to find out who had done it. He suspected a family friend who'd once made a lewd comment about Frances while they were all at a pool. Frances didn't want to make her father feel any worse, so she steered the conversation in a different direction. She wanted to make it safe for him to share his truth and for her to share hers. As she later told me, "I needed him to know that I benefited from learning more about my childhood, that this was about me."

When their conversation ended that day, she worried that her father would walk away. However, he responded in the most positive way he could.

They cried together.

"I felt like a heavy weight had been lifted off of me. I felt liberated," Frances told me. She had begun the hard work of moving her block.

A few days later, Frances's father texted her; "I wish we had had that conversation earlier."

She replied, "Me, too."

Frances and her father continued to have real conversations for the next few months, conversations that evolved and strengthened their relationship.

Then came devastating news. Her father had been diagnosed with terminal brain cancer.

4. Forgive Them

Many people define forgiveness as: "I need to stop feeling angry at (or resentful of) the person who hurt me." As a result, too many of us associate forgiveness with letting go of what the other person did or said and moving on. However, genuine emotional forgiveness usually involves more than that. It requires you to replace your negative emotions toward someone who has offended you with compassion and empathy.

You need to understand why someone may have said or done what they did by putting yourself in their shoes. This allows you to forgive them.

It's not often easy.

First, you may feel ready to forgive—until you're in the conversation. If the other person apologizes and you keep ranting about everything they did wrong, you probably haven't examined why you are so upset and how their actions made you feel. You also may not have acknowledged the hurt the person caused you.

In either case, you are telling the other person, *I hold you responsible not just for what you did to me but for how I reacted and responded to what you did. I hold you responsible for my unhappiness*. If you write this down or say it out loud, you should be able to see that it is not valid. Only you can control your reaction, and you shouldn't hold the other person responsible. If you find yourself here, go back two steps and take more time preparing for your forgiveness conversation.

If you haven't taken ownership of your ability to control your reaction, ask yourself what I ask myself in the same situation: "What could I have done differently to change the situation? What's my role in this? Why am I, in this case, still ranting? What's happening *for me*? They apologized, so what's my deal?"

If it's still hard to forgive, you may not have tried to understand the other person by empathetically listening to them or considering their childhood environment. When you hold on to a grudge, you hold tight to your idea that you are right and the other person is wrong. You prevent yourself from seeing anything other than what you want to see. Forgiving can seem much easier if you try to understand the other person's perspective and show empathy for their situation. Dr. Enright says this requires you to substitute the negative emotions you have been feeling with some positive emotions of compassion for the offender's situation. You try to understand why they might have said or done what they did, what they might have been suffering with themselves, and you begin to reframe the offender not as evil but as a human being.

Remember: Forgiveness is not about letting the offender off the hook. If a crime is involved, forgiveness is about something other than whether justice takes place. You'll probably never forget what happened or excuse the other person from their actions. Forgiveness is about what happens inside you, not what happens to them.

Forgiveness is not a sign of weakness. I see it as a rare sign of strength.

You start to offer goodwill to the person within the limits of how much you trust them. If the action was abuse or involved deep trauma, you may just lessen your resentment toward them. (I have learned that some people benefit from counseling during this phase. Such a partner can help you see what you need to see.)

Forgiveness can also be hard when you worry that the traumatic event can happen again. Trust may have been broken, which may change your expectations of the other person. However, since forgiveness is not the same as reconciliation, you can still choose to forgive and let go of your anger and resentment—on your own. Reconciliation occurs between people. Reconciliation means you trust the other person again, which can only happen when both people engage in mutually trustworthy behavior. You may forgive someone yet have no intention to reconcile because you don't trust them, or because it would be unwise or unhealthy for you—e.g., they might abuse you again or they committed another crime against you or someone you love.

Sometimes, when you attempt to forgive someone, you might characterize them as inferior, which may or may not be accurate. For example, if someone criticizes your input, you may characterize that as ignorant, fearful, or paranoid. This may or may not be accurate; however, it protects you by making you feel better about yourself and justifying your actions. Still, it does not help you in your goal of true forgiveness. Please do not do this.

If you forgive those who've hurt you, you free up energy to accomplish other goals. If you're constantly or consistently ruminating about that person, you won't move on to where you could be. Remember: You don't have to love them or even necessarily interact with them; you just need to understand them and then move on.

Choosing not to forgive is a waste of energy.

When you've chosen to forgive, you should start to feel relief, as if you've been released from an emotional prison of unforgiveness, bitterness, resentment, and anger. You may start to find meaning in the suffering you endured, which can sometimes give you a new purpose in life.

Forgiveness is worth the effort. A lot of research links forgiveness to many different health benefits, such as lower anxiety, depression, psychiatric disorders, mortality rates, and stress relief. When you carry negative emotions, especially over an extended period, it causes a constant release of stress hormones like adrenaline and cortisol, which are linked to the previously mentioned health conditions. For yourself, forgiveness is about getting rid of the anger and bitterness that can harm your well-being. You let go of that anger and replace it with compassion. You let go of resentment and any desire for revenge, even if the offender deserves it. You give the gift of acceptance, understanding, generosity, and love to the offender.

With this gift, you help to heal yourself.

Frances received this gift when she finally chose to forgive her brother. It took place in a somber moment, in the aftermath of her cancer-ridden father being placed into hospice care. Unexpectedly, her brother showed up one day to help bathe their father.

Frances was touched. "You have no idea how much that helps," she told him. Then she went deeper—a real conversation spoken from a deep place, a conversation she'd long prepared for, even though she didn't need many words.

She looked her brother in the eyes and said, "I need you. I need you in my life. You are all I have left, and I want to have a relationship with you. I am grateful you are with me in this."

After taking care of their dying father that day, they told each other, "I love you."

The next morning, her phone buzzed her awake at 4:30 a.m. She heard her sister-in-law first, frantic, then a male voice grabbed the phone and said, "I'm Sheriff Jones. Am I speaking to Frances?"

Frances said yes even though she had no idea what was going on.

"Your brother suffered a cardiac arrest this morning. He's been rushed to the hospital."

Frances wept.

Her brother would die later that day.

Six days later, her father passed away too.

5. Forgive Yourself

If you have processed your block and forgiven the person who hurt you, you may feel a freedom you've never felt before. The event that caused your obstruction may not even come to mind, not because you're still in denial, but because you've overcome it. Many people who go through this process discover that part of the weight of the block they carry is related to what they did or didn't do. So you may need to accomplish one last step: relinquishing your feelings of guilt and shame and choosing to forgive yourself for what you did or didn't do—e.g., *I didn't tell my father that I was being abused and I needed him* or *I didn't stand up for my mother when my father was hitting her.*

Forgiving yourself is not easy. For instance, if you have grown to love or respect the person who's hurt you, and you don't have a loving relationship with yourself, you may be able to get past their mistake more easily and find it difficult to forgive yourself. However, forgiving yourself may be even more important than forgiving others. It's a critical step to having a better relationship with yourself, a prerequisite for better relationships with others.

The best advice for forgiving yourself is to remember that we are all human beings and, thus, not perfect. We usually do the best we can at the moment. Your goals should be to learn from your mistakes and celebrate that learning, and rather than looking backward in chastisement, look forward to bettering yourself.

While Frances remains devastated by the loss of her family members, she's also grateful for the real conversations she had with her father and brother. Those talks and Frances's acts of forgiveness were instrumental in helping her overcome the block that had been in place since she was a child.

"I have peace," she told me. "I have overcome the losses and grief because I had those conversations. I can now express my feelings. I am more forgiving—less judging. I no longer run scenarios about what could happen if something escalates. Now I can see the patterns in people's behaviors, call them out, and give voice to them. Sharing my stories builds my confidence, especially when I can help people who need to hear them. I am an open book. I am comfortable sharing. I do it if I need to say something on someone's behalf."

She loves to look at interpersonal relationships like a puzzle. Through her keen observation skills and courage to speak the truth, she helps employees at large and members of her team learn how to deal with their struggles. When someone else gets angry, rather than worrying about what she did wrong, Frances has begun to say things like "You seem angry. What's going on with you?" For example, she seeks to know if their purpose aligns with their work, or if they're wrestling with an issue with their boss. Ultimately, she's asking, *What's this about, really?*

Frances, now fifty, is very proud of the growth she has witnessed in herself. That includes stepping into a new executive role as head of talent development in her company. The puzzles she loved about numbers when she was younger have become one of her superpowers as she's applied the same concept to people.

While she had learned to embrace vulnerability at work by sharing her childhood experiences with strangers, Frances began to feel like she was cheating on her husband. She'd told her male colleagues about her abuse, but not her husband. "It was affecting our relationship," Frances told me. "Everywhere else, I felt liberated and could conquer the world. But at home, my guilt skyrocketed."

She recalled one particular night on the couch next to her husband, the both of them watching TV as on any other regular night. Except this time, she was noticeably upset, then she got more upset that her husband wouldn't ask her what she was so upset about. So she went to bed. The following morning, she told herself, *Come on, Frances. You owe it to him. He's not going to judge you. He loves you.* She recognized that she needed to have a conversation with him too.

Back on the couch, she finally confided in her husband: "There is something I need to tell you." As she relayed the details of what had happened to the young girl she once was, she wept. Transported back in time, she relived the horrors of when she was six so that her husband could know her at a new, deeper, and much more vulnerable way.

After letting her speak, he held her and just repeated all he knew to say. "I'm sorry. I love you. I'm sorry."

It was a breakthrough moment for them.

However, Frances didn't stop there. She then told her son about that experience and lessons about how he needed to honor women's boundaries.

Her son was stunned when Frances told him the story. Then he hugged his mother.

"He told me how sad he was that I had kept this story hidden for my entire life and carried it alone," Frances told me.

Now freed from her self-imposed silence, Frances has blossomed.

"I am a better human," she told me. "I am a better mom. I am a better spouse. I am a better aunt. I am a better niece. And a better leader because of all this."

Confrontation is hard. Forgiving is often harder. However, in my opinion, they may be the most rewarding actions you can take to overcome what's stopping you from living a full and purposeful life, both in your job and at your home.

As we turn to the final act, I want you to think about how far you've come and the challenging work you've accomplished. It's often not easy to look back at your childhood and give it the full consideration it deserves. Thank you for doing that work.

Just like a good story, everything comes together in Act III. You've recalled your cast. You've identified your environments. You've discovered your blocks and have overcome them—or you have a plan to do so.

So what's left?

How to transform those family patterns into real conversations that create meaningful change in your job and in your life.

ACT III

The Role You're Destined For

You've done the hard work of examining your childhood so you can transform your family patterns. If you discovered a block, you've removed it, or you at least have a plan in place to do so. So what's next?

Act III is about improving your life and your leadership right now. You can do this through learning to have real conversations—the kind that go beyond surface-level facts and figures and get to the heart of every matter. The kind that produce results, even if there's conflict. And the kind that enhance relationships.

Once you establish and hone this capability, you will become a more *referentially powerful* leader. By that I mean others will learn that they can trust you because of how authentically and vulnerably you show up at work and at home. Sure, you may land the promotion you've had your heart on for years, but the benefits are much greater than a new title and a bigger paycheck. You will become someone that others want to follow or emulate simply because of who you are. You will become an inspiring leader and a more capable human. And there's an amazing trickle-down effect from your workplace leadership to your home life that so many of my clients have told me was a surprising benefit.

In the following chapters, I'll provide practical next steps. This is the same way I coach all of my clients. Though these steps may seem deceptively simple, I encourage you to consider them deeply and choose to fully incorporate them into your life. You may even want to start a journal that documents your progress as you begin using these proven tools.

If this is Act III of your life, let's make it showstopping.

[11]

How to Have a Real Conversation

Curt Welling knew his company was on the precipice of disaster. A bad decision at this critical juncture could result in the demise of a well-loved nonprofit that had long provided humanitarian help across the globe. As CEO of Americares, it was his job to ensure that didn't happen. Yet, in the aftermath of the Great Recession of 2007, he didn't feel like he had many viable options.

Countless organizations had been caught in its devastating wake, and particularly philanthropic organizations. During Curt's tenure, Americares was entirely supported by others' philanthropy—no endowments, no direct government assistance. As fears of a deepening recession spread, their funding sources had suddenly been cut off. By 2009, their contributions and revenue had dropped by about 30 percent. Enough, as Curt knew all too well, to kill the company.

Knowing that hard decisions were ahead of him, he called his top leadership team together. When they heard just how desperate the situation was, they were stunned, even paralyzed. Curt tried to stay upbeat as a way to model leadership, even if the ship was going down. Still, no solutions formed. As the meeting ended and several leaders stood up to leave, his CFO—let's call her Lori—spoke up. She put words to what many in the room were likely thinking but were too scared to say: "You're all naïve. We're not dealing with reality here."

The conference room went quiet.

In the throes of a make-or-break moment, their typically quiet and guarded CFO had let her true opinion be known to everyone. The room held its breath to see how their CEO would respond. Lori filled the silence. "If we leave now, we'll be back in a few weeks and the situation will be worse."

Faced with such blunt truth, Curt nodded. "Lori's right. We cannot nip and tuck our way through a crisis like this. Lori, what do you think we should do?"

"We need a plan, Curt."

The team sat back down and discussed their options, none of which were good. They spent an hour developing a plan. Ultimately, they were forced to lay off a third of their staff, which pained Curt and the leadership team tremendously. On a positive note, they also spent a lot of time thinking about Americares's values and, in light of them, how they should go about letting so many of their employees go.

Curt would be the first to admit that his reaction to Lori would have been much different years earlier, before he and I had worked on his ETL (which he was very skeptical about!) and before he had recognized the influences of his childhood on his leadership style. Before he could accomplish more at his job, he had to accomplish work within himself. Yet since he'd done that hard work, he was prepared for Lori's courageous and direct (yet necessary) awakening.

Lori had also been working with my colleague Martha on overcoming her guardedness and how to be vulnerable at work. That she had chosen to speak up in that pivotal moment was a personal breakthrough for her. Years later, Curt would observe, "I'm quite sure that conversation preserved Americares through the crisis."

Their bold, authentic, vulnerable interaction is what I call "a real conversation." It led to company-saving results, yet it required one woman's bravery to just get real, both with her colleagues and with herself.

In a business context, having a real conversation means that opinions and perspectives on both sides of the conversation are expressed honestly, with no fear of rupturing the relationship between the participants. Even when it will mean individuals challenging their superiors' perceptions and decisions, they speak their truth. They are genuine and authentic. They drop any pretense or protective shield they may hold and disclose what is in their head *and* in their heart. They embrace their vulnerability so that the conversation can enter the realm of uncertainty, which leads the participants to generate unexpected possibilities and outcomes.

Boldness and bravery are essential to enter this realm. Participants in real conversations are willing to share a part of themselves that they keep hidden. Real conversations require mutual vulnerability and intimacy. This element of simultaneous self-disclosure makes conversations more compelling, stimulating, and meaningful.

When you have these real conversations with individual leaders who build their self-awareness in this way at scale, huge performance and cultural goals can be achieved. Recall Tom Linebarger, whom you met in the Prologue and whose origins were in the Matriarchy. In 2009, Tom was promoted to president by the company's Board of Directors, with the hope that he would become chairman and CEO two years later, which he achieved.

Jill, whom you've also already met, was his HR leader. While she was quite faith-based, Tom was an atheist. Jill didn't know if they would align from a values point of view. Her core values included winning together, vulnerability, and faith. She wondered how she could work with and achieve great things with this new leader. Two prior leaders had questioned whether her decisions would be biased by her faith. As challenging issues arose, I wondered if Jill and Tom would be vulnerable with each other in order to find a successful way forward for their company.

Tom had several strong values too, including justice and fairness. He also wanted to have fun and work hard with people he cared about, while addressing the company's issues. He loved solving big problems, one of which was growing the next leadership level at Cummins. So, while Jill and Tom's values were not the same, they had integrity about their principles and aligned their goals for Cummins. This made Jill realize that even though Tom didn't share her faith, he did share an aspirational worldview to make Cummins a successful organization by developing exceptional leaders at all levels. Jill saw that Tom would support her vision of developing anyone classified as a leader at Cummins. She wanted all of them to see themselves as leaders and invest in their own development. In line with her values of winning together and accountability, her goal was for all the leaders to collectively change how they were leading, to see themselves as leaders, and not to wait for their managers to make every decision.

Tom was on board, and Jill wanted to orchestrate it. Tom became so supportive of Jill for two reasons: First, they were united in their aspirations for the company. Second, Jill and I focused on turning her Model Home strengths as a Values Crusader into an essential ingredient of her success as a leader.

When I asked Tom how he'd worked with Jill in the early days of his CEO tenure, he said, "I had a deep respect for Jill's capabilities and found her smart and caring as a person when she was my colleague. Thus, I was heavily tilted toward finding a way to work with her. Her values always aligned with mine, especially deep caring about our hourly workforce and standing up for the rights of our people versus letting bureaucracy reign." Jill's faith wasn't a factor for Tom, yet because she was quiet and unwilling to participate on his leadership team, he wondered if she would make it.

While Tom remained as committed an atheist as Jill was faithful, they became true partners. Together, they created an inspiring leadership culture at Cummins. Working with me and my firm, they built nearly twenty-five high-performance teams globally and transformed Cummins's top three hundred leaders using my authentic leadership process. Using what Jill had learned, we built a leadership development experience for ten thousand leaders so they could become more self-aware and start having real conversations in every sphere of their lives.

What all this shows is that you can have fundamental differences interpersonally—and you will. Tom's and Jill's values are just one example. Once you get transparent and have a real conversation with each other about whatever is facing you, you can likewise achieve amazing results.

You also learn how to harness the strengths of each person's environment to engage better in real conversations. Tom grew up in the Matriarchy, just as I did, and Jill grew up in the Model Home. As we worked on their company's cultural transformation, we had numerous conversations about goals and opinions, including our own as individuals, those within our relationships, and how to support the employees in their world. As individuals, Jill had the strength of a Values Crusader and fought for the rights of others. As the initiating sponsor of the leadership transformation and as a matriarch's son, Tom actively partnered and depended on us. As a matriarch's daughter, I was a Driver and held responsibility for the quality of the leadership and organizational change processes we were working toward. Tom and I also saw all the problems to solve and were determined to achieve them. Jill always figured there was a way to address them. We all shared a goal of excellence. We discussed how to harness our individual strengths. We dealt with shared values and conflicting values. And we provided feedback to each other on our developmental issues. We had numerous challenging conversations, sometimes fun, sometimes emotional. Yet they were always real.

You can too, and they could very well lead to results you could only imagine.

These kinds of conversation don't happen as often as they should, both in the workplace and at home, and for myriad reasons. Yet, after experiencing real conversations, you'll never want anything less. Over the next few chapters, you're going to learn the proven steps for having real conversations. Your inability to hold real conversations may be holding you back from your full potential as a leader and a human.

Thinking any differently is naïve.

How do you have real conversations?

I'm so glad you asked.

[12]

Create Psychological Safety

Simply put, Jeff and Tony weren't getting along. Both were successful, accomplished senior leaders in their company, fully capable of leading their people well. Yet when it came to working with each other, and especially when hard decisions had to be made, they could barely stand to be in the same room. Because of their status within the company, their failing relationship had ramifications far beyond a tense working relationship. Communication broke down, if it even happened at all. Their teams began to struggle. Other higher-ups took notice.

Both leaders knew something had to change, and quick.

Jeff and Tony needed to have a real conversation, one that pulled no punches and got to the source of their conflict. They both understood that the company's success depended on them learning to work well together. What they didn't understand was that to get there, to be able to talk to each other without a filter and from the depths of their humanity, they needed a new environment. After working with thousands of leaders and hundreds of executive teams, I've discovered that *psychological safety* is the key to unlocking real conversations. It's the magic. It's the first and most necessary step that I believe too many leaders look past or never even consider.

Psychological safety, most importantly, is about creating an environment in which everyone in the room feels free to say what they think and feel emotionally and aren't afraid of reprisal. They are at ease raising and discussing interpersonal tensions, providing behavioral feedback to direct reports, peers, and bosses, and debating political, social, or business issues. There is no fear because they know there are no repercussions for sharing their truth with those involved. Psychological safety allows team members to be courageous and take risks. They will speak up, disagree openly, and raise all their worries and concerns. Employees feel free to admit mistakes, bare their underbelly, and be vulnerable. When psychological safety is present in the workplace or at home, it creates a more innovative, stronger community because it's a safe space to share thoughts and ideas without judgment.

These conversations are also intimate. The word *intimacy* means different things to different people. Some may feel discomfort when hearing the word (especially if you're a woman like me and you're all too familiar with people making unwanted advances). Others might feel congenial warmth as they think of the intimacy between two friends or colleagues. In the context of real conversations at work or at home, I define intimacy as *closeness*, *familiarity*, or *friendship*. As you read through this chapter, keep those words in mind.

According to the Gallup Organization, which created the Gallup Q12 Survey on employee engagement, one of the most significant impacts on a person's morale is whether they have a "best friend at work." We lose something powerful if we hold back from having dear friends at work. Most of us crave these connections with the people around us, including those in the workplace. My goals in having a real conversation with someone includes sharing personal feelings and worries, being truthful, and being warm, all while honoring physical and emotional boundaries.

Ultimately, becoming a better leader is intimate work because it involves genuinely caring about another person and continuously thinking about how you can help them in their situation. Simply put, Jeff and Tony were not thinking about how they could help each other.

So I helped them.

How I Create Psychological Safety

Come be a fly on the wall during my meetings with Jeff and Tony. You'll get a glimpse of how someone with many years of expertise creates safe environments so that real conversations can take place. Then, in the following section, I'll provide you with a step-by-step guide so that you can begin deepening relationships beyond what you may have thought was ever possible.

I met Jeff alone first. I'd heard that he was more upset by the situation and so I'd initiated this intervention. While I always prefer to meet my clients in person, we met virtually due to our schedules and locations. Since I was at my house, at least my home office conveyed the kind of informality I prefer for creating a psychologically safe environment. I purposefully choose warm, approachable colors and comfortable textures to create an inviting environment.

My first step to connect with Jeff was by being genuine, warm, and vulnerable as we started our virtual meeting. Following the guidelines of my head, heart, hands check-ins, I shared what I was nervous about, excited about, and struggling with. I also said that I'd happily refer him to another coach on my team if he didn't feel any chemistry with me or that he could trust me. I wanted him to know that who he works with was as much his choice as mine. I needed him to maintain the power in the situation.

Jeff thanked me and told me that another one of his colleagues had spoken highly of working with me. He said he was approaching our conversation in the spirit of "Why wouldn't I trust you?"

This certainly made me feel happy. I liked him and it was a good start. Still, we had work to do to build trust with each other.

I promised that our next meeting would be at his office, even though that would require considerable travel from me. Yet I knew that in our next meeting I'd be coaching him through building his Emotional Timeline. I wanted him to see that I'd listened and heard him say how important it was for him to have face-to-face, in-person interactions. I wanted him to know that I would be responsive to his needs in the future. I was also sure to turn off my phone so that no distractions would interrupt us. Over time, Jeff became a role model of being present for me. He turned off his phone, closed his door, and told his admins not to disturb us.

As I was building my relationship with Jeff, I was doing the same with Tony. I needed to learn what they thought about one another—what they were struggling with in their relationship and what needed to change. I also wanted to start getting to know both of them so that I could help them when the time was right.

Obviously, I spent time doing an Emotional Timeline with each of them. Both leaders needed to know that I would support them as they shared details of their lives, experimented with new behaviors, spoke their truth, or pushed back on each other. They needed to know that I cared about both of them and would jump in and help them, even when they screwed up. In fact, each wondered whether he was at fault. Tony recalled consistently telling his team not to partner with Jeff's people. Was he to blame for their tension? Jeff recalled that he wouldn't share people or financial resources with Tony. Both felt guilty.

During our work together, complications soon arose. The company's CEO, Marvin, whom they both reported to, wanted me to share my views on whose fault it was. This was a no-go for me. If I was going to build trust with Jeff and Tony, I couldn't turn around and blame one of them. I sat down with the CEO and bluntly explained my position. "If that's what you want from me, I'll fire myself." Fortunately, Marvin recognized my actual role in the process and said, "I get it. You're here for Jeff and Tony's development as leaders, not the assessment of them."

When I next spoke to Jeff and Tony, I explained what had happened. I emphasized how much I treasured their privacy and that I wouldn't share their stories with anyone unless they wanted me to and they were present. I assured them that nobody would know the details of our work together unless they revealed it or if they authorized me to.

They nodded, and I could tell they believed me. That was reassuring. In that moment, I had chosen to act out of professional love for my clients and not out of fear for losing my job.

Tony was very worried about his wife's frustration with him not being around, and he felt guilty for not being able to attend his children's events. Jeff's mom was terminally ill, which consumed Jeff with worry. How both

Tony and Jeff were showing up at home was concerning them. Since my work is about caring about the whole person, I wanted them to know we would prioritize talking about these challenges too.

I told Jeff and Tony that the next step in our process was to arrange a three-way conversation between the two of them and me.

They were confident that I knew a lot about personality theory, and I had lots of insights about each of them based on their Emotional Timelines. They knew that the connections I was drawing between their life stories and what was showing up in their personality results was valid enough to listen to. Over time, they also realized that they needed to build their competence in listening skills, vulnerability, feedback, and conflict to help their teams through this moment of tension. Next, we needed to talk through each of their recollections of the events, assumptions, and inferences they were making about each other, and the resulting emotions they were feeling about one another. However, they needed to be ready to give that kind of feedback to each other. Another form of competence and skill on their parts! I was creating a true sense of psychological safety for Jeff and Tony. If I didn't do this well, Jeff would never have the trust or courage to share his authentic self with Tony and vice versa. Plus, I wanted them to focus on growing as leaders, not on who was right.

Tony wasn't quite ready. He needed to look in the mirror first.

I wasn't surprised. I'd seen his defensiveness very early on. I couldn't tell him, though, until he could hear it. However, I knew Tony to be a data guy. He respects facts. To challenge him to change, I'd have to prove to him why. So I shared interview data from others about his defensiveness and common defensive personality characteristics, like his level of guardedness and containment of his emotions. When he saw the data reflecting the truth he didn't want to admit to, he softened.

Tony and I then worked together to prepare for our meeting with Jeff. I coached Tony on how and what to be vulnerable about, such as his health concerns, his family, and other personal matters. While we discussed some complex issues in Tony's life, I needed to convey unconditional support and love. I needed to focus on building that sense of safety for Tony as we approached that crucial meeting with Jeff. I also needed Tony to be ready to be vulnerable.

When the meeting day came, I was confident in Tony's readiness. I smiled when Jeff kicked off the meeting by looking at Tony and saying, "We already know each other well." I hear this a lot.

Just wait, I thought to myself.

When it was Tony's turn to share, he explained how he grew up in The Nest. "I was surrounded by unconditional love and people I cared about. We talked about everything. This is why I am so direct today and shower my people with care."

Jeff nodded his head and said things like, "Oh," "Ah," or "Hmmm," as he began to see the connections between who Tony was as a leader and his childhood environment. When I hear these sounds, I know meaningful insights are being gained.

Over the next ninety minutes, Jeff and Tony had a real conversation for the first time about their childhoods and how they affected their leadership. Both gentlemen were vulnerable and authentic, and the conversation was sometimes touching and intimate.

When they were through, Jeff said, "This was a great meeting. I learned a lot."

Afterward, Tony approached me and said, "That was actually fun."

I flew home that night on an emotional high. We had held the meeting in Jeff's location. All that work creating psychological safety had led to a moment that could change the course of Jeff and Tony's relationship and their teams' ability to achieve amazing results.

This is what gives me genuine joy. When people speak their truth together and their outcomes change for the better.

How You Can Create Psychological Safety

If psychological safety is my secret sauce, what are the ingredients?

When you set out to intentionally create an environment of psychological safety, I encourage you to proceed sequentially through the list of suggestions that follows, for the first time only. However, as you become more familiar with these techniques, you will find yourself using them "out of order" or even simultaneously. When you are adept at this, you'll find yourself bouncing around, applying what is necessary for the situation. Employ them as you see fit and always use your emotions as data to guide your next steps. This is not a checklist to be accomplished. It's a map to help guide your way. Sometimes you may not start at the beginning, so to speak. So use your intuition to know which step is your next right step. When in doubt, always return to the foundational elements of psychological safety: warmth, vulnerability, and friendliness. Start with a smile.

I offer these steps for when you'll need to establish psychological safety in a one-to-one setting—even with a superior. You may be skeptical that you can create psychological safety when a power differential exists, especially when a boss or senior stakeholder's dysfunctional behavior intimidates you. Remember: You cannot control how someone responds; you can only regulate your behavior. Just try. Assume goodness and do not judge. If someone demonstrates anger or defensiveness, that's on them, not you. (Refer to the tools within this book on how to deal with anger or denial, in Chapter 11.) Typically, if someone reacts this way, they are going through something. Don't take it personally. Try to help them through whatever they are facing. The steps to creating psychological safety listed here work. You have to be patient and persistent.

Every suggested step has one goal in mind: to ensure that the real conversation you want to take place will happen in a psychologically safe environment. The most challenging part of a meaningful conversation is done beforehand. When you do this prep work well, you've set the stage for true connection.

Meet in an Informal Environment

Choose a place where the other person can relax and examine their thoughts and feelings comfortably. To me, living rooms are ideal. They have couches and a place to put down your coffee or tea. No boardroom tables to separate you. If you're limited to your workplace, try to grab a room without glass walls so no one can see in. If you are in a conference room, do not sit across from one another. Sit at the end of the table and have your colleague sit next to you on the side of the table. Strive to find comfy chairs. Today, some offices have them for collaborative discussions. My clients know that having water or drinks and tissues is my go-to. Set a scheduled time and length to meet, with as few distractions as possible.

Note: Sometimes you have to have a tough conversation immediately and do not have time to plan your environment. Not to worry. Imagine a bubble around you and the person or people you are with. Look into their eyes and don't move. Be there for them. I call this the *safety zone*.

Model What You Want to See Through Warmth, Friendliness, and Two-Way Vulnerability

Psychological safety starts with relationship building. It begins with *warmth, friendliness, and a smile*. You enhance your relationships by being *transparent* about your feelings, from what excites you to what anguishes you. You model *vulnerability* in order to discover two-way vulnerability. I view this starting place as my foundation, my place of comfort. The head, heart, hands check-in is an excellent technique to build trusting relationships at the beginning. If you genuinely want to make your colleagues feel psychologically safe, you will need to check in and ask them how they are feeling in the environment and why they're feeling that way. Then you'll need to reciprocate with the same kind of emotional vulnerability. Tell them how you're feeling in that moment and why you're feeling that way. (Remember: Fine isn't a feeling!) If you're honest about what you are feeling first, your partner will be transparent too. These check-ins work!

Be Fully Present and Engaged

Your partner needs to know that they are the most important person to you in that moment. (Remember the bubble.) Being fully present requires empathetic listening and mindfulness, two characteristics I'll discuss in the next chapter. I mention them here to underscore how truly focused I want you to be on the other person when you're having a real conversation.

When possible, be actually physically present. The other person also needs to know that you are focused on them and not distracted by technology or tasks. Put your cell phone away, and not just on do not disturb!

Don't Judge

Your job is not to evaluate. Rather, *assume goodness* and seek to *understand* the other person's actions, thoughts, and beliefs. Most people are good people. They're probably already judging themselves, as are other people. They need your support. You want and need to help them, so put the judgment next to your phone—buried in your pocket.

Maintain Confidentiality

Jeff and Tony needed to know that I wouldn't share what each of them told me about the other. Likewise, your partner needs to know that you will keep your conversation private. The information shared with you will go nowhere, including your family members, partner or spouse, colleagues, or friends. Nowhere, and I mean it!

Provide Unconditional Support

Ensure that the other person knows that you care about them—even, and especially, in their failure. That's the epitome of unconditional. No matter what they've done, you choose to support. Providing this kind of help really means acting out of love. The opposite is acting out of fear, which typically happens when you're thinking about yourself and your own performance. *Am I coming across as competent? Do they think I'm smart?* You're more concerned about your image rather than their situation or their feelings. When you act out of love, you encourage the other person to experiment, to talk to someone directly, and to examine their intentions. You'll sit with the person selflessly to listen as they speak. No matter how much your ego shows up, stay focused on helping the other person be successful.

Appreciate the Whole Person

For someone to grow as a human being, all their life roles must be considered, not just who they are as a leader. How one behaves as a parent, spouse, sibling, child, relative, community servant, and friend must also be looked into. At times, something that happened at home or with a friend can dominate the conversation, and that's okay! It's helpful because you will be able to link the way the other person is showing up with their friend to how they are behaving at work.

Show Your Competence and Skills

Your partner in dialogue needs to know that you have the competence and skills they need to resolve something and help them. As you role-model how interpersonal situations are handled well, their competence can also improve. They learn vicariously through you. If you do not know how to handle a specific situation, seek expertise from someone you know who is strong interpersonally, like a Human Resources person. If you or your colleague are struggling, sometimes counseling is a great solution to handle more challenging situations.

Pace the Conversation

You need to know how quickly or slowly to push someone to see and address the relationship issues they are dealing with or the conversations they need to have. You'll get better at this over time. Pacing is both about science and art. I am making judgments all the time. As a coach, I see the issues very, very early on. The person, though, may not be ready to hear my views or own their role in the situation. I must be patient and wait so they can internalize it. Do the same with the person who needs your help. Offer it—but at the right time and in the right way.

This can feel like walking a tightrope one careful step at a time. The skill is in finding the right pacing, how quickly or slowly you need to push someone to see and address the issues they need to deal with—regardless of how quickly you can see for yourself. As I say when I coach team members, "Timing matters. A person needs to be ready."

Become a Mirror of Truth

If you can tell that the other person isn't "getting it," challenge yourself to speak the blunt truth they need to hear. Yes, you'll get nervous. Your stomach will tighten. Your initial thought may be *They're not going to like this.* But remind yourself that the goal—psychological safety so that a real conversation can happen—is worth your present and momentary fear of rejection. I call this becoming a mirror of truth. You hold up a mirror so that the other person can see a truth about themselves they've been ignoring for too long.

In an upcoming chapter, I'll give you further tools on how to give feedback, i.e., how to be a better mirror.

As you begin to use these steps to create psychologically safe environments for real conversations to take place, give yourself grace. Start by using one or two of the steps above to see how they affect your conversations. As you become more confident in using these steps, add more. Make it a point to practice the steps in *all* of your conversations. You'll be amazed at the depth of relationships that form in the process.

Psychological Safety in Action

With Jeff and Tony, the onus was on me to create psychological safety for them. However, that's been my job with all of my clients for decades. The relevant question for my clients is: Can someone without extensive training and experience create psychological safety for the people they work with?

That's where Curt's story comes back into play. He's an excellent example of a leader who evolved from relying only on his "thinking" skills to being able to create psychological safety for his team so they could all enjoy the benefits of real conversations. Even when Curt announced layoffs at Americares, he understood that the organization was bruised and its people were feeling uncertain. He shared the tough news about the layoffs by embracing it with transparency, empathy, and compassion. That moment revealed the deep change that had occurred within him, from a leader who always had the right answers to a CEO who could tune in to his team's emotional needs.

Of course, to see why Curt was once so staunchly stuck in his head and assured of his rightness, we have to look back. As is typical of children raised in The Model Home, Curt's parents instilled in him a deep sense of right and wrong early on. On a particularly memorable day when he was seven, his parents told him not to leave the house. As he recalled, "I was given boundaries in our neighborhood. Our neighborhood was made up of blocks and quarter-acre lots, and there was a drugstore about four blocks away. I was never supposed to leave the block without being accompanied." Bored at home alone, Curt walked to the neighborhood drugstore a few blocks away. He grabbed a newspaper from the newsstand in the front of the store and brought it home to give to his father.

When his father came home, he asked Curt, "Where'd this paper come from?"

Beaming, Curt replied, "Well, I walked up to Chilson's and I got it for you."

"Well, you know you weren't supposed to leave. . . . Number two, it's not your newspaper. Did you pay Mr. Chilson for it?"

Curt replied, "No, no. It was on a rack outside."

"Well then, son, you stole that newspaper, so we are going up there now."

Curt's father made him go back to Chilson's, give Mr. Chilson the newspaper back, and apologize to him for stealing the newspaper.

Curt never forgot the lesson and knows that his father wasn't tyrannical. He was just values-based.

When Curt began his career working for financial institutions like First Boston and Bear Stearns, the deep sense of fairness and honesty instilled by his parents sometimes worked against him. He was a Values Crusader in a culture that prioritized making money above all else. Curt found himself in trouble with other leaders from time to time when he shared his opinions or questioned unethical decisions. He starkly remembers when he challenged his friend and colleague Oscar on an issue that he thought wasn't in the best interests of a client or the firm. Oscar gave Curt a withering look and told him, "It must be hard work to always know what the right thing to do is."

As Curt would later admit to me with a sarcastic laugh, "I didn't always endear myself to others." I experienced this too when I first met him. Curt had just made a significant career transition, leaving the world of finance to lead Americares. In fact, he was replacing the organization's founder.

I was asked to attend a retreat in the Adirondacks for about thirty of their global leaders. My role was to teach the attendees the importance of modeling authentic, open, accessible, and approachable behaviors—e.g., how to have real conversations. The challenge was getting Curt to grow in the work first. He needed to build his self-awareness and experiment with being more vulnerable. As the leader and role model of this work, he had to demonstrate the behaviors before the rest of his organization was expected to, so they believed he meant it when he said it was important.

During one exercise, my partner Martha and I co-facilitated a public feedback circle in which we asked each person to share positive and negative constructive feedback with a colleague. I watched as a young woman engaged with Curt. She paid him a nice compliment and gave positive feedback. Then, when she was asked to provide negative feedback to Curt, she suddenly burst into tears. She was terrified by the notion of challenging her boss.

So I intervened. I asked Curt to go for a walk with me. I wanted to explain to him how his physical stance, facial expression, and tone adversely impacted his people.

As soon as we started walking, I bluntly said, "You're an intimidating person."

I immediately saw his blood boil. His face turned red, and he puffed out his chest. "I am not an intimidating person!" he shouted.

I calmly replied, "You don't understand your personality's impact on other people."

Looking back at that moment, I recognize I could have delivered my feedback more effectively. Yet my words had their intended result. They stayed with Curt. While he was initially skeptical of the work I'd asked him to do, he became more self-aware of the downfall of his learned communication skills. He couldn't speak to his colleagues in a cause-driven nonprofit world the same way he'd spoken to his peers in the investment banking world, or how he'd learned to talk with his parents while growing up.

He would later tell me this insightful self-revelation: "We had people on our leadership team who were primarily introverted. And now they had an extroverted corporate leader who had been used to managing many high-priced, high-octane financial services people who were outcome oriented and lived in a corporate culture that damned empathy. I was not aware of the impact of how I was showing up as their leader."

With time, Curt overcame his lack of self-awareness and gained knowledge about how his behavior affected others. He learned how to create an environment of psychological safety where Lori and others could share their points of view without fear that he, as the CEO, would punish them for speaking out. "I became a different leader and person than I was years before," Curt told me. "I had gone from being impatient about hearing what people wanted to say to me to encouraging them. We had come together as a group, and we shared respect for each other and made progress in being more open."

It's no accident that Curt most recently worked at Tuck Business School, where he taught future leaders about the values of self-awareness, authenticity, and real conversations. As he told me, "One of the gratifying things is I've been able to develop relationships with a small but significant number of students who I've been able to help in some way." He's also introduced the practice of a head, heart, hands check-in to the community theater group he helps run as another way to better connect with the people in his life by having real conversations. All in all, Curt said, "I've changed how I think about relating to people, whether it's a relationship with a colleague, superior, or student. Part of that has to do with understanding how I come across. More importantly, I want to understand and discover their perspective and what they're all about."

In other words, Curt seeks real conversations.

As you lean in to real conversations, please keep the following tips in mind:

1. **Focus on building psychological safety for the other person.** You may be upset about something that happened previously; however, if you want the end result to succeed, you must focus on the other person's heart and feelings first. Check in: Ask them how they are feeling and why. If it helps to put them at ease, share your feelings first.
2. **Always begin by building relationships.** Start with warmth and a smile. (Watch your friends who grew up in The Nest for how to do this well.)
3. **Pay attention to your body's visceral responses to tune in to what you are feeling in the moment.** This is both an art and a science. Keep experimenting as you practice and make moves.

[13]

Listen Empathetically

When learning here about the importance of creating an environment of psychological safety, you heard a reference to *listening empathetically* to the other person in order to be fully present. Those are two simple words that I don't want you to gloss over. Listening empathetically is about much more than just hearing what the other person is saying.

For example, my client Chip is a well-respected and beloved senior leader in a construction materials company. I always looked forward to working with him as I appreciated his equal parts business knowledge and emotional intelligence. At a leadership behavior workshop, he slowly walked across the room toward me. As he got nearer, I could see how red his face was. He wiped at his eyes in that way guys do to try to hide that they've been crying. Who could blame him? He'd missed facilitating a group at the workshop because his stepfather was in hospice. He was struggling with whether to leave the workshop to be by his mother's side in Florida, to help her through the end of her husband's life.

In the few seconds that it took for Chip to walk over to me, I recalled the lessons my parents had taught me about how to listen—especially my mother's when she was at her best. As a little girl, I followed her everywhere. I'd watch her work with mentally challenged children, or wait in line talking to others as they signed up for graduate school classes, or meet with high school students as a teacher and school psychologist. When she really listened to someone, she physically adjusted her height and seat so that her eyes met theirs. She smiled, leaned forward, and went into a zone.

As Chip approached me, I smiled, leaned forward, and zeroed in on him alone. Despite the crowded room, this moment contained just him and me. Very slowly, I asked, "How are you?"

His dam burst.

With tears in his eyes, I knew he was ready to share. I immediately moved into empathetic listening mode. I had to be intentional about it and wanted to. I had to choose to move away from my default modes of listening.

How You Listen

Throughout the day, you use seven distinct levels of listening. (We all do.) You cycle through them depending on the circumstances, the person talking, and whatever else you're thinking about. Because you cannot listen full throttle twenty-four hours a day, seven days a week, you'll move to lower levels of listening throughout your day. That's okay and completely normal. For example, you may listen deeply at work yet not effectively at home, or vice versa. Whether you were listened to as a child affects how well you listen as an adult. You may use one level of listening more than another simply because of the environment you grew up in. We'll get to that later in this chapter.

Your goals today are to become aware of when you use the different levels and how to get better at the highest levels of empathetic listening and active listening. Most importantly, because empathetic listening is essential for building psychological safety, I want you to become a master at it. Let's discuss the seven main levels of listening through Jayne's story.

Jayne is a high school principal who recently remarried. She and her husband have a four-year-old daughter together, and her husband's teenage children from his previous marriage live with them. As you can imagine, Jayne is busy with continuous meetings at school. She has many stakeholders: parents, kids, teachers, school counselors, administrators, not to mention her family. Let's imagine her day and the levels of listening that occur around and within her.

The first level is *passive listening*. (This could also bluntly be called not listening at all.) Jayne's teenage stepchildren demonstrate this. Jayne will ask: "Did you do your homework? Do you need any help?" But, like many teenagers, they don't respond. They may have heard her voice, yet they're not paying attention.

The second level is *pretend listening.* Jayne's been guilty of this after a long day of work. Her passionate four-year-old is excited to tell her mom everything about her day. However, all Jayne's energy and attentiveness can muster are "Uh huh," "Sure," and "Right, honey." Jayne's listening enough to respond without ignoring her child. Yet it's not true listening. It's a one-way conversation that you're trying to make sound like a conversation. (Let's be honest: How many times have you done this in the last week? I know I have.)

The third level is *selective listening.* Jayne sometimes finds herself doing this at work, especially when it comes to teachers complaining about curriculum, board members badgering her about the budget, or parents whining about their kids' playing time (in every sport). In these moments, Jayne already has a firm stance on the issue at hand. She's made up her mind. She may hear what the others are saying but she's not influenced by it. And so she hears what she wants to hear.

The fourth level is *attentive listening.* This is only slightly better than selective listening. Jayne has so much data coming at her every day and so many decisions to make that she can only process so much (honestly, true for all of us). Consequently, she can take in facts yet have no mental or emotional capacity to take in anything else. This may occur when a salesperson is trying to pitch her, or when her superintendent has brought her troubling news. She listens for the content only and ignores nonverbal signals. She listens to achieve her purpose. Attentive listeners seem like they're engaged. However, more often than not, while the other person is talking they're concocting their reply. An attentive listener is often looking out for their best interests first, asking themselves, *What's in this for me?*

The fifth level is *gotcha listening.* Attentive listening can quickly turn into gotcha listening, sometimes also referred to as "listening to refute." You listen only to find the flaws in the speaker's argument without making any effort to see what is right in it and without any concern for how relevant the "errors" are to the point the person is trying to make. Jayne has to interact with another competitive principal in her district who always wants to show her up. He consistently points out how his statistics around college acceptances are better than hers. When Jayne isn't her best self, she listens for and points out the faults in his numbers. (Wouldn't you?!) This kind of listening "proves" that the listener is superior to the speaker. And the gotcha listener doesn't even have to point out the flaws to feel that they are superior to the person they're speaking with.

The sixth level is *active listening.* When you're trying to help someone solve problems analytically, you're employing active listening. You tune in to their verbal and nonverbal cues, seeking to understand them, while putting aside your judgments and assumptions. Jayne actively listens at work when the decisions are high-stakes, like changing the curriculum. She must understand the reasoning behind switching directions, the pros and cons of doing so, and what has been done historically. She must also understand how different stakeholders feel about the change (in this case, the feelings are facts, not the result of empathizing with them). She'll ask questions to clarify points, mirror back what she hears, summarize the points she takes away, and so on. Jayne is quite good at this, and it's one of the main reasons she'd been promoted so quickly.

Most leaders I've worked with over the years have been excellent active listeners. That's how they solve problems. By using active listening techniques, like *summarizing* what someone shared or *inquiring* to understand a situation, they can quickly assess the facts of a situation. That leads to a more robust knowledge of the issue and the ability to brainstorm better solutions.

But active listening has some serious limitations, like only eliciting factual answers and revealing surface emotions. Plus, it's not always helpful in creating a real conversation. To have true, vulnerable, authentic conversations, you must strive for the highest level of listening. It's often the most demanding, yet also the most rewarding.

The seventh level is *empathetic listening.* Author Steven Covey refers to empathetic listening as the highest form of listening because you take everything in—the other person's words, their emotions, their facial expressions, and the feelings behind their words. Empathetic listeners try to put themselves in the speaker's shoes and feel directly what the other person is experiencing emotionally. This evolved leader is using emotions as data. This enables the listener to influence and be impacted by others in an atmosphere of caring and problem-solving based on assumed goodness in one another. And this is a critical step toward engaging in the final two steps of having a real conversation: frank feedback and healthy conflict.

The Two Listening Levels to Strive For

Extraordinary leaders learn to listen both actively and empathetically. They also quickly come to realize it's impossible to do both at the same time. Your brain can only handle one or the other, so you must consciously choose your mode of listening. Active listening solves problems and deals with business issues. Empathetic listening tunes in to others' emotional needs, resolves relationship issues, inspires people, and drives change. Empathetic listening, at times, involves techniques used in active listening as you encourage the speaker to continue or ask clarifying questions, but you go beyond just the superficial facts to the underlying emotions. You may need a lot of practice to understand where to strike the balance. The more you understand the different levels and make the appropriate choice, the more you can focus and listen effectively to the situation.

The following examples will help. When I first worked for Unilever Home and Personal Care over thirty years ago, Ann Kirk, who worked for me, showed me a variation of this. First, let's look at what *not* to say when you're actively listening. If you grew up in environments like Slings and Arrows, The Maze, or Sounds of Silence, you may have heard these lines from the characters in your environment, maybe weekly or even daily (which I imagine was very difficult for you). As a result, you may be echoing these phrases as a leader today purely out of habit. Or maybe you've chosen to show up differently because you didn't like how you were spoken to long ago. (Good for you!) Or you're modeling what your parents modeled because that's what their parents modeled to them. Regardless, know that you can break these simple patterns once you're aware of them.

What Bad Listening Sounds Like

Ordering	"You must tell him about ______."
Threatening	"You better, or else."
Preaching	"The right thing to do would be to ______."
Interfering	"I'll go talk to him for you."
Judging	"Why are you so argumentative (stubborn, controlling, etc.)?"
Blaming	"It's your fault."
Accusing	"You lied to me." "You started it."
Generalizing	"You always ______." "You never ______." "That's typical."
Personalizing	"You're too introverted/extroverted."
Diagnosing	"You're just trying to get attention." "You're being defensive."
Denying	"It's not my fault."
Distracting	"That's nothing—wait till you hear what he said to me. . . ."

- Which of these, if any, do you use now as a leader?
- Which may have stemmed from someone in your childhood cast?
- How are these phrases preventing you from having real conversations?

Now let's see what active listening sounds like. Children from environments like The Nest, In the Shadows, The Matriarchy, The Model Home, The Phantom Limb, and The Nomad can demonstrate active listening behaviors when they are rested and interested. Children from The Maze, Slings and Arrows, and Sounds of Silence can learn active listening if they overcome blocks. This might look and sound like:

What Active Listening Sounds Like

Encouraging	"Tell me more about ______." "I'm interested in why you said that."
Clarifying Facts	"When did that happen?" "Who else was there?"
Soliciting	"What suggestions do you have?" "What do you think needs to be done?"
Agreeing	"We both believe in forgiveness." "Let's communicate that we are in agreement about the timeline."
Supplementing	"Let me build on that." "Yes, *and* . . ."
Inviting Collaboration (through open-ended questions)	"Why?" "How?"
Responding	Nonverbally: physically leaning in, nodding, smiling. Verbally: "I hear you."
Summarizing (explain what you heard)	"Let me see if I understand what you said." "Is that correct?" "Am I getting it?"

- Which of these do you use now?
- Which do you wish you used more often?
- How could adding any of these phrases to your conversational repertoire increase the likelihood of having more real conversations?

Finally, let's look at how you can turn active listening into empathetic listening. In other words, what does empathetic listening sound like? Then we'll look deeper into how to prepare for, and how to have, an empathetic conversation (no matter your propensity for having them).

What Empathetic Listening Sounds Like

Acknowledging	"I can see you feel angry about that." "I can appreciate why you feel that way." "It sounds like you are feeling ______."
Normalizing	"That sounds like an appropriate response." "I think I would have felt the same way."
Mirroring	Notice posture, breathing, and silences, and mimic them—e.g., quiet your voice, breathe slowly, open eyes wide, etc.
Recognizing, Validating, and Appreciating	"By sharing the employees' survey responses, I now understand how they feel. Thank you!" "I appreciate your willingness to be honest with me." "Thank you for taking the risk to talk with me."

I believe we all can improve our empathetic listening. As you become more comfortable with moving into that level with people in your life, seek to incorporate one or more of the aspects or phrases above. Then see what develops.

If that still makes you nervous, here are my tried-and-true tips on becoming a better empathetic listener.

How to Listen Empathetically

Empathetic listening isn't necessarily easy. As we've discussed, it comes more easily to some than to others simply because of how they were raised. Some people have personality characteristics oriented toward tuning in to the emotional needs of people. Others don't. That doesn't mean you're off the hook if the cards were stacked against you when you were young. Anyone can become better at listening empathetically to others if they'll allow themselves to be vulnerable and to seek a true human connection with another person. Here's what I've found to work for me.

Listen for Your Cue

Empathetic listening is the highest form of listening because it requires you to prioritize people, not results. That's probably one reason why a majority of us aren't as intentional about this kind of listening as we should be. It can distract us from achieving our goals, yet I have found that empathetic listening deepens relationships unlike anything else, and therefore positively impacts results later. If you want to experience a breakthrough with a coworker, a boss, a spouse, a family member, or a friend, seek to be an empathetic listener.

To do this, you have to know the signs that someone is ready for that kind of conversation. For instance, a person's body language, a person's hesitance to speak, or just the mood in the air often reveals their intent to have more than a surface-level conversation. I can always tell that someone needs me when they cautiously look into my eyes and ask, "Do you have a second or a few minutes to talk?" or "Can I share something I am struggling with?" That's an easy cue.

Also, tune in to facial affect, body language, and tone of voice. Does the person look sad? Are there tears in their eyes? Are they looking down and sitting by themselves? Are they not talking to anyone? Is their voice quiet and monotone? Would they prefer you leave them alone?

Clear Your Mind and Give Your Undivided Attention

Clearing your mind and solely focusing on the other person requires mindfulness. The father of mindfulness, Jon Kabat-Zinn, defined it as "paying attention, on purpose, in the present moment, and non-judgmentally, to the unfolding of experience moment to moment." Mindfulness lets people slow down, become present, and tune in to the situation. To understand what the other person is feeling and why is a hallmark of an effective leader. Your relationships will deepen when you learn how to clear everything else from your mind, give others you are speaking to your undivided attention, and never dismiss what someone is saying or doing.

To set your mind on being mindful, do this: Imagine your head as an empty vessel you calmly wait to fill with the other person's story. You want to clear any work-related technical issues from your mind. Don't let your mind wander or let your eyes look away. (Turn your phone off too!)

When I looked into Chip's reddened eyes on that memorable day, he became the most important person to me at that moment. Not only was that true; I also wanted him to know it. Everything around him blurred. I was in what I call a "zone" with him. I didn't fidget, look away, yawn, or interrupt. He then told me how difficult the last month had been and how sad he was. I felt it.

Put on Their Shoes

Imagine what it would feel like to be the other person in that moment.

When I was talking to Chip, I asked myself, *What must it be like to be him right now?* I thought about my dad and how heartbroken I would be if he were in hospice care and I were thousands of miles away from him. I thought about how my husband John would feel if his stepfather were dying. I viscerally felt pain in my stomach. Then I imagined Chip sitting by his father's hospice bed, talking kindly to him and listening deeply to his mother. I could see that happening because I knew that's who Chip is—very kind, and with an empathetic face.

Listen Beyond the Words

Throughout the conversation, pay attention to facial expressions, tone of voice, pace, and breathlessness. Notice which words are emphasized or said several times. What mannerisms did the person show? Maybe their arms were flailing. Maybe they spent their time looking at the floor. These nonverbal communication signals are information.

I asked Chip what the tears were about, what he was most sad about. He was hunched against my table. Did he not want to let others hear what was going on? Maybe he was embarrassed or trying to be private.

Assume Goodness

As I listened, not everything Chip said was clear. Not all of it made sense to me. However, you must avoid the laziness of snap judgments when listening empathetically. A simplified version of a Carl Jung quote aptly describes why we're prone to this: "Thinking is difficult, that's why most people judge." Instead, when you're listening empathetically, assume goodness. In your body language, in your pauses, and in your words, strive to convey this: *You matter to me. I'm not judging you. I want to know how you feel and what you went through and are going through.*

Most people are good characters. I understood that Chip and his family were going through a genuine hardship. Hearing about it linked our shared mortality and humanity. I wanted him to know that. I felt sad for Chip and his mom.

Choose Silence over Solutions and Never Dismiss What They Feel

When you listen empathetically, stop what you're doing and tune in. You cannot simultaneously listen empathetically and actively solve problems.

As we talked, Chip paused at certain moments. He was quiet. I knew he was processing what he was feeling and remembering. At other times, he was crying. It's essential in those moments to remain silent. Let there be silence. Maybe hand them a tissue. Do not think about how to reply. Just be still. Don't comment on how you feel or redirect the conversation.

This isn't easy. It makes so much sense to want to help when you're seeing someone you care about struggling. I assume that you'll want to help. You think you should talk. Don't! Just wait. Waiting allows the other person to process what they're going through. If you speak, they won't be able to tune in to their visceral feelings. In the case of Chip, I needed to let him deal with what he was processing quietly and to let him know that experiencing his feelings, even in front of me, was okay. I knew he would never forget that I let him do that.

Often, when people share something emotional they are going through, they say things like "I should have done what I thought." Or "I didn't handle that well." Or "I was selfish, and I could have been a better son." It's essential to empathetic listening that you don't dismiss what they're saying or doing. Avoid platitudes. Don't say, "It's not that bad" or "You'll feel better tomorrow." Instead, acknowledge what they're saying. When Chip said, "I feel despondent. I wish I could have done more," I just nodded. Then I acknowledged what he'd shared: "Of course, you're sad, Chip. If you weren't, I would worry."

When I felt that Chip was waiting for a reply, I finally asked, "What else do you wish you had done? Tell me." Remember, if you care about someone, you inquire about what they are feeling. You ask open-ended questions to learn more. If you start preaching, you stop listening empathetically. I wanted to know what Chip was feeling. I was in it with him.

Check Your Body Language and Facial Expressions

Sometimes, your face and your body can belie your best intentions. Be intentional about keeping them in check when you're empathetically listening. Be authentic and use your body language and facial expressions to convey that you're listening. So long as it makes sense for your cultural context, consider focusing on maintaining eye contact (even if the other person looks away), leaning in, having an open body language, and showing that you're physically relaxed.

After Chip approached me and I knew he needed a longer talk, we sat down. I made sure to lean toward him, just as my mom had modeled for me. I touched his arm to show how much I cared about him and that I felt connected to what he was going through. For the rest of the day—and even now as I remember it—I felt drawn to him.

To listen empathetically, you need to listen for the other person's cues. Then clear your mind and focus all your attention and energy solely on the other person. Try to walk in their shoes. Think about what it's like to be them. Listen to their verbal and nonverbal cues. Assume goodness. Don't listen to judge or to agree or disagree. Choose silence over solutions. Don't let your body language or facial expressions betray your intent. Your job is to take everything in: their words, their emotions, their facial expressions, the feelings behind their words.

To listen to them so well that you can viscerally feel what they're going through.

In other words, to empathize, as one human to another.

Later that day, after Chip had returned to facilitate his tablemates through some emotional group discussions, he told me that he felt energized by his role. He was glad he was there for his mom and equally proud of the meaningful role he'd played helping his table members talk about their personal joys and challenges.

How Your Home Environment Influences Your Listening

Now that you have a better understanding of how to listen well, let's consider how your home environment may have strengthened or weakened your listening skills. Some people got an early lesson in empathetic listening. Certain childhood environments, like Homes of Stability, help leaders develop that strength right from the start. Yet leaders who come from Homes of Trauma can also evolve into excellent empathetic listeners for different reasons.

In this section, I'm going to review how each type of childhood home environment affects a person's ability to listen empathetically. I ask that you read through each setting, even the ones that you didn't grow up in. For those, ask yourself if a coworker, a family member, or a friend may have come from that type of home. Then consider how they listen to you today. You may just discover a new way to listen *to them* to engender better empathy.

And, of course, always consider how the type of home you grew up in has either encouraged or discouraged your own ability to listen empathetically. Then hone those specific aspects of yourself that you know could be better.

If You Were Raised in The Nest

You were raised in a home of deep, unconditional love. Your parents were highly interested in your emotions and wanted to hear what you had to say. They were deeply involved in helping you solve problems and emotional issues. They modeled the highest form of listening.

Today, as a leader, you tend to love to listen both actively and empathetically to others because you want to solve problems that affect the performance of a company. Like your parents, you want to help others solve their problems and emotional issues. You use all forms of listening based on your typical energy and stress levels, and all forms of listening tend to come easily to you.

To that end, Nesters can be pulled into too many people's issues and concerns. Because you love to help and other employees see how good you are at listening well, you get slammed with solving everyone's issues. You need to empower others by coaching them to be better listeners and encouraging them to solve their own issues. If not, you may get overwhelmed resolving everyone's problems, and the organization can become too dependent on you. When stressed, you may get irritated because people are not performing up to your standards. If you have heard too many excuses, you may stop listening. Make sure you understand why they aren't performing before you stop listening.

If You Were Raised in The Model Home

You were raised in a stable home with parents who paid a great deal of attention to your behavior. So their observation skills were quite high, which is helpful in listening. They probably wanted to ensure that you were acting in line with values that were important to them. Parents in this environment tend to use both active and empathetic listening to help guide your choices around behavior, through open discussion. They also use attentive listening when observing your behaviors that reflect certain values, maybe to catch you doing things right or wrong. You probably had real conversations about what were appropriate and inappropriate behaviors. However, some of these parents are judgmental in their observations, and this can lead to a child being annoyed by the constant nitpicking. Children in this case stop listening altogether.

As an adult, your ability to empathetically or actively listen will be even higher if your parents taught you the importance of values like respect, fairness, compassion, inclusion, and the golden rule. These values tell you to care about others, so you listen to do that. The specific values that are emphasized can affect your level of listening. For example, if financial stability is most important to you, you may attentively listen during discussions about money and passively listen during not-for-profit discussions.

At your best, when your physical energy is high and your mental energy is positive, you want to empathize with others, understand them, and actively solve their problems—especially with values violations. However, if you become stressed or triggered—especially if someone else isn't living up to the values you consider vital—you can move into more destructive listening behaviors—e.g., selective listening or even gotcha listening, to catch someone saying something that you can then righteously attack. At your worst, you'll shut off your empathy out of annoyance. You'll need to build your self-awareness about which type of listening you do when different topics are discussed, see if you need to get stronger on some, and build your ability to assume goodness about other people's intentions even if their values don't align with yours—or you will tune out.

If You Were Raised in The Matriarchy

Your mother likely cared deeply for you. Still, she may have been over-extended in her life due to her responsibilities. As a strong woman, she may have been more focused on execution than tender loving care. She may have most often resorted to pretend listening, passive listening, or not listening to you at all simply because she didn't have the mental or emotional capacity to do so after a long day. And when she could listen well, active listening would win out over empathetic listening because she was focused on solving problems more than growing a relationship. Yet, when space allowed, she did momentarily listen empathetically.

Today, you may model a similar propensity to stay in the shallow end of the pool, fearful to wade into more meaningful conversations via the higher levels of listening. Make sure you are building your muscles in all levels of listening and understand when each is most appropriate.

If You Were Raised in In The Shadows

You grew up with a larger-than-life figure in your home who felt like your center of gravity—whether you wanted that or not. The way you responded depends on how you felt about that person. Either way, you became a great observer of that person's behavior and the behavior toward them of those who were around you.

If you were tired of that person getting all the attention, or you felt that they were just "too much," you may have been stuck in the lower levels of listening—e.g., pretend, selective, or not listening at all. Gotcha listening could also have been a mainstay as a small way to assert some dominance over their dominating personality. For example, your proud and narcissistic father may say, "Thanks for the compliment, but I don't deserve it." And you reply, "Yeah right, Dad. You *love* hearing that."

However, if you were proud of or in awe of the person, you respected them and wanted to please them. Consequently, you strove to actively listen because you wanted to glean their knowledge, or even become like them. This holds especially true if the beacon of your life had specific expectations and explicit instructions for how you should speak and act around visitors and the type of person you should become (which was likely very similar to themselves). Of course, if you didn't respect them, you probably selectively listened.

Most adults who grew up In the Shadows are exceptional listeners because that's how they met expectations. If you were raised in this environment, your goal may be to please others and perform. The bigger challenge for you may be engaging in conflict and providing feedback (two of our essential topics in Act III). One caveat: If your parent's desire for attention annoyed you as a child, when you see similar desires in other adults, you may move to lower levels of listening. Watch out for this!

If You Were Raised in The Phantom Limb

Due to death or divorce, you lost a parent or a parental figure. This can temporarily negatively affect anyone's listening ability. You may have chosen to shut down and not listen at all. Or you may have become a passive listener because that's all your mind and body could accommodate during your grief. It can feel like you are numb. Selective listening eventually came into play as your life continued past your loss.

But with time and healing, you may have intrinsically learned to lean on empathetic listening as you worked through your grief with your other parent, or with a sibling or other close family member. And because you were hurt deeply by this loss, you noticed when others were struggling. You wanted to take care of others.

Today, you tend toward selective listening and active listening because you want to help others. And since your grief has never fully left you, you're on the lookout for when others are struggling, which makes you quite capable in the empathetic listening realm.

Emotionally tuning in to everyone else's needs can be draining. You need to take care of you. I want to ensure that your needs are listened to and heard. Who is doing that for you?

If You Were Raised in The Nomad

Because you and your caregivers moved around so often, everyone was likely focused on assimilating into the new environment. This may have led to more limited listening to you and your needs. You and your parents may have been more focused on listening to others to determine how to integrate. What kind of listener you became and what level of attachment you developed is probably due to other caregivers who would have focused on you, such as a grandparent or a nanny.

You became a self-reliant lone ranger and emotionally distanced. So while others may not have listened well to you, you probably became an empathetic listener for others because you desired to connect with them. You longed for friends wherever you resided, and you enjoyed meeting and entertaining people. You wanted to be liked. Consequently, you became adept at deciphering facial expressions, body language, and tones of voice. You sought to get to know the core of a person. And you figured out how to do this in many different situations and environments.

Today, you're just as adept at reading people. You seek to understand others' needs, likes, and dislikes. People know you're a safe place because you're a strong active listener. You're often ready for empathetic conversations.

However, remember that you also have needs. Allow other people to listen to you empathetically and actively, and ensure that they do. You need to let people in and make sure they are hearing *you*!

If You Were Raised in The Maze

You were oftentimes uncertain about what to expect from the parent who struggled with alcohol. Their relationship to you could have ranged from doting and caring, to angry and vengeful, to completely oblivious. And it could have changed day by day. You may have wondered if you were even loved. If you loved your parent, you may have exercised active or empathetic listening as a way to help them. However, you may have defaulted to selective listening or pretend listening because you didn't want to get into trouble. Maybe you were sick and tired of daily dealing with their drama, so you selectively listened for only what you absolutely needed to know in order to go on with your day. Outside of your home, you may have used active listening to maintain a positive reputation for your family home or to resolve issues with the law that your inebriated parents caused.

Today, you may be quite adept at using all of these modes; however, you may still stick to the lower levels of listening in order not to engage in conflict or provide feedback. Still, you can turn on your empathetic listening mode when necessary—especially if you see someone else in pain. Whether you use your skills or not will depend on whether you feel psychologically safe to speak your mind. At work, your boss may get frustrated if you do not share your views, etc. That's what they pay you for, correct? So make sure you work on overcoming any block you have and building your ability to share your voice!

If You Were Raised in Slings and Arrows

You tried your best to survive each day, unsure of what kind of abuse you might have to endure. Whatever helped you make it through your day is what you internalized. For example, if you were sick of being treated poorly, you may have used gotcha listening and raising your voice to get back at the other person in the only way you could. Or you may have resorted to pretend listening since much of what was said to you was degrading or disrespectful. You may have often felt like you didn't have a voice, so why use it?

However, you may have had a parent, sibling, or other family who had to endure the same slings and arrows from a particular person in your household. In your discussions with them, they may have modeled for you what active listening and empathetic listening are like. If you didn't get rewarded for employing those higher-level listening techniques as a child, you likely didn't practice them.

Today, you're capable of all the lower levels of listening because those techniques helped you survive. You may want others to feel respected since you weren't, so you employ active and empathetic listening. Still, you may need to be more intentional about using these techniques with *all* people. Those who are bullies seldom if ever listen to anyone, so they don't employ the higher forms of listening. In the end, what you use depends on how much you grew from your experience. Beware: If you become too strident about how people *should* behave, others will stop listening to you.

If You Were Raised in Sounds of Silence

Most often, you were likely scared that you would be sexually abused again. Consequently, you became keenly observant of your surroundings so that you could avoid your perpetrator. You listened attentively and actively out of necessity, maybe even hypervigilantly. You learned how to listen with your eyes because you were constantly surveilling everything.

Today, you may be a deep feeler and excellent listener. You cannot *not* listen. Your drive to empathize with others in pain may even be a core characteristic of your personality. At work, because your listening skills are very high, you may take on too many issues for people who are suffering. You need to ensure that others are also tuning in to the needs of colleagues, not just you.

The environment in which you were raised dictates much about how you typically listen to others. However, you may have also learned how to employ the higher levels of listening in your work or just as a result of getting older. In the following questions, I'd like you to think about how you listen based on the seven levels of listening and how your childhood home environment has affected your default modes of listening.

For each listening level (passive, pretend, selective, attentive, gotcha, active, empathetic), ask yourself:

- Does this describe me?
- How often do I listen in this particular way?
- Whom do I most often listen to this way? Why?
- In what environment (work, home, etc.) do I most often use this listening level? Why?

Consider which listening level you default to in general, then ask yourself:

- What about my childhood is causing me to show up this way when I listen to others?
- Do I need to talk to someone from my past about my childhood environment to get more details?
- How is this listening level preventing me from having real conversations?

As you move forward with becoming a better empathetic listener, please remember to do the following:

1. Quiet your mind. Clear your head of analytic thoughts and tune in to the visceral responses in your heart.
2. Be insatiably curious to learn what is happening to the other person.
3. Recognize that other factors like stress will negatively impact how well you listen. When you're at your best, you can hear much better!

[14]

Engage in Constructive Conflict

Psychological safety? Check.

Listening empathetically? Getting better every day.

Speaking your mind when you know the other person doesn't share your opinion? Not so much.

Almost always, real conversations will involve conflict. Why? Because real conversations involve real humans, each of whom has their own needs, perspectives, worries, and talents. Consequently, as the number of people in the room increases, so too will the likelihood of conflict. That's why the best leaders need to know how to handle conflict well. Teams discover solutions they could never have arrived at without capably working through their conflict. Plus, successfully navigating conflict one time often makes it easier to do the next time, while also replenishing the relational reservoir of trust, vulnerability, and authenticity. (In fact, when you look at successful conflict in hindsight, there's a certain kind of beauty to it.)

To have real conversations, you *must* become comfortable with constructive conflict. I define *conflict* as any situation where your concerns, needs, or desires differ from another person's. Initially, they appear incompatible. Note too that I'm specifically speaking to conflict over content, versus interpersonal conflict. Conflict pertaining to content is about important topics or issues. Interpersonal conflict occurs when tensions or challenging dynamics exist between individuals or groups of people. (Facilitating interpersonal conflict is an entirely different book!)

Since I want my clients (and you) to go beyond surface-level conflict resolution, which rarely leads to beneficial results, I will teach you to engage in *constructive conflict*. This is where you have passionate, unfiltered debate around issues of importance to your team, family, community, or the world. The issues can be business, technical, political, or social. Constructive conflict levels up how you relate to others, even when they seem against you.

Conflict is fun to watch in a play. That's what garners our attention and propels the story to its conclusion. Without conflict, books and films and TV shows are boring. However, when you're the central character, conflict becomes something much different and much more personal, which is why many people fear even healthy conflict. They just don't have the tools to handle conversations that turn against them.

In this chapter, I'm handing you my toolbox.

In a typical day as an executive coach, I was asked to facilitate a team discussion. The executives were struggling with how to downsize headcount. They were frustrated with Chuck, the leader of the process, and needed help separating their frustration from determining the best process. The work wasn't going well. Feeling defensive, Chuck had been taking out his frustration on his boss and colleagues.

Chuck is an apt name, I thought. He was chucking around accusations left and right, casting aspersions on his manager Joe and outright demeaning his coworkers Indira and Srikanth. He wasn't engaging in healthy conflict, so I cut him off and held up a metaphorical mirror.

"Chuck, you just blamed Joe for what's been going wrong. And then you spoke badly about Indira and Srikanth. Remember: A team only improves if you identify what *you* need to do differently to fix the situation."

Unfazed, Chuck replied, "Pam, I'm not blaming them. I'm just telling you the facts."

I thought, *Really?*

I took a breath and looked squarely in Chuck's eyes. "Let's start with you and the environment you grew up in. Let's talk about what behaviors were role-modeled for you in your home and how that has impacted how you engage in discussions in the room today. I am happy to hold up the mirror and give you feedback on what I see of you in the room."

Chuck looked stunned. I could tell that the first step for successful conflict was dawning on him. It's just like what they tell you at the beginning of every flight: "Secure your own mask before helping others." In other words, you have to work on yourself first.

Unsurprisingly, people often tell me that their teams don't engage in real conflict. Most are terrible at it. They usually blame the group leader for not creating the right environment, or they point a finger at their colleagues for being conflict-averse and not speaking their truth, or they blame the workplace culture. Most skip their own role when explaining why the team isn't successful.

However, to have healthy conflict, you must be willing to point the finger at yourself first. The best place to start is by discovering the connections between how you experienced conflict as a child and how you choose to approach conflict today.

How Your Work Environment Influences How You Handle Conflict

Bring your most recent workplace conflict to mind. Maybe it was on the lower end of the conflict spectrum, where a coworker said something dismissive and you didn't reply because you didn't want the conflict. Or maybe it was on the higher end, a business decision with high stakes that you and your CEO were on opposite sides of and that you argued extensively about. From relatively small-time to very consequential, conflict is still conflict. How you show up in handling one kind is often how you show up handling the others. So no matter the intensity of your most recent conflict, the lessons I'm about to teach you will work.

As you reflect on the type of conflict you face at work, consider these questions:

- How do you engage (or not engage) in conflict? What do you do or say to either step up to conflict or steer yourself away from it?
- Check in with your feelings. Do you get excited, invested, defensive, angry, or turned off when engaging in conflict with someone? Remember, emotions are data, and you can increase your self-awareness around conflict if you start with noticing.
- Do you clarify the issues you are trying to solve?
- Do you fear speaking your truth, so you avoid a conflict, or do you lean in and courageously argue with someone over your point?
- Do you assume that you are right and the other person is wrong about the topic, or just doesn't have the facts, or just doesn't understand?
- When you use conflict tools you know, how do you feel? Confident? Fearful? Courageous? Uncertain? Timid?

Your workplace environment affects you just as your childhood family and friends have. At work, you have relationships that impact you, and your behavior is influenced by what happens there. It is essential to look at your current or prior work environment for clues about why you show up in conversations the way you do. Let's get more granular.

- How do you handle conflict with your boss?
- Peers?
- Direct reports?
- Do you engage in conflict with these groups differently?

When engaging in conflict, some people show up exactly the same way, whether interacting with their boss, peers, or direct reports. They feel equally comfortable with all three.

Some leaders think it's their responsibility to present different ways of seeing things to their boss, so they engage in conflict with their boss freely. They think, *That's what I'm paid for.* Others are afraid to challenge their manager. Still others wait to be asked.

With peers, I have seen that relationships and interpersonal styles play a role. Ken, for example, is very close with his boss, Mark. Ken knows when Mark is ready to hear a challenging point of view and when he isn't, so he modulates how he shows up and when to raise an issue. Ken, however, loves to debate points of view, so he does this freely with his peers daily. Ken's peers, however, have enough challenging issues to solve, so they avoid getting into conflict with their peers on tough issues unless they have to.

- Has anything significant at work affected how you deal with conflict?

You might have a boss who loves to hear what you have to say, so you are encouraged to speak your mind all the time. On the other hand, not all bosses are encouraging. Consider Bill, a kind, good-hearted leader who cares deeply about doing a good job. He once worked for a tough manager who was abrasive and condescending. Every time Bill spoke up about an idea, his boss told him some form of "That's stupid," "That won't work," or "You, of all people, should know this by now." Bill developed what is commonly called, in psychological terms, learned helplessness. He believed anything he would say would be wrong, so he stopped trying. He was eventually transferred to another job at the same company. Sadly, as a result, he rarely shared his views in his new role, so his boss thought he added no value and Bill was fired.

- What would you change about how you deal with conflict at work today? For example, do you avoid direct conversations when you're upset and wish you didn't?
- What role do you play in conflict on your team? Are you the facilitator, clarifying or restating the issue, or are you raising or creating the problem?

The questions in the preceding section should help clarify how you show up at your work when conflict arises. Now let's investigate why you engage in conflict that way.

How Your Childhood Environment Influences How You Handle Conflict

To reveal the connections to your childhood, consider these questions:

- What kinds of discussions took place in your childhood home?
- How were differences of opinion handled?
- Were you actively invited into and engaged by your parents in challenging conversations—e.g., The Nest?
- Or was your home one where people thought children should be seen but not heard—e.g., Slings and Arrows?

If you were often asked what you think and believe, and especially why you think and believe that way, you were granted the opportunity as a child to practice articulating your point of view, how to defend your opinions, and how to modify your views in the face of persuasive evidence. As I've witnessed with my clients who had such an upbringing, the more you were asked to actively share your thoughts, opinions, and beliefs as a child, the more comfortable you are doing so as an adult. I have seen many variations of this. For example, only children who are encouraged to read a lot and share their ideas often have parents who are teachers or diplomats. Or parents who are engineers or psychologists might engage in profound conversations about the underpinnings of things with their children. The parents may deeply listen to each person's perspective or want to enter an enriching debate. Families with many kids actively involved in sports and other physical activities may banter or tell funny stories about the day's activities. Each child offers a different perspective, providing them all with a framework for dealing with multiple opinions on a single subject. They may laugh at various points of view or yell at each other—and then go back to carefree playing the next minute.

Now let's focus on how your parents dealt with each other:

How did your parents handle disagreements between them?

Did these disagreements occur in public or private, in front of you or behind closed doors?

Did they tell you, or did you infer, that they believed in transparency, so they shared their conversations with you?

Or did they not want to burden you with their issues, so they discussed them privately?

Did you ever see them yell at each other? What did this teach you?

If it was in public, did they argue constructively, and were you impressed with how they did it?

Did you want to emulate their process?

What did you learn about conflict resolution from them?

Watching your parents engage in conflict (or not) can provide a treasure trove for fascinating learning. Day-to-day life is filled with conflict opportunities, and what your parents let you witness (or not) affected your skills and attitudes about conflict. If your parents saw conflict as a good and healthy thing, they probably wanted you to see their arguments and the techniques they used. Sometimes they worked and sometimes they didn't, which was fine. They wanted you to experiment. They wanted you to see all of this, so they did it in front of you. But if they thought conflict was unhealthy or a bad thing, they probably hid it behind closed doors. You may not know what to think about conflict today. Their attitude and behaviors around conflict formed yours. Maybe they loved conflict so much and argued or debated so often that you vowed you never would!

My son Ryan once told my husband and me, "You guys are funny. When you argue, you go around and around on the same point. Don't you teach this stuff?!" Ha! We're all human and he was right! My point: If you talked about how your parents dealt with conflict, that's even healthier, especially if you made changes!

Now let's look at the different roles you learned to play in conflict when you were a child. Read through the following list and see which roles could have described you when you were young:

- **The Facilitator** ensures everyone is listened to and their ideas are heard.
- **The Observer** watches people's body language and facial affect. They listen to words so closely that they effectively record the discussion.

- **The Cheerleader** inspires or lifts others up, instilling a belief that anything is possible with direction.
- **The Truth Teller** has no fear of being direct. They want intellectual purity, and they get to the facts.
- **The Antagonist** loves to make trouble and instigate tense talks between people.

Consider the following questions:

- Which environment did you grow up in? As a result, what role did you play when conflict arose? Or what characteristics did you take on?
    - Were you a Facilitator trying to get each person in your family to speak their mind directly and ensure they felt heard?
    - Were you an Observer who watched what happened in the room and could summarize everyone's words, body language, and patterns of thinking and feeling?
    - Were you a Cheerleader who tried to lift and inspire others to believe they could have a productive conversation?
    - Were you a Truth Teller who forced people to clarify facts?
    - Or were you an Antagonist trying to create trouble or drama? ("Oh, you should hear what so and so said!")

Here are a few examples of how your childhood environment influences how you may show up during conflict today.

- If you grew up in Sounds of Silence or The Maze, you were likely very observant of body language, tone of voice, and interpersonal dynamics because you had to protect yourself from your abuser while growing up. So today you are good at facilitating conversations because of what you see in behavior. That is, of course, if you speak your truth.
- Children of The Nest may default to cheerleading because they want to inspire and lift their teams to solve issues. They assume goodness, so they won't be antagonistic. They may facilitate or

clarify issues to solve—anything to be helpful. If those raised in The Nomad are interested and want to attach to a group and feel valued and included, they might cheerlead, clarify issues, or facilitate as well. Whatever works!
- Children of In the Shadows may be facilitators and truth tellers for a different reason: They want to shine a light on others. They want to help other individuals see their own uniqueness and have conversations about themselves in a safe way. If coaches have helped Illuminators see their greatness, they want others to experience that same wonderful feeling.
- Those raised in Slings and Arrows may become antagonists. They have seen trouble their entire childhood. However, if they worked through blocks related to their childhood, they may be truth tellers about what is happening and cheerleaders of others to ensure they are heard. They want the cycle of pain and anger they experienced to be broken. In a way, they gain the strength of another environment, The Model Home. They become Values Crusaders who fight for the rights of others.

The final question to ask yourself to see how you related to conflict as a child could be the most difficult:

- How did your parents and other key adults handle traumatic or difficult events when you were growing up?

How trauma was handled early in your life has a significant impact on how you later engage in conflict. If you were sexually abused when you were young, and your parents found out about it and stood up for you, you learned that you can have agency to stand up for yourself. If you were raised in The Maze and were often yelled at by one parent, and your other parent didn't help you in those moments, you may have suffered low-self-esteem issues and fail to stand up for yourself now. These are the most likely environments in which trauma happens. However, it happens in other environments too. Yet, whatever the circumstances, if you were of a certain age and witnessed someone address the trauma, you learned positive behavior, you realized that people can overcome things if they have real conversations.

As you'll remember, your home environment also includes a larger cast of characters that affected you. When it comes to learning how to do conflict well (or not), our relatives and friends often teach us much.

How Your Childhood Cast Influences How You Handle Conflict

Now let's turn to the role of your childhood peers in how you show up in conflict as an adult. For some, peers serve as a surrogate family—whether because their family situation is difficult or because their friendship group is incredibly close. Consider these questions:

- When there was a disagreement or a "fight" between your friends, how did you handle it?
- What role did you play when there was conflict in the group? Were you a facilitator or an instigator?

Julie, whose parents divorced when she was young and was therefore from The Phantom Limb, was always part of a trio of girlfriends. She now works in a large financial consulting firm. When we last spoke, she remembered being very busy in her work when she was younger, just like she is today. As children, her friends would bicker, and she'd try hard to get them to listen and hear each other. She facilitated their relationship like she did the relationship between her geographically separated parents throughout her life. Julie was so successful that after fixing the relationship between her friends, the two friends bonded and Julie's connection to them vanished. This made her sad. But at least she felt productive for improving their relationship (an attempt at finding humor in the story).

Some children avoid fights between friends as it reminds them of the tension in their own homes. Others are antagonistic because that's what they've witnessed. They may think it's funny to instigate conflict. Or some kids will observe and comment toward the end.

- Were you ever bullied, or did you ever bully someone?
- What did you do when someone was being bullied: stand up for the person, remain quiet, or walk away?

Being bullied as a child is humiliating. Period. I was heartbroken when I heard about Fred, a high school basketball player on Long Island. Fifteen minutes before the starters went onto the court for a game, members from the other team pulled him into a bathroom, threw him into a shower, and verbally abused him. Fred already had confidence issues as he was from the In the Shadows environment.

Still, Fred was faithful to his team. After the bullies left, he gathered himself to get ready to run onto the court. His teammate Weston immediately grabbed their coach and told him what had transpired. The coach approached the ref. They stopped the game and told the other team's coach what had occurred. The coaches brought both sides together. When the other team's members were forced to say what happened, they denied it. Weston called them out and said, "You're lying."

Fred learned a few lasting lessons that day: While there are thugs in the world, there are good people too, who will stand up for you when it matters most. And when someone is bullied, Fred needed to stand up for them, just like his friend had stood up for him.

- How do you handle conflict with friends now?

Typically, the pattern of how you show up in conflict as an adult mirrors how you dealt with conflict with your friends as a child—unless you purposely chose to act differently.

As you use these reflection questions to examine how and why you show up in conflict the way you do, look for common patterns across categories. Did you show up with your friends like you did with your family? Or differently? What about how you show up at work today? What parallels do you see?

My hope is that as you connect the dots across every act of your life, you'll start having aha moments that lead you to meaningful breakthroughs.

Conflict in Action

To change how you show up in moments of conflict today, you need to understand *why* you show up in a particular way and then choose to get better at constructive conflict. An example may help provide a mirror. Let's return to Georgia's story from Chapter 7, of having been raised in the multiple home environments of The Maze, Slings and Arrows, and Sounds of Silence. By the time she and I began working together, she was already an accomplished leader with a long list of titles, including becoming the first female plant manager in the United States, if not internationally, at Southern California Edison. Additionally, she later started and became the president of Midwest Generation. She'd served on boards for eleven different companies. It was in her role of SVP Worldwide Operations in her late forties that she became adept at diplomacy and influence, which was evidenced in how she led her teams and handled conflict. In our work together, she connected the dots as to *why* she was so good at it.

In her multiple home environments she had learned to speak up and fight back for her beliefs and values early, like when she took on a city administrator who refused to let her play baseball with the boys. At the same time, she learned to fear her father's drunken—and often racist and sexist—outbursts and rages. As a young adult, she left her first husband because he exhibited similar behavior. Georgia also hated the way her mother, who'd grown up in a strict religious household, always refused to talk about anything that might feel emotional or embarrassing inside the family, like Georgia's traumatic experience with her brother raping her in their backyard.

The cumulative effect of Georgia's life experiences as a child and her second act as an adult shaped her decision to speak up if something needed to be said when an issue crossed her ethical boundaries—no matter how uncomfortable everyone involved might feel. Her childhood experiences also helped Georgia develop a keen sense of empathy for others, especially anyone whom she felt had been subjected to racism or sexism in the workplace.

When she entered the workforce, she initially felt her role as a leader was to keep quiet, even if she disagreed with someone—something she learned from her mother. Yet she realized that she wanted to be a different kind of leader and parent. She didn't want to perpetuate the pattern of not speaking up when she felt someone had been wronged. She chose not to live her life in silence anymore. She had become an Assertive Diplomat.

"I didn't want someone to be shunned for being different," Georgia told me. "I hated seeing people singled out for being poor or fat. I felt the pain of that."

As a result, Georgia earned a reputation as a straight shooter who could sometimes rub people the wrong way. By bluntly speaking her truth, like when she witnessed blatant sexism, Georgia sometimes triggered defensive reactions among fellow executives or board members. While that approach ensured she got her point across, it didn't always sway the other person's opinion or change their mind.

"Surprisingly, my mouth didn't get me fired early in my career," Georgia told me as she laughed. "I was prone to throwing Molotov cocktails in my twenties and thirties. Being told not to talk about something like sexual harassment made me crazy. People would tell me to let something lie, but I couldn't walk away from it. There's no way I can live with myself if there's a conflict and I don't address it. But I learned continuously and changed over time. When I turned forty-nine and became a CEO, I mellowed. I knew that I had to change how I engaged with others if I was going to be successful and get things done."

Successful leaders like Georgia share two characteristics: They're self-aware and they're not afraid to alter their standard operating procedures—especially when it comes to the necessary soft skills of dealing with people. She already had the tools. She just wanted to know why they were working and how she could hone them. Georgia's approach to conflict had partly evolved from her increased awareness of what she had learned to practice as a child. For instance, when she created her Emotional Timeline, she drew dramatically high and low lines that reflected the turbulent events she had experienced.

"That was my first aha moment," Georgia told me while holding on to her ETL, which she has kept on her desk for years. "I stepped back and recognized I was soldiering through life without context, and suddenly, I had some context about why I felt the way I did. It made sense of why I was so passionate about those issues."

She recognized ways to improve her approach to conflict both at home and in the workplace. When Georgia engages in conflict now, say, when she's challenging her fellow board members over whom to choose for a firm's next CEO, she uses empathy. She customizes how she talks to her colleague to get her point across while minimizing the chances of escalating the conflict, even when she might have powerful feelings about the issue.

One time, she felt the board was giving too much airtime to a male CEO candidate while shortchanging a more qualified female candidate. Georgia had potent feelings about the issue and spoke up on behalf of the female candidate. Before she spoke, though, Georgia paused and thought about who her audience was. "It didn't change my courage to confront issues," Georgia told me. "That's in me. But sometimes, it doesn't serve me well. I needed to think about my delivery and how I could change my words and approach an issue differently. I really think that the skill I've developed over time that has helped me be so much more effective is finding ways to reframe the conflict issue without it losing any of its oomph. That has been a skill I've consciously tried to develop, and it has benefited me enormously."

Georgia has learned to take some time to think about what she knows about people, including what they may have learned from their childhood, before she speaks with them. This includes considering what she knows about their beliefs, their values and ethical boundaries, and what motivates them or doesn't. As she told me, "It's like taking a drama class where you do character analysis to help you play the role. What do I know about Bob, and what does that tell me about how I can get my point across to him so that he will receive it? It's the same message in a different package."

By combining her courage to tell the truth with empathy for others, which is rooted in what she practiced as a child, Georgia has become a more effective leader. Even better, she now coaches other female leaders on how to take similar actions in their careers, deal with discrimination in the boardroom, and lead their businesses.

How to Engage in Constructive Conflict

Here are ten tips I've found most useful for having conversations that don't fear conflict. I've used these steps for decades with some of the world's leading leaders, men and women with strong personalities and stronger opinions. When you choose not to fear conflict, you'll be amazed at what opportunities lie in wait for you on the other side.

Starting the Conversation

1. **Lean in to the conflict.** Engage in conflict in both *mindset* and *behavior*. Don't hope it will go away on its own or assume that others understand without you explaining. Some people see conflict as a good thing because it leads to more innovative solutions. Strive to emulate these role models versus those who fear it.
2. **Clearly state the problem you're trying to solve.** Cut the small talk and say this at the beginning of your conversation. Be direct. Everyone comes to a conversation or conflict with what they believe the real issue is that they need to solve first. Remember the global pandemic that started in 2020? Some people wanted to figure out how to make masks or more ventilators. Others wanted to figure out how to get enough cash to keep their business afloat. The world was shutting down. Keeping employees safe and their families informed

were also important issues to address. All of these issues mattered, but you had to choose one at a time!

3. **Be prepared.** Come to the conversation with relevant data and facts. Conflict can be messy, so help the team be as efficient as possible. Do your homework. Determine what data would help you resolve the issue and bring it with you. Don't be one of those people who show up waiting for others to fix the situation. Be proactive and participate.

Having the Conversation

1. **Be transparent.** Explain why the subject has come up, what you know about the problem, and how you feel about it. So often people wait to be invited into the conversation, even though they are in the room! Share what you know about what happened, how people feel, how you feel, who is involved, who is affected. Share what you know freely. You're trying to fix this.
2. **Look for common ground, alternatives, and compromises.** Find the win-win territory. Collaborating to find a positive outcome for all involved is challenging and takes time. You have to slow down, empathetically listen to what is important to each person, and be as flexible as possible. Find points of alignment. Say yes to them, so that you can move on to those compromises. A small yet effective way to achieve this is by saying "and" rather than "but." Saying "but" often negates what was just said, whereas saying "and" validates the prior point and builds on it.
3. **Appreciate their differences.** Be aware that others have different styles of communication and different perspectives, and that this adds value to the conversation. Remember: With diversity, conflict is endemic. You *want* conflict. Ask each person for their views about issues, and if their style aggravates you, turn up the patience!
4. **Employ empathetic listening. Inquire about and acknowledge their feelings.** Use the highest form of listening. Inquiry is about asking open-ended questions to hear and understand what someone else feels and thinks. Don't just advocate or share your view. In America,

most of us spend 95 percent of our time talking in advocating and just 5 percent inquiring. Strive for 50 percent of both. Heck, facilitators spend the majority of time inquiring. You learn a lot this way. When you hear other people's feelings, acknowledge them out loud. Don't miss the opportunity to connect on a deeper level.

5. **Ask for help and/or offer to help.** Don't hold back. Ask! If you hear that the other person is struggling, take time to help. Likewise, don't struggle on your own. Reach out. Remember: be authentic and choose vulnerability. Too many people don't ask for help when they need it. They are afraid to bother others. Here's a secret. Most people love to be asked to help. It makes them feel valuable.
6. **Own your role in the problem.** When a problem exists, usually both sides have a role in it. Ask yourself: Why is this issue still unresolved? More importantly, what did I do personally that may have led to this moment? What can *I* do to fix this? Then lean in and fix it!

Ending the Conversation

1. **Close with a plan.** Don't end the conversation without an agreement for next steps. Most of my clients find this step incredibly tedious and boring. The fun part is the debate and finding solutions. Remember: A lot of people love conflict. And (not *but*) if things are going to change, you have to write down a timeline: who will do what and how you will know if you are successful.

As you move forward, please remember:

- The next time conflict finds you, choose to go in prepared.
- Stand up for yourself *and* make space for the other person.
- Remember who you were while choosing who you want to be.

[15]

Provide Constructive Feedback

After you've created a psychologically safe environment, after you've chosen to listen empathetically, and after you've successfully navigated any necessary conflict, now you're ready for the final step of having a real conversation: how to give (and receive) constructive feedback. Of all the relational tools I teach, this is the one that generates the most angst in my clients. I find myself answering an endless number of questions like:

- "How do I give feedback upwards without making my boss angry?"
- "How do I handle denial or anger?"
- "What if they ask me for more examples and I don't have them?"
- "How do I give feedback to my direct reports versus my peers?"
- "What if I am wrong about my view?"
- "How do I give my spouse or children feedback?"

In the following pages, we're going to define helpful feedback, learn how to give constructive feedback in a four-step process, and then consider how your childhood has impacted how you offer feedback today.

No matter your skill at this, I believe there's always room for growth.

What Is Constructive Feedback?

At my firm, we define feedback as the direct, specific, timely, and honest disclosure of personal behavior observations to improve the performance of another individual or to advance a shared goal. When you are direct, you do not sugarcoat anything. You don't soften the message. You speak about what you see and get to the point quickly. This is linked to specificity. People need to be told exactly what they are doing in detail so that they can "see" it. Too often, people say things like "You're really strategic" or "You're a nice person." Honestly, that says nothing. You need to describe what the person actually did: "You walked into the room to where the speaker was and stood in front of him." To me, timely means within twenty-four hours, or as soon after the event as possible. You need to say specifically what you saw a person do, be honest about how it makes you feel, and do it soon!

A common misunderstanding is that feedback is only negative. Feedback can be positive or negative. The critical element is that it's *constructive* and is designed to help the person be better. That might involve pointing out how something can be done better (constructive negative) or encouraging and praising someone for what they do well already, which reinforces good behavior (constructive positive).

Feedback is fuel for development, both for individuals and for relationships. Yet many of us struggle to do it well. Don't get me started on why too many companies only conduct *annual* performance reviews. I believe that one of the most critical skills of a leader is giving and receiving feedback *daily*. If that's a stretch for you, start small by incorporating the steps from this chapter at a pace that works for you. Make daily feedback—both giving it and receiving it—a long-term goal.

That's why I believe everyone should give each other behavioral feedback, even if you didn't learn how to in childhood. Whether team members have input for their colleagues, or union employees on a production line need to provide feedback to their supervisor, or early career managers need to give their peers feedback—they are all equally accountable for improving one another if they want to win as a team. Every leader is responsible for pointing out what they see in other people's behavior, mindset, and attitude in order to build the company's capabilities and help individuals thrive.

First, we need to discuss how to give constructive feedback. When you see how this ought to be done, you'll be better able to assess whether it was modeled for you as a child, including what step (or steps) of the process you may have never witnessed.

How to Give Constructive Feedback

When I discuss giving feedback with my clients, I always run them through this thought experiment. If I hand you a fuzzy piece of a baby blanket, what words come to mind as you hold it? My clients have said *baby*, *soft*, and *unconditional love*. Then what if I ask you what people come to mind. People will say *mom*, *grandma*, or *aunt*. Now, if I hand you a piece of sandpaper, what words come to mind as you hold it? They'll say *rough*, *coarse*, or *refinement*. What people come to mind? They say *dad*, *coach*, or *boss*.

Then I ask, "Would you rather get feedback from a blanket or from sandpaper?"

Most of my clients opt for the blanket.

Then I tell them it's a trick question. The truth is that we need both, and preferably from both the men and the women in our lives. Personally, I compare it to how my mother treats me. She loves me unconditionally and will speak the truth to me. I know that she wants the best for me and wants me to be my best self because she loves me. And so she doesn't hold back her truth. I need both her blanket and her sandpaper.

Let's see how this plays out in a real-life example between a teacher and her principal. Angie has taught second grade in the same elementary school for over three decades. Her students love her, and parents beg the administration to allow her to teach their kids, especially the children and even grandchildren of her first set of students. The administration also respects Angie because of the structure and tough love she provides to special needs children. Over the past decade, her class has held the most special needs children in the grade, more than any other classroom. Angie truly loves her kids, and when she's close to the brink, she will say: "It's a lot!"

One of Angie's students, a remarkable young boy named Mark, had lost his parents and lived with his grandmother. He was severely depressed, and Angie was apprehensive about his mental health and stability. She was worried that he might even hurt himself. She worked a long time to build an attachment with the boy and was overjoyed when, after three months, he came up to her and hugged her. A big step! She then worked out a special reward with the school's custodian to continue his progress. If he did his assignments, Mark would spend fifteen minutes once a week helping the custodian sweep his favorite room.

On a Monday, Angie revealed Mark's reward to him. He was so excited that he hugged her once again. However, at that moment, the new principal unexpectedly walked into the room and announced, "I'm taking Mark out of class this morning for a treat. There's a craft I'd like him to help me create."

Angie couldn't believe her ears, especially after all of the work she'd done with Mark and how much she knew he wanted to help the custodian. She thought, *Why did Sally have to walk in now?* Still, she respected her new boss and allowed her and Mark to leave without saying a word.

In the aftermath, Angie stewed. Her main goal had been to help this young boy feel safe and loved and grow in his confidence. She thought about how bad behavior by a boss can cause a distraction. To get back to helping the child, she knew she had to deal with the behavior quickly. At the end of the school day, Angie walked down to the principal's office and asked for a moment of her time. Sally agreed.

Let's use this example to learn and practice the four-step method for providing constructive feedback.

1. Convey Positive Intent and Set the Context

When you start providing someone with feedback, you want to create a psychologically safe moment so the person can hear you. Ideally, you are conveying that you care about making the person successful. You could say that you are aware they are working on improving their leadership in some way, or you could mention the situation and why you want to discuss it. Many times, but not always, it is also a good idea to ask if it's a good time to speak. If you're nervous, say so now.

Angie said, "Sally, you mentioned that you would appreciate feedback whenever we see something. I would like to talk to you about what happened in my classroom this morning. Is this a good time to discuss it and share some feedback?"

Sally responded, "Sure!" (Sally had encouraged her teachers to share feedback when they had it.)

Angie genuinely conveyed her appreciation and said thank you in return.

2. Describe Specifically What the Person Did

Explain precisely what you saw. Don't make any judgments or draw any conclusions. This is when you strive to be direct and specific.

Angie told Sally, "This morning, I was about to send Mark out with Mr. Joe for a long-awaited reward. The plan was for Mark to clean for fifteen minutes a week with Mr. Joe if he got all his assignments done. He was about to walk out of the room, and you walked in and told me, in front of Mark, that you were taking him out of the classroom because you had brought him a craft as a treat. You took him with you to make it."

Notice how Angie recounted the facts like a journalist. She made no judgments about Sally's actions in retelling what happened.

3. Describe the Impact on *You* Emotionally

You're seeking to speak the answer to this question: When the person did __________, how did it make *you* feel, and why? For example, you could say, "I felt ________ emotion because . . ." This step is what makes people listen to you. Give voice to the impact of the action on you. Make sure that you share how it made you feel, *not* how it might have made others feel. You only know how you feel; you cannot speak for someone else. And if the person receiving your feedback wants to discuss it further, you cannot answer questions on another's behalf, only on your own.

After Sally nodded her head, Angie continued. "Sally, I felt two emotions. On the one hand, I was *grateful* that you cared about my student and took time out of your weekend to do something for him. On the other hand, I felt *annoyed* because I was trying to give him structure and we had a plan. He was excited about the reward he was getting. In the end, he didn't get that reward today, and he showed up late in class, so he missed the morning work, which was disorientating for him."

Angie admitting her gratefulness for Sally's gesture suggests that Angie was genuinely appreciative and wasn't trying to control the situation or be selfish. She saw the good in her principal. However, saying she "felt annoyed" may have temporarily hurt Sally, yet it shows how serious the situation was to Angie. I call that temporary hurt an "ouch." Most feedback models suggest discussing the impact on someone by saying something like "It made me lock my door and scream." I tell my clients that sharing an emotion is like a hook. It forces the listener to tune in.

4. Recommend a Potential Solution

It is super-helpful to have a feedback provider brainstorm ways of doing things better, because they have personal experience with the person they're giving feedback to. So, for this step, first think about what would be most helpful and share the answer to this question out loud: *What should be changed or repeated in the future and why?*

Angie said, "Next time, can you please ask me what my plan is for my student and support me? I would appreciate it. I am also happy to hear your suggestions if you think I am not on top of it."

Sally responded, "Angie, I am sorry I disrupted your class and room. It sounds like I made things harder for you. I am sorry. I was trying to help. And no, I do not think you are not on top of it. I was inserting myself and not being helpful. I apologize."

When someone tells you you've hurt their feelings, it is best to apologize quickly. You can discuss it later. You may disagree with the feedback the person gave you. It doesn't matter. Apologizing will defuse the situation and help the person feel heard.

A key lesson Angie learned is that it is *your responsibility* to be precise when you deliver feedback. You need to provide examples of behavior that the person can see. So share the feedback as soon as possible after the incident and describe the specific behavior. It is your *right* to feel what you feel. The person you are giving feedback to does not need to agree with you. Your feedback is based on your feelings, beliefs, and values. This is your perspective, and it's valid.

If you are waiting for someone else to provide feedback to a person you should be giving feedback to, don't wait. If this world is to improve, you must start with yourself and lean in to giving (and receiving) constructive feedback at the office and home. For example, I treasure the fact that my daughter Adriana is incredibly honest with my husband and me about how we show up. She always gives us feedback; some isn't easy to hear, but it's real. It comes down to whether psychological safety exists or not. When it's present, we will tell someone else the truth. We will be candid with love because we care about one another.

Giving Feedback Close to Home

Providing constructive feedback is challenging in regular business situations. Imagine if your company was a family-owned business and your mother was your boss, your siblings and cousins members of the leadership team. This would add a whole other dimension to giving feedback. It might seem confusing and risky; however, I promise you it can be done.

Consider Julie, who is from the In the Shadows environment and worked for her family's business. Growing up, Julie often followed her mom around and watched her speak to large audiences of employees, suppliers, customers, and family members. She frequently struggled to differentiate herself from her mother. It wasn't surprising that, while incredibly smart and charming, Julie also struggled with confidence issues. She recalls a memorable time when her mother told everyone in the room that they must give each other constructive feedback. *Really?* Julie thought. *Do I have to tell my mother in front of others how she can improve? Oh, Lord.*

When the time approached for her mom to retire, she asked Julie if she would like to become the next CEO, or at least be considered. Julie had young boys in elementary school and didn't want to miss time with them. Still, she recognized the fantastic opportunity. She liked helping her family and challenging herself, yet she was conflicted. She told her mom, "This is an important and serious question. I need to go think about this and talk to Peter."

Julie spoke with Peter, her husband, and they decided she should hire a coach to help her decide if she wanted to be a CEO: me. We went through the leadership development process described in earlier chapters. She created her Emotional Timeline, we analyzed her personality through inventories, and we explored what was most important to her by considering her values and ethical boundaries. We learned that Julie loved to lead and achieve something significant on behalf of others. She started to dream about how her leadership would be different from her mother's.

To help answer that question, I did a 360 assessment where I interviewed fourteen people in her life, divided among peers, direct reports, her boss, senior stakeholders like the Board of Directors, and her husband. (Yes, her husband! No one knows us better than our spouses and life partners, although in this case, her boss is her mom!) That's the beauty of a complete 360. People at home can show us how we show up there. Comparing our behavioral patterns between work and home deepens self-awareness. It shows a true 360-degree perspective on a person's leadership.

Do you know how you show up at home?

Julie was alarmed when she heard from her 360 that she was not vulnerable about who she was as a leader or as a human being. She learned that she either avoided conflict or just chose to engage in it privately. The biggest shocker was that her team at work said she needed to get *significantly* better with giving constructive feedback as it was affecting the performance of the business and making employees cynical about whether leaders called out poor performers. She thought she had been strong at this. Her 360 participants said:

- "I've rarely seen Julie give behavioral feedback. If she attempts to, she gets short with people and doesn't use the four-step method.

She doesn't describe bad behaviors, how they make her feel, or share solutions."

- "She only compliments people and tells them what she likes about them, as opposed to positive feedback–what they should do more of because they are so skilled."
- "We have had performance issues in this company for years because she and her mom don't deal with them. She doesn't care. She lets people do whatever they want to."

Yikes, Julie thought. *I have work to do.* She didn't like hearing the hard truths. Still, she leaned in to it. She took a week off to reflect on what she'd learned about herself.

Julie realized it was true. She did struggle with giving constructive feedback. She's soft-hearted and tunes into the emotions of others, so she would confuse giving constructive negative feedback with making others feel like they weren't loved. I remember a time she had to tell her aunt that she couldn't go to the Caribbean because of a brewing crisis in her part of the business. The aunt told her that she would handle it when she returned. Julie said, "No, it has to be done now, or we could lose this business." Her aunt begrudgingly agreed and understood. Even saying that had been really hard for Julie.

Her 360 and an examination of her Emotional Timeline began her journey in constructive feedback, which was very uncomfortable for her. Still, she recognized the value of doing this well. In fact, when she became CEO, she required that everyone in the company go through the same training. She worked with her head of HR to embed these skills in the company. Today, Julie is a fantastic role model for providing feedback to her colleagues. She gives constructive feedback to her aunts, uncles, cousins, and other family members in the room. "It never gets easier, but it changes things!" she told me.

Time and time again, I have seen leaders change just like Julie. And it inspires them so much that they decide to expose everyone in their company to constructive feedback. If giving helpful feedback is so transformative, why do so many of us struggle with it, especially when I believe so many of us desire more helpful feedback in our lives?

I'll give you one guess.

Too few of us learned how to give and receive constructive feedback in our childhood environments.

How Your Childhood Environment Influences How You Give Feedback

As a child you may have been taught to respect your elders. Don't be "fresh" or talk back to them. In other words, you were trained not to give your parents or grandparents feedback on their behavior because *any* feedback was deemed disrespectful. And so you may have unknowingly carried that reticence to speak out into your work environment today. A boss is like a parent, so why would you challenge their behavior, especially in public?

This lack of practice helps explain why leaders are scared and anxious to speak their truth about what they see. They worry that saying what they believe is true will harm their relationship with the person receiving the feedback. However, this approach often has a different effect. Leaders don't understand that while delivering feedback may hurt for a moment ("ouch"), people appreciate honesty.

Regardless of whom you give feedback to, it's crucial to recognize how your childhood influences your delivery. To do this well, you need to think about where your trigger points might be activated and get ahead of them.

- What forms of constructive feedback were given in your home?
- Did your parents catch you doing things well and point it out?
- Were they specific about what they saw you do?
- Did they share how it made them feel emotionally when you did something well?
- Did they say they were proud of you?
- Did they offer you suggestions for getting better if you did something wrong in their eyes?

Now let's look at how each home environment may have contributed to how a person experiences feedback today.

If You Were Raised in The Nest

You may have often experienced psychological safety when speaking your truth as a child, so you know how to create a secure environment for others to hear feedback. You invest time in setting the proper context and making people feel respected. Today, you may say things like "I care about you and want you to succeed. Let me share some feedback to help you improve." You realize how important that sort of feedback is, yet you prefer to give positive feedback. For example, when people leave my client Kristi's office, she always says something positive and uplifting, as if they've visited her home and she's sending them off with well wishes.

If You Were Raised in The Model Home

You likely enjoyed an idyllic environment. Since you may have emulated certain elders, you observed their behaviors and could talk about how those behaviors made you feel. They gave you a lot of feedback, which normalized doing the feedback model. You may have even liked hearing their feedback (which is unusual!). You may be adept at tuning in to behaviors and using emotions as data more than others. However, you may sound judgmental in your observations or solution recommendations if the person's values are dissonant with your own beliefs.

If You Were Raised In the Shadows or The Nomad

These environments share a commonality: They were centered around one of the parents' or grandparents' jobs or roles. However, there's a difference when it comes to feedback. If you come from In the Shadows, you may have been very in tune with what your parents and guests were doing. You could, if asked, describe behavior. However, you may have dismissed how it made you feel. Why? Because you were taught: to prioritize focusing on guests and others rather than yourself. If you come from The Nomad, you're likely good at building superficial relationships, so you can also set the context and explain what you see a person doing. You'll focus more on the positive attributes to compliment them and build the relationship rather than choose to articulate how they can be better.

If You Were Raised in The Matriarchy or The Phantom Limb

Due to divorce or the death of a parent, you may have taken on the role of the missing spouse (whether intentionally or not). Children from these backgrounds become good listeners and spend a lot of time reassuring (which is not feedback) and offering suggestions (versus solutions). As adults they are more direct about how their behavior is probably affecting others (which of course they shouldn't be doing; they should only share feedback from their own perspective).

If You Were Raised in The Maze, Sounds of Silence, or Slings and Arrows

You likely suffered shame. You didn't feel valued. You feared sharing what you saw behaviorally, and you might have been terrified to say how it made you feel. Today, you most often won't offer suggestions on how things could be better until you feel more secure within yourself, or validated and protected by others in your home or workplace. Also, if angry, you may deliver feedback destructively. However, if you address your block, your confidence builds, your anger dissipates, and you can later speak the truth. Because you felt unsafe in your home, you became very observant. Long-term, this will enhance your ability to give feedback. when you feel safe to do it.

Using the following table, consider how your childhood environment has affected your ability to provide constructive feedback today.

Environment	Step 1: Provide Context and Convey Positive Intent	Step 2: Describe Specific Behaviors	Step 3: Impact on You Through Emotions (I feel X because . . .)	Step 4: Solutions
Stable Homes				
The Nest	Positive, supportive environment	Shares a lot of specific constructive positive feedback; If you believe the constructive negative feedback will be helpful, you will push yourself to mention it	Shares positive emotions more	Provides suggestions in a constructive way
The Model Home		Attuned to what people do / don't do; Can sound judgmental if person's values differ	Can probably describe how it makes you feel	
The Matriarchy		Takes on the role of life partner—very direct over time		Offers solutions, spends time reassuring
Homes of Complexity				
In the Shadows		Pretty observant of behavior; Shares if asked	Not tuned in to how you feel	
The Nomad	If it helps the person, you will share, as it will help the relationship	Points out the positive behaviors to build relationships	Very complimentary	
The Phantom Limb		Takes on the role of life partner—very direct		Offers solutions or suggestions; Spends time reassuring
Homes of Trauma				
The Maze		Observes a lot to protect yourself	Probably won't talk about it or will say it badly through anger; Learned to predict the parent's mood	

Homes of Trauma (*cont.*)				
Slings and Arrows	Mostly negative—feel shame or little value	Won't share what you see, or if you are angry, you may deliver it poorly	Would be afraid to talk about how you feel	Doesn't necessarily feel valued enough to share unless you have overcome your block
Sounds of Silence	Can provide context	Sees a lot!; If you've overcome blocks, you can deliver feedback well to help others—otherwise you will remain shut down	Can express emotions	And offers solutions

Feedback in Action

John Replogle has enjoyed a remarkable career leading values-based organizations like Unilever, Burt's Bees, and Seventh Generation. He's renowned for his ability as a leader to connect with people and inspire them to reach new heights. But before he reached his full potential, he had to unlearn some of the lessons he'd been taught as a young man, especially about using feedback to help the people around him thrive and grow. To accomplish this, he had to look far into his past.

When John was a child, his father was the dominant figure in his household. Both of John's parents were well educated. However, his disciplinarian father constantly challenged John and his four brothers to excel in school and sports. His childhood environment was a blend of The Model Home and Slings and Arrows. The only way to earn praise was by winning. Consequently, John embraced that spirit of competition.

He excelled in school and began his career at the prestigious Boston Consulting Group before moving on to leadership at the global beer company Guinness. He brought that same level of competitiveness to work with him. "I had a model of how I thought about operating," John told me. "I had a high need to be one of the smartest guys in the room and to be the one who found the answer and drove the solution."

When I met John at that point in his career, I saw his competitive nature emerge when he dealt with colleagues or team members—especially when he needed to deliver or receive feedback. He could become very short, use four-letter words, and lose patience. As you might imagine, people receiving John's feedback didn't often respond well.

Yet, as I worked with John, exploring his childhood and the kind of environment he was building with his wife for their children, I saw him evolve into a more self-aware leader. "I realized I was carrying a big shield," John told me. "I didn't feel loved or fully affirmed as a kid. So my shield was being 'right.' It took me a long time to put that down and find other ways to build connections, affirmation, and ultimately a team."

With my help and that of several mentors inside the organization, as well as his wife, Kristin, who modeled unconditional love in a family, John began to appreciate the critical role of feedback in building solid relationships with his team members. But it required unlearning deeply ingrained lessons from his childhood, his early career, and even from business school, about driving decisions and striving to be the smartest person in the room. By leveraging his team members' rich and diverse range of wisdom and experience, rather than his insights alone, he achieved better outcomes for everyone.

John said, "The old me would have stood in front of people with a marker and a whiteboard, written a solution, and then demonstrated the proof points about why what I was saying was right. At first, it was a struggle to sit on my hands and not be the first to speak out, and listen instead. Over time, I became comfortable with not having the 'right' answer or the solution. Rather, I learned to listen and let others shine. It took me a long time to practice being okay with being wrong and vulnerable."

A key moment in John's leadership growth came when he built sales teams at Guinness in Great Britain. He intentionally sought to create powerful emotional bonds and trust with his team by being open and vulnerable. "We started to practice understanding what each of us was going through in life beyond what we were doing at work and to bring that into the workplace," John told me. "You must be willing to reveal yourself, expose yourself as you truly are, warts and all, and put it out there and make it okay to do that. It's about building trust with each other and spending the time to get to know each other. When you build trust and safety, it's incredible how quickly people will open up and come together."

Growing up, John practiced competing with his brothers. Now he was learning and practicing instead how to collaborate with a new set of brothers and sisters in pursuit of the greater good of the team.

While John was making great strides in building his UK-based teams, he knew he was facing a difficult decision regarding a manager named Mike. Mike ran a call center in London, and his employees, 80 percent of whom were women, had filed multiple complaints about his gruff, command-and-control leadership style. John knew he needed to muster the courage to intervene.

Mike was physically imposing, standing at least six feet four inches tall and was built like a brick wall. He was also a well-known local rugby star, and he led his team like they were all on the rugby pitch. Mike would push them to improve their numbers, such as call times and customer satisfaction scores, as if they were trying to win a game. Yet the harder Mike pushed the team, the worse they performed. And the worse the team performed, the louder and more aggressive Mike became toward them.

"Mike was struggling at his job, and people could see it," John told me. "He was creating a fear culture."

John's challenge was that Mike reminded him in many ways of how he had led earlier in his career. Now John had to give Mike feedback on his leadership style and ask him to change it—or there was a risk that Mike would lose his job.

Mike had been very successful on an actual rugby pitch with other men. That approach was deeply ingrained in him, but it wasn't working with a predominantly female team. He couldn't just show up as a masculine, domineering figure. Instead, he needed to create a safe, secure, and vulnerable environment for his team.

"I knew this would not be easy feedback for him to receive," John told me. "Mike needed to go through the hard work of understanding that how he showed up wasn't working. Many cared about Mike as a person. However, he had never gotten any feedback before, and I had to give him some of the harshest, most direct feedback I've ever given anyone in my life." Fortunately, as John described it, he had "put some money in the Mike relationship bank." He said that "Mike knew me to be someone who was working on myself. He knew I had a personal development agenda and was open to feedback. I demanded feedback from my team." John also knew Mike, his family, his history, and what mattered to him.

"Mike had grown up much like I had, in a demanding family," John told me. "He didn't have an affectionate relationship with his father. He found rugby to be a great outlet and release for him. In many ways, I could frame the feedback so that Mike could understand, relate to, and see it as helpful in his journey."

To give the necessary feedback, John went to Mike's office in a vast building wing where up to fifty team members were based. John sat at a small round table and asked Mike to sit across from him, in front of his team but with his back to the door. "I didn't want his team to see his face," John told me.

John and Mike then spent the next hour talking—and crying.

"I had to be vulnerable in expressing to Mike how much I wanted him to succeed," John told me. "But I couldn't let him off the hook. I told him I was holding him accountable for how he needed to come back to me with a plan to change how he led. I wanted him to think deeply about it. I told him I had his back and he would fail only if he didn't try to do things differently."

John talked to Mike about how managing people by the numbers wasn't helping them show up with a smile in their voice on the phone. Mike needed to catch them when they were winning and not just losing. What helped is that the team wanted Mike to succeed. They were all honest about what they were going through to help him evolve as a leader.

John said, "That was a huge gift they gave Mike by opening themselves up so that he didn't feel alone. That was a beautiful moment and not something I had ever experienced with my brothers."

To his credit, Mike leaned in to becoming more aware of how he was showing up as a leader. He was a team player, so he learned to see his role as uplifting the team's spirit and using language to support that. Mike also worked with his wife, who became a coach for him. After a year of hard work, he had become a different person and leader. He'd shifted from a rugby team captain to a captain of a customer service organization.

"Mike is one of my heroes," John told me. "He excelled through this period of change and self-discovery and stayed with Guinness for years and years after that."

This story is one of many that has impressed me over the years with how John has created psychologically safe and intimate environments in the workplace where people don't just accept feedback from their peers; they demand it. As he once told me, "I believe in using feedback as fuel, but feedback is much more on the how than the what. You need to show that you care about someone as an individual, their growth, and their family. That pulls everyone closer to where you can create a family-like environment at work. But it takes time, courage, vulnerability, and trust."

As you move forward, please remember:

1. If you care about someone, you will give them feedback and genuine relationships will improve, not worsen. This will be easier for people from more positive environments like The Nest or The Model Home and The Matriarchy, so let's learn from the kids who grew up there. Providing feedback works and will enhance relationships.
2. The hook is telling someone how their behavior made you feel emotionally. It makes them want to change.
3. Creating psychological safety occurs in Step 1 of the feedback model, setting the context. Regardless of the childhood environment you are from, start with warmth and a smile. Be vulnerable about how you want to help the person.
4. Your view is valid and worth sharing. Whether your parents welcomed feedback when you were young or punished you for it, share your truth. It is your responsibility to be clear about what you see and your right to know what you see.

[16]

Real Conversations in Action

Outside the hustle and bustle of the resort town of Myrtle Beach, there's a lovely lake surrounded by a park. It's a peaceful place. People come there to relax and enjoy family time together. As Rob and his father watched the sun glinting off the water, they sat at a picnic table and talked for three hours about their complex history.

It was their first real conversation.

Rob had worked hard to reach this point. He'd spent months, even years, laying the groundwork to create a psychologically safe space, to listen empathetically, to engage in conflict, and to provide constructive feedback where he and his father could talk about their challenging past in a truthful and vulnerable way.

Rob could never forget the most pivotal moment of his Act I, with his dad in a starring role as the antagonist. In fact, he even told me that he remembers it like a scene out of a movie, so crystal clear is it in his memories.

After he arrived home from college, Rob and his parents sat at their kitchen table. His dad, as usual, was prickly and argumentative. With a military background, he could be domineering and aggressive. In contrast, his mother was a saint who would never say a bad word about anyone. However, that didn't mean she didn't stand up for herself, and particularly with her husband.

An argument erupted between his parents. Rob's father threatened his mother, saying, "If you don't do what I'm saying, I'm going to slap you."

She replied, "I'd like to see you try it."

Rob's father then reached over the table and slapped her across the face.

Rob lost it. He grabbed his father and was about to hit him, until his mother grabbed his arm, pleading with him to stop.

Rob yelled at his father: "I thought you never hit a woman!" Then he stormed out of the house. He slammed the door behind him and cried. He told himself, *I don't need this relationship.*

He returned to college and kept his parents at a distance, rarely seeing or talking to them for years. He was ashamed of them and about what had happened that day. He never told anyone about that moment—until he shared the story with me.

When I first met Rob, he was one of several high-potential leaders I had been hired to coach in an Authentic Leadership program. As I do with all my clients, we began by embracing their vulnerability and sharing in a group setting their highs and lows from their early lives.

Rob later admitted that he wasn't prepared to do what I asked. As someone who had never worked with a therapist, he had rarely shared any of the details of his childhood with anyone, including his by then ex-wife. "I was super nervous," Rob told me about that day we met. "I had never been through a deep examination of myself. I heard that you would push me to go deep."

While his fight-or-flight instinct told him to run, Rob stayed. He knew that future company leaders were expected to complete this work, and Rob was ambitious. He was also curious about what I was trying to do and just how I'd accomplish that with him. So he decided to stick it out.

That was the first step in Rob confronting his block.

On the first day of Rob's executive development group session, each person had thirty minutes to share a brief overview of their childhood, as well as their greatest joys and sorrows. "I never thought I would have shared some of the things I shared," Rob told me. "But listening to the other stories was heavy. And that helped to open me up."

While I had asked everyone to share their biggest sorrow, Rob felt the need to share what he considered his most significant failure—the end of his first marriage. He blamed his upbringing and how his family acted with each other for his divorce. However, sharing his emotions about those difficult memories eventually had a freeing effect and helped him better understand the role he'd directly played in his marriage. "I never intended to speak about these things out loud—ever," Rob told me. "And certainly not think about why they happened or how that changed who I am or how I show up at home and work. I never made any of those connections."

Another pattern emerged when Rob and I worked on his ETL a few weeks later. He shared a story about how he'd excelled in high school and college football. However, his father would also ask Rob disrespectful questions about his teammates' race. Recalling those remarks, Rob said he "was ashamed and felt guilty. I thought I was doing something wrong because I didn't stand up for them."

In college, Rob's parents never showed up to watch any of his games. Worse, when he experienced a catastrophic injury that required extensive surgery, they never visited him during the several weeks he spent in the hospital. He was devastated, mainly because his grandmother had made the trip alone even though she was ill and didn't have a car. Why hadn't his parents come as well?

And then his next major negative moment on his ETL appeared: the unforgettable dinner when his father slapped his mother.

As we discussed his childhood memories, I asked Rob, "How did your father grow up?"

He shared that his parents had come from large families. Then he remembered that his father's father had abandoned the family when Rob's father was just seven years old.

I paused to let Rob think about the ramifications of that history. Then I asked, "Do you ever have any empathy for your father because he grew up without a dad?"

Rob was speechless.

He'd later tell me, "That question floored me. I hadn't ever thought about it that way. I was so angry toward my father that I had never looked through that lens. I never gave him the benefit of the doubt. I never asked questions." Recognizing how he was carrying the trauma of his ancestors, Rob began to walk toward forgiveness. "It was a turning point for me," he said. "I knew I could either sit around and complain about things and blame others or deal with it. I needed to hold myself accountable and change how I showed up."

Rob was naturally empathetic to everyone around him—everyone except his father. He decided he didn't want to remain angry any longer. He called me soon after our meeting. I don't think he even said hi. He just said, "Pam, I'm ready to talk to my dad."

I hoped he could hear my smile. "That's great, Rob. Why now? What are your goals?"

"I had an epiphany." After his divorce, Rob had remarried, and they were building a life together with children. That's when he realized his kids had no real relationship with their grandparents. "As wonderful as my mom was, I was trying to protect [my children] from my relationship with my dad. But I was hurting them by keeping them away. Plus, speaking to my dad will help me achieve peace in my heart, no matter how he reacts."

The line went quiet.

Then Rob said, "I want to let it go."

I smiled even wider at his breakthrough, yet I knew he still had significant work to do. I cautioned him to ensure he had a plan and knew his goals for their conversation. I asked him to consider what he wanted to accomplish and exactly how he would do it.

Rob did an exceptional job of scripting out how his conversation with his father might go, doing his best to anticipate what he'd say based on his dad's answers. "I am good about writing things down," Rob told me. "As an introvert, this helps me. I wanted to respect my father and ensure I did it well, regardless of the conversation's direction."

Rob had a plan.

The question was, how would his dad react?

Rob was brilliant and methodical in how he went about creating psychological safety for his father. He spent months putting his plan into action, and he made sure that every step he took was a safe next step for his father. For instance, Rob purposefully texted his father first, which gave his dad the option to reply or ignore Rob's outreach.

Rob texted, "I want to talk. I have questions that I would like to ask."

His father texted back, "Sure."

To Rob, that text was like seeing his father take a tentative step back toward their relationship. Now he could proceed to the next phase: a phone call. Rob later filled me in on their call. "I told him that my company was investing in me as a leader, and I wanted to learn more about my childhood and his childhood and how these things affect how I show up. I also wanted to know because I wanted to become a better husband and father to my kids."

Rob was worried that his father would yell at him or hang up. He didn't do either. His father said, "I'd be happy to talk. I think it's great that you are doing this."

His father felt safe enough to take another step closer.

Rob's response is what you might expect if you were in his shoes: "I was shocked and a little embarrassed that it had gone so well versus what I had scripted. I was learning that once people are asked, they want to know more. They begin to ask you, 'When can we talk again?'" (As I've witnessed time and again with my clients who need to have similar conversations, many parents crave these kinds of conversations with their children and would do anything to take care of them. They just need to be asked.)

After texting and talking, Rob felt comfortable enough to make his biggest ask: "Could we meet?"

That's when his father took literal steps toward healing their relationship and found himself sitting across from his long-estranged son at that lovely lake surrounded by a park in Myrtle Beach. At that picnic table, Rob further ensured his father's psychological safety by reminding him that they were there because Rob was "doing some leadership work" on himself. Because Rob placed the focus there, his father could feel relief that their discussion wasn't going to be about him or his past shortcomings.

Then, in that safe space that Rob had laid the groundwork for over many months, he walked his father through his Emotional Timeline—from his best moments to his worst.

While Rob's father denied making racist remarks, he did remember the incident in the kitchen. "That was a real low point in my life," he admitted. He said he immediately regretted his actions and had never again struck his wife. "If you don't believe me, ask your mother."

Rob felt the emotions of that day rise in him, but he kept steady. Then he brought up how much it had hurt him that his parents hadn't come to visit him in the hospital after he had back surgery. "I was prepared for a fight," Rob said. "But it didn't go that way. He reacted very differently."

Rob's dad looked down at the ground and was silent for a minute. "That was the biggest mistake in my life. Both your mom and I wanted to go, but I said we didn't have the money. The money shouldn't have mattered. That was a bad decision."

Looking back on the moment, Rob said he "was a little surprised at how open he was. The fact that he apologized. And he asked whether there was anything more he could share that would be helpful. I never expected that level of empathy or listening from him. Having that conversation was so liberating."

They continue having tough conversations today. His parents even came to stay with Rob's family for six weeks—something that would never have happened earlier. Now Rob's parents have begun building a relationship with their grandchildren.

Rob admits that his relationship with his father will never be adorned with rainbows and flowers. However, the hate is gone, and he can share what's on his mind and ask his dad questions about his childhood, something he would never have done before having that first real conversation. He also recognizes that his parents changed over the years. They now help others and support underrepresented groups. "My pain and hurt did not allow me to see this," Rob admitted. "It's an entirely different relationship than it used to be."

When Rob learned that his father didn't have a role model for being a good dad or husband, it humbled him to think that his own childhood had been better than what his dad had experienced. Building empathy for someone for whom he once had such anger was liberating for Rob. It's helped him understand the value of vulnerability and empathy as a leader. As Rob told me, "I never really understood the power of sharing. I always thought leaders must be strong and never show their weaknesses. I was completely wrong. Leadership strength is about sharing your entire story. Times where you were wrong or that you failed. Your worries, your fears, and your joys. Here's where I have failed. Here's who I am and why I show up the way I do."

One shift Rob made was to ask different questions of the people he works with. Rather than asking about superficialities, he uses empathy and emotions as data to connect with people and share his observations. People who grow up in a Slings and Arrows environment, as Rob did, often develop the strength of respecting others and trying to find ways to connect with them on a deeper level.

For example, Rob remembers when one of his team members—let's call him Tim—started attending virtual meetings with his camera turned off. This surprised Rob because Tim was always very social and talkative in meetings. Something didn't feel right, so Rob reached out to see how Tim was doing.

During their conversations, Tim mentioned struggling with some issues at home with his wife. That was Rob's cue to share his divorce story and how he'd learned from that experience. Tim then opened up more about how he had been sexually abused as a child and how those issues had begun to impact his marriage.

Rob connected Tim with their company's employee assistance program so Tim could get professional help. Rob also stayed in touch, checking in on Tim to see how he was doing.

One day, Rob received a call.

"Rob, I wanted to thank you for listening to me. I learned that I was depressed. I was watching a movie that featured sexual abuse, and it triggered me." Tim went on to explain that he had since shared with his wife what happened to him as a child—something he had never told her or anyone else—and that they were working on healing together.

While emotional healing is complex and is the result of hundreds of variables, I like to see this moment in this light: Because Rob had learned how to overcome his generational trauma, he was able to help someone else overcome his.

Since this work brought out his greatness as a human being, Rob has been promoted several times. His story shows what is possible when leaders embrace transparency, tune in to their emotions, move past their embarrassments, learn to connect deeply and meaningfully, and start having real conversations with everyone they know.

Imagine what our world would look like if we all learned to lead like this.

Exit Stage Left

The single greatest reward I have as a coach is to hear how my clients have grown *outside* of their professional lives. At first, they'll exclaim, "What have I done to my kids? What kind of environment have I created?" Over time, as we accomplish our work together, their tone changes. They start to tell me, "I wish I would have done this work years ago so that I could have impacted my children even more." I love hearing their stories about how our time together has affected the home environment they're purposefully creating for their children.

For instance, I fondly remember working with Amy. She grew up in The Phantom Limb after having lost her mom when she was a young girl. She never got the opportunity to practice giving positive, constructive feedback to her mother about what her mother meant to her. And she never had the chance to receive feedback from her mother. She had long struggled with both giving and receiving feedback in her family environment. Yet, after committing to the process I laid out in this book, Amy has now embraced coaching her two teenage daughters in how they deliver and receive constructive feedback.

"We're on this journey together as parents and children," Amy told me. "Now, when I see something, I'll ask my daughters, 'Are you open to feedback? I want to share something with you, but I'll wait if it's not a good time. If it is, here we go.'" She's come to understand that there's a time and a place to engage in feedback (and certainly in the world of teenage dynamics). By finding the right time, when her daughters feel psychologically safe to talk, she has taught them how to defuse a situation rather than amplify a potentially emotional situation.

"There's a helpful control element to it," Amy told me. "And typically, it gives them the right mindset to hear the feedback I want to provide. I have this mantra with them and have had it their entire life: 'I will do anything for you. I will work incredibly hard for you and to the extreme, but I won't work harder for you than you.'"

What inspires me about Amy and many other leaders I have worked with is that they have taken the lessons they've learned about the influence of their childhood and decided to pay it forward in ways they hope will help their children.

As you consider all of the implications of what we've discussed, consider the further implications of how changing your life could positively change the lives of those nearest to you. Only your imagination can limit your impact.

As our time together draws to a close, I'd like to tell you one more story from my childhood. I'll never forget when I saw *Little Women* on Broadway. Louisa May Alcott wrote it in the 1860s, yet it is as relevant now as it was then. I watched the March sisters—Meg, Jo, Beth, and Amy—working, playing, and loving completely. I saw them grow from childhood to adulthood, dealing with the joys and sorrows of being young women. Then I experienced their pain when their father loses all their money, leaves home, then falls ill. His wife comes to his aid, leaving the girls to fend for themselves.

Meg and Jo work to support the family, but it isn't easy. Meg, the oldest, is beautiful and traditional. Jo is a hotheaded tomboy who writes. Beth is a peacemaker and pianist and cripplingly shy. And Amy is a materialistic artist who longs for fine society. When their mother is called home because Beth, all of thirteen years old, develops scarlet fever and dies, my heart broke for the little women.

After the curtain closed and the play ended, I'd been on an emotional roller coaster for at least three hours. In the silence of the patrons shuffling out of the room, I thought about how I hadn't seen my specific life represented on stage, yet I still saw myself. The idea of losing a sibling or child was heartbreaking for me. Family is everything to me. I kept thinking: *Life is fleeting. I don't have much time. You just don't know how much time is left to live your life fully. You certainly don't know how much your behavior and your life is affecting or impacting those around you.*

Remember the ripple effect when someone throws a stone in the water? Consider how Beth's death changed Jo's life. When Beth dies from the lingering effects of the scarlet fever she contracted years earlier, Jo vows to live her life with more care and consideration for others, just as Beth would have.

For a few hours, because of the characters, the setting, and the compelling and emotional story, I experienced moments of self-revelation, even as I laughed and cried. I hope that, after spending tens of thousands of words with me, you may feel the same.

Even if the feelings that came up were difficult, I hope you've come to see them as necessary to feel so that you can continue to make waves in your life.

In taking a front-row seat to your life, you may have recalled people and moments you haven't thought about in decades. I hope that brought back more warm memories than cold. I hope you felt joy for the child you were and empathy for what they had to endure. And I sincerely hope that you experienced a number of aha moments, where you saw an indelible, unmistakable connection between the child you were and the leader you are today.

As you realize we all have areas for development, I hope you'll seek help to grow yourself wisely. Of course, you may reach out to me at manfredocurtis.com for personal coaching. However, you could also consider talking to a counselor or a trusted mentor. Your goal shouldn't be to overcome your shortcomings as soon as possible. Your goal should be to start that journey as soon as possible. Take your next best step to become the person you want to be—the person that "childhood you" always dreamed you could be.

You may need to revisit the various home environments and decide which one most describes your upbringing, the home you grew up in. Remind yourself about all your amazing strengths. You may need to talk about your memories with your parents, siblings, or other loved ones who knew you as a child, to learn more about the facts of your life. I'm willing to bet that exploration will reveal so much about you that you were never aware of before.

For some of you, your next best step might require the hard work of overcoming a significant block. Consider rereading Act II and slowly ruminating on what may be blocking you, as well as the person, or people, you need to speak to in order to move past that block. Make sure you articulate your goals for the conversation and build a plan for psychological safety. Then make your plan, even if it takes years, and follow that plan.

Others may need to live in Act III for a time, to truly learn how to speak your truth and have a real conversation. Again, don't forget the secret sauce! Work through the simple four steps for constructive feedback that are by no means simple to put into everyday practice. Then begin incorporating those steps into all of your relationships. Maintain smart boundaries, but be willing to risk vulnerability and authenticity and just see what happens. Even though the stories throughout this book have shown you what's possible, I still believe you'll be amazed at what can happen in your leadership and your life.

The play of this book may be over, but yours has truly just begun.

Don't wait.

Be your best self now.

With Gratitude and Love

I am consumed with love and appreciation for the amazing people behind this book. It's difficult for me to articulate how grateful I am to each of you, but you know I am. This was a dream—to share what I have learned from my work with executives with people around the globe to change their lives. Each of you helped me accomplish that, and I will forever hold you in my heart for these specific reasons.

To those who helped me launch:

Eileen Schneidman: For your endless optimism and belief in the importance of this work. You see everyone's gifts, including mine. Thank you for fostering the kickoff of this book by reaching out to your college friend, Jeanne McIntire, who connected us with Leslie.

Leslie Stevens: I will never forget that wonderful lunch in New York where you offered to connect me to Pattie.

Pattie Sellers: You graciously invited me to speak to Fortune's Most Powerful Women, and you connected me to Scott Greenstein and Rory Belfi at SiriusXM, who initiated and produced my show, *Corner Office Confidential*. You also introduced me to Todd Schuster of Aevitas Creative Management, who formalized a book launch.

Todd Schuster: Thank you for valuing the work and saying, "There is definitely a book in here!" Those words propelled me, from providing example proposals to most importantly introducing me to Jane, my agent extraordinaire.

Jane von Mehren: You above all have been by my side through it all. You have held my hand and kept me safe the whole way. Pushed me. Consoled me. Taught me. Made me grow. I owe you so much. While writing a proposal was no easy task (synthesizing thirty-five years), it is our deep friendship and partnership that I cherish.

There is nothing more important than the power of connections.

To my main writing coaches and editors:

Darren Dahl: From that first meeting in Asheville where the metaphor of the play was born, to teaching me how to find and tell a story, and just plain making me get the ninety thousand words on the page—with kindness.

Blake Atwood: For helping me find and articulate my voice, strengthening my structure, and teaching me how to write a book so it is compelling and engaging—with patience and empathy, especially at deadline time.

I have learned so much from you both and trust you implicitly. Thank you.

To my amazing Manfredo Curtis team and associates:

I know that I'm blessed to work with the best people in our industry: You! Your wisdom, compassion, and emotional intelligence draw others to you, including me. I always want to hear your insights because they are illuminating. Working and playing with you has made me better. I am most touched by your generosity of time.

Allen Hammer, PhD: My go-to expert. For your full read of the earlier manuscript (Phew!), challenging my views, and helping me refine my perspective throughout!

Sarita Bhakuni, PsyD: For reading the environments and offering your view as a clinical psychologist, especially around The Maze.

Eva Kant, LCSW-R: For sharing your wisdom about The Sounds of Silence.

Kiki Cahn, MBA: For your research and ability to enhance the tools we use to help our clients through your thoughtful and practical words, some that are shared in this book.

Geno Schnell, PhD; Rob Devine, MA (and Al): For your humor about environment names. Thanks for the laughter!

Martha Morris Graham: who I first met in 1999. Our joint work included rich conversations about our shared interests and perspectives in this work. Initially a loving mentor to me, then a colleague. I worked for you. You worked for me. Our joint work included wonderful conversations that helped me develop my approaches today. I am so grateful.

Dayna Macari: For somehow helping me to organize and run my work life and personal life while I wrote this book.

Rachel Kleffman: Your insights about editing and writing came at just the right moment.

Pam Cunningham: For your clever, multiple attempts to name this book! And **Aaron Clar**, for your compelling and beautiful videos.

To my clients and friends, some named, some not:

I am moved by your willingness to share your stories to help others. This required interviewing you multiple times, lending pieces of your own words, reviewing and editing, not to mention having real conversations about putting your personal story out there. Thank you for your trust in me. Thank you to Tom Linebarger, Curtis Welling, Matt Levatich, Sara Levinson, John Replogle, James Schacht, Earl Newsome, the Yoder family, and Georgia Nelson. And thank you to the partially named, like Amy, Chip, Jill, and Rob, and the renamed or unnamed, for your belief in the importance of this work and your personal support of me.

To my publisher and amazing Simon & Schuster team and connections:

Stephanie Hitchcock: "You got me with hello!," not to mention your phrase "Woot-woot." Thank you for your genuine desire for collaboration, insightful feedback on the manuscript, flexibility, and wanting to make this great because you love the content.

Karina Leon, Michael Trudeau, and all the people involved who I haven't met, including that anonymous person who came up with the main title that we love, and to **Kimberly Harrington**, who taught me so much about titling.

Paul Slicker, my publicist: Thank you for your hard work, and I look forward to seeing the impact of our work together.

To my family and closest friends: So many of you provided me with endless encouragement, support, and interest in this work. I appreciate all of you.

For Guy Manfredo, who, while unnamed in this book, is and always will be my big brother. Thank you for loving me and reminding me that when a goal is in front of me, I am determined and focused. I needed that.

My nieces and nephews, especially Katie Manfredo and Andrew Thomas, for offering up environment names or sharing your personal experiences.

My godson, Nick, whose humor and protective love pushes me to keep going.

My sister-in-laws, especially Liz Manfredo, Beth Curtis-Thomas, and Julie Dudones, whose endless support on this endeavor, especially when pulling my hair out, meant the world.

My dearest friends, Melissa Elmasry and Dina Gumins, whose consistent, genuine interest and listening ears warmed my heart.

My mom and dad, for being the best parents I could ever hope for.

My husband, John Curtis, Jr., PhD, for being my sounding board in selection and assessment and for validating my observations of your personal environment. Most importantly, for ensuring I was focused on the most important thing through these writing years: our life together. I love you.

And for **Christopher**, **my daughter-in-law Anna**, **Ryan**, and **Adriana**, for inspiring me to want to be a better mom. I cherish and love you more than anything.

Appendix: The Emotions Library

Moving From . . .

Fear → **Love**

Angry	Upset	Confident	Caring
Despairing	Sad	Intrigued	Excited
Depressed	Hurt	Optimistic	Enthusiastic
Disappointed	Embarrassed	Compassionate	Happy
Rejected	Aggravated	Proud	Grateful
Confused	Agitated	Hopeful	Relaxed
Distressed	Irritated	Content	Joyful
Scared	Insecure	Secure	Admired
Worried	Perplexed	Worthy	Buoyant
Annoyed	Nervous	Inquisitive	Inspired
Anxious	Drained	Curious	Exhilarated
Cranky	Frustrated	Engaged	Jubilant
Frazzled	Shocked	Relieved	Safe
Overwhelmed	Apprehensive	Surprised	Amazed

Notes

Introduction

xvi *an HR leader with referent power has employees who open up to them:* John French and Bertram Raven first identified and classified types of power in their 1959 paper, "The Social Bases of Power." Their model has since been expanded.

xvii *I've modeled this book after the essentials of a three-act play:* As a longtime entertainer through song, I find that this structure marries a personal passion (performance) with a professional passion (leadership development). As you're working through this book, I hope you'll also see opportunities to combine passions you may have lost from childhood with what fires you up today.

xviii *I use this head, heart, and hands method:* Thank you to my friend and colleague Martha Morris Graham for first sharing this technique with me. It's transformed how I do business and has helped my clients strengthen their emotional muscles.

Chapter 2: Meet Your Childhood Cast

19 *attachment theory suggests that . . . the most secure children experience psychological attachment to their mothers:* Attachment theory is a psychological framework that describes how we form emotional bonds and relationships early in life, and how that continues to affect us throughout life. John Bowlby originated the theory, while his colleague Mary Ainsworth tested it through empirical studies. David J. Wallin covers this well in his book *Attachment in Psychotherapy*.

20 *Dr. Gary Chapman's five love languages:* Gary D. Chapman. *The Five Love Languages: How to Express Heartfelt Commitment to Your Mate* (Nashville: Lifeway, 2010).

Chapter 5: Were You Raised in a Home of Complexity?

74 *Linda Hoopes, PhD, the founder of Resilience Alliance:* Linda Hoopes, *Prosilience: Building Your Resilience for a Turbulent World* (Dara, 2017). If you haven't read her book and are concerned about your level of resilience, I strongly recommend it.

Chapter 6: Were You Raised in a Home of Trauma?

81 *the age at which the trauma occurs is the age to which the traumatized person will always return:* Toni Luxenberg, Joseph Spinazzola, and Bessel A. van der Kolk, "Complex Trauma and Disorders of Extreme Stress (DESNOS) Diagnosis, Part One: Assessment," *Directions in Psychiatry* 21 (2001): 374.

84 *You were raised by someone with alcoholic use disorder:* To be clear, I have not worked with executives whose parents had drug addictions. Their children may have, but not the parents, so I do not claim to be able to talk about drug addiction.

86 *Children of The Maze also tend to be the Hero:* Sharon Wegscheider-Cruse, *Another Chance: Hope and Health for the Alcoholic Family* (Science and Behavior, 1989). The Hero is one role out of six (The Addicted, The Enabler, The Scapegoat, The Hero, The Mascot, and The Lost Child) found in families who have an alcoholic in their midst.

86 *Heroes put a lot of pressure on themselves:* Sharon Martin, "How Addiction Impacts the Family: 6 Family Roles in a Dysfunctional or Alcoholic Family," *Psych Central*, May 15, 2017, https://psychcentral.com/blog/imperfect/2017/05/how-addiction-impacts-the-family-6-family-roles-in-a-dysfunctional-or-alcoholic-family.

87 *"They have difficulty expressing their feelings and loving themselves":* Martin, "How Addiction Impacts the Family."

Chapter 9: What's Stopping You?

138 Bill George, the previous CEO of Medtronic, was the first to coin the term "Authentic Leadership" in his book *Authentic Leadership: Rediscovering the Secrets to Creating Lasting Value* (Jossey-Bass, 2003). He focuses on *what* people are here to do and *how* they want to lead through values. I focus on *why* they can or cannot live or lead authentically and teach them how to release what is blocking them.

Chapter 10: How to Confront—and Maybe Even Forgive—the Ones Who've Hurt You

147 *Dr. Bob Enright . . . created a model to help you forgive someone who has hurt you:*

R. D. Enright, *Forgiveness Is a Choice: A Step-by-Step Process for Resolving Anger and Restoring Hope* (APA Life Tools, 2001).

159 *research links forgiveness to many different health benefits:* Kirsten Weir, "Forgiveness Can Improve Mental and Physical Health," American Psychological Association, January 2017, https://www.apa.org/monitor/2017/01/ce-corner.

Chapter 12: Create Psychological Safety

171 *It's the first and most necessary step:* Honestly, I thought I was the only one with the secret; however, I learned that the term "psychological safety" was coined by Harvard Business School professor Amy Edmonson. Amy C. Edmondson, *The Fearless Organization: Creating Psychological Safety in the Workplace for Learning, Innovation, and Growth* (Hoboken, New Jersey: John Wiley & Sons, 2018).

172 *Gallup Q12 Survey on employee engagement:* "Gallup's Q12 Employee Engagement Survey," Gallup.com, 2025, https://www.gallup.com/q12-employee-engagement-survey.

Chapter 13: Listen Empathetically

191 *Author Steven Covey refers to empathetic listening:* Stephen R. Covey, *The 7 Habits of Highly Effective People* (Simon & Schuster, 1990).

195 *"paying attention, on purpose, in the present moment, and non-judgmentally, to the unfolding of experience moment to moment":* Jon Kabat-Zinn, *Wherever You Go, There You Are: Mindfulness Meditation in Everyday Life* (Hyperion, 1994).

197 *"Thinking is difficult, that's why most people judge":* This simplified version is widely quoted online. Jung's actual words are, "Thinking is difficult, therefore let the herd pronounce judgment!" *The Collected Works of C. G. Jung*, vol. 10, *Civilization in Transition* (Princeton University Press, 1964), 344.

Index

abandonment, feelings of, 74, 75
abuse. *See* Slings and Arrows; Sounds of Silence
achievement, in The Nest, 36–37
Act I. *See also* blocks; childhood; childhood cast; childhood settings
  and Emotional Timeline, 8–11, 15, 133–134
  example of impact of, 245–246
  example of sharing experiences from, 246–247
  importance of understanding impact of, 1
  role in leadership, xiii–xv
  in three-act play, xvii
Act II. *See also* blocks; confronting people responsible for blocks; identity
  blocks related to, 137–138
  connections to childhood, 107–109, 111–116, 126–127
  and Emotional Timeline, 8, 11–12, 15, 134–135
  in three-act play, xvii
Act III. *See also* constructive conflict; constructive feedback; empathetic listening; psychological safety; real conversations
  and Emotional Timeline, 8
  leadership work in, 163–164, 256
  in three-act play, xviii
active listening, 190–194
addiction. *See* The Maze
adult life, early. *See* Act II
aggression, in women, 53–54, 55
"aha" moments, 133, 135
alcohol-addicted parents. *See* The Maze
Alcott, Louisa May, 254–255
alternatives, in constructive conflict, 224
Americares, 165–166, 181, 183–184
anger
  in conversations of confrontation, 155
  dealing with feelings of, 75–76
  as preventing progress on blocks, 147, 148–149
antagonists, 216–217
anxiety, 73
anxious attachment, 78
apologizing in response to constructive feedback, 232
appreciating differences, 224
appreciating whole person, 180
asking for help, role in constructive conflict, 225
Assertive Diplomats, 90–91, 92–93, 99
assuming goodness, in empathetic listening, 197

attachment
anxious, 78
avoidant, 68, 69, 78, 87
dealing with issues with, 70, 78
disorganized, 78
secure, 36, 78
attention, in empathetic listening, 195–196
attentive listening, 189
"Authentic Leadership" questions, 138
authentic self, xxxii–xxxiii
avoidant attachment, 68, 69, 78, 87
awards, and Emotional Timeline, 10

bad actors from childhood, 25–26. *See also* confronting people responsible for blocks
balance
and children raised in multiple settings, 101–102
defining, 54–55, 56
behavioral feedback. *See* constructive feedback
beliefs, 112, 124–125
blocks, 129–142, 256. *See also* confronting people responsible for blocks
in children from Homes of Complexity, 61, 75–76
in children from Homes of Trauma, 82, 86, 91, 97
emotional loads as, 140
example of, 129–132
guiding lights for discerning, 136
identifying, 132–136
overcoming, 141–142
tied to home environment, 138–140
ways people understand, 136–138
body image, 96, 97
body language, 198
boosterism, 54, 56
bootstrapping, 50
bosses, handling conflict with, 212, 213
boundary crossings, sexual, 94
bullies and bullying. *See also* Slings and Arrows
children of Slings and Arrows becoming, 90, 91
influence on handling of conflict, 219

caring for others, and performance, 39
cast, childhood. *See* childhood cast
Chameleons, 69–70, 71–72, 78
Champions of Women, 51–52, 54, 56, 57–58
Chapman, Gary, 20
character, focus on in The Model Home, 43
cheerleaders, 216–217
childhood. *See also* Act I; blocks; confronting people responsible for blocks
and beliefs, 112, 124–125
connections to Act II, 107–109, 111–116, 126–127
and constitution, 111, 116–120
experience in, 112, 123–124
and motivation, 111, 120–122
real conversations about, 176
role in leadership, xiii–xv, xxiv, xxvii–xxviii, xxxvi
situation in, 112, 125–126

and skills, 112, 122–123
Tom Linebarger example, xxx–xxxiii
childhood cast, 17–29. *See also* confronting people responsible for blocks
connections to Act II, 108
dad, 20–21
emotions related to, 28–29
grandparents, 23–24
identifying blocks related to, 133–134, 135–136
implications of, 114–115
influence on handling of conflict, 218–220
mom, 18–20
parents, 21–23
secondary characters, 25–28
siblings, 24–25
childhood settings, 256. *See also* Homes of Complexity; Homes of Stability; Homes of Trauma
blocks tied to, 138–140
categories of, 32
children raised in multiple, 101–105
ground rules for work related to, 32–33
importance of revisiting, 31–32
influence on empathetic listening, 199–207
influence on giving feedback, 236–240
influence on handling of conflict, 214–218
commitment
of children of The Nomad, 70
in children of The Phantom Limb, 74
common ground, in constructive conflict, 224
compassion, role in forgiveness, 156–157
competence, showing to enhance psychological safety, 180
Complexity, Homes of. *See* Homes of Complexity
compromises, in constructive conflict, 224
confidence
in matriarchs, 51
role in resilience, 74–75
confidentiality, maintaining, 179
conflict. *See* constructive conflict
confronting people responsible for blocks, 143–162
choosing whom to talk to, 150–151
example of need for, 143–146
example of success in, 141–142
feelings that will prevent progress, 146–149
forgiving them, 156–160
forgiving yourself, 160–162
general discussion, 162
having conversation, 154–156
setting goals and planning for safety, 151–154
steps in process for, 150–162
connection, role in resilience, 75
Consistent Stabilizers, 85–86, 88, 99
constitution, 111, 116–120
constructive conflict, 209–225
and childhood cast, 218–220
and childhood environment, 214–218
example of improving, 220–223
general discussion, 225
tips for engaging in, 223–225
and work environment, 211–213

constructive feedback, 227–252
and childhood environment, 236–240
defined, 227–229
example of improving, 240–244
in family-owned businesses, 233–236
four-step method for giving, 229–233
general discussion, 244
content, conflict pertaining to. *See* constructive conflict
context, setting in feedback, 230–231
conversations. *See also* constructive conflict; constructive feedback; empathetic listening; psychological safety; real conversations
of children of The Maze, 86–87
to confront people who harmed you, 154–156
and Emotional Timeline, 9
Covey, Steven, 191
creativity, role in resilience, 74–75
cues, and empathetic listening, 195
Cummins Inc., xxiii–xxiv, 41–42, 45, 51–52, 62, 64, 167–169
cynicism, 75, 76

dad, recalling and describing, 20–21. *See also* parents
daily feedback, 228
data, emotions as, 3–5, 12–14
death, childhood experiences with, 72. *See also* The Phantom Limb
decoder ring concept, 126–127
denial
in conversations of confrontation, 155
as preventing progress on blocks, 147–148
depression, 73
determination, in matriarchs, 51
development areas
for children of In the Shadows, 66
for children of The Matriarchy, 54–57, 60
for children of The Maze, 86–87, 88
for children of The Model Home, 45–49, 59
for children of The Nest, 39–40, 41, 59
for children of The Nomad, 71
for children of The Phantom Limb, 75–76
for children of Slings and Arrows, 91, 92
for children of Sounds of Silence, 97, 98
differences, appreciating, 224
difficult events. *See also* Homes of Complexity; Homes of Trauma
and Emotional Timeline, 10
handling of by parents, 217–218
direct feedback, 227–228, 231. *See also* constructive feedback
disorganized attachment, 78
distractions, eliminating, xx
divorce of parents during childhood, 72–73. *See also* The Phantom Limb
Drivers, 52–54, 57

early adult life. *See* Act II
embarrassment, 84
emotional abuse. *See* Slings and Arrows

emotional loads, as blocks, 140
Emotional Timeline (ETL)
and constructive conflict, 222
emotional presentation as data, 12–14
example of, 5–7, 247
help with creating, 8–12
how to create, 7–8
identifying blocks on, 131–132, 133–134
implications of childhood for, 112
information revealed with, 14–15
real conversations about, 250
reviewing, 33
Tom Linebarger example, xxx–xxxi
emotions. *See also* head, heart, and hands check-in
acknowledging in empathetic listening, 197–198
of children of The Nomad, 69, 70
in conversations of confrontation, 155
as data, 3–5, 12–14
describing in constructive feedback, 231–232
forgiveness and relief from negative, 158–159
learning to not run away from, xx–xxi
need for leaders to access, xxviii–xxx
need for men to identify and share, 56
preventing progress on blocks, 146–149
related to childhood cast, 28–29
related to conflict, noticing, 212
role in identifying blocks, 132, 133–134
empathetic listening, 187–207
general discussion, 206–207
influence of home environment on, 199–207
as level to strive for, 191–194
and levels of listening, 188–191
and psychological safety, 178–179
role in constructive conflict, 224–225
tips for, 194–199
empathy
in conversations of confrontation, 155
role in forgiveness, 156–157
role in real conversations, 247–248, 251
engagement, and psychological safety, 178–179
Enright, Bob, 147, 157
environments, childhood. *See* childhood settings
ETL. *See* Emotional Timeline
expectations
of children of In the Shadows, 66
in The Nest, 36–37
In the Shadows, 62, 63
experience, 112, 123–124
expressing anger, 148, 149

facial expressions, in empathetic listening, 198
facilitators, 215–217
family
changing behaviors in, xxxiv–xxxv
importance of in The Nest, 37
traditions of, and Emotional Timeline, 9
family-owned businesses, constructive feedback in, 233–236

father, recalling and describing, 20–21. *See also* parents
fear
acting out of, 179
behind other emotions, 4
feedback, constructive. *See* constructive feedback
feedback assessment, 360, xxiv–xxvii, 234–235
feelings. *See* emotions
FIRO-B assessment, 116, 130
forgiveness
forgiving people who harmed you, 156–160
forgiving yourself, 160–162
uncovering phase of, 147
foundational areas. *See* identity
Freud, Sigmund, 148–149
friendliness, modeling, 178
friendships
of children of Slings and Arrows, 90
of children of The Maze, 84–85
of children of The Nomad, 69
handling conflict in, 218–220

girls, impact of The Matriarchy on, 52–54
goals, when confronting people, 151–154
goodness, assuming in empathetic listening, 197
gotcha listening, 190
Graham, Martha Morris, xxiv
grandparents, recalling and describing, 23–24
grief, dealing with feelings of, 75
guilt, 95
Guinness, 240–244
Gwen, Gena, 46

Hammer, Allen, 116
happy home settings, 36, 39–40
Harley-Davidson, 113, 114, 118, 125
head, heart, and hands check-in
about childhood cast, 28
and Emotional Timeline, 10–11
and preparing for leading role, xviii–xxi
and psychological safety, 178
help, asking for and/or offering, 225
helplessness, learned, 90, 213
Herman, Alexis, xxiv
Heroes, 86–87
home-related blocks, 137–138
Homes of Complexity, 61–77. *See also* In the Shadows; The Nomad; The Phantom Limb
blocks tied to, 139
general discussion, 77–79
influence on empathetic listening, 202–204
influence on giving feedback,
versus other childhood settings, 32
Homes of Stability, 35–60. *See also* The Matriarchy; The Model Home; The Nest
blocks tied to, 138–139
general discussion, 58–60
influence on empathetic listening, 200–202
influence on giving feedback, 237, 238, 239
versus other childhood settings, 32
Homes of Trauma, 81–100. *See also* The

Maze; Slings and Arrows; Sounds of Silence
blocks tied to, 139–140
general discussion, 99–100
influence on empathetic listening, 204–206
influence on giving feedback, 238, 239–240
versus other childhood settings, 32
Hoopes, Linda, 74, 75
"hydraulic theory" of anger, 148–149

identity
beliefs, 112, 124–125
of children of The Maze, 87
constitution, 111, 116–120
effect of living In the Shadows on, 63
experience, 112, 123–124
implications of childhood for, 111–116, 126–127
motivation, 111, 120–122
situation, 112, 125–126
skills, 112, 122–123
idols, in The Model Home, 44
Illuminators, 63–65, 66–67, 78
In the Shadows, 61–66
blocks tied to, 139
children of as leaders, 63–66
development areas for children of, 65–66
influence on empathetic listening, 202–203
influence on giving feedback, 237–238, 239
influence on handling of conflict, 217
versus other Homes of Complexity, 61
as primary childhood environment, 63
reflection questions, 66–67
takeaways from, 77, 78
inferior, characterizing people who hurt us as, 158
informal environment, and psychological safety, 177–178
informal power, xvi, 46
inquiry, role in constructive conflict, 224–225
inspirational nature of stable childhoods, 39–40
interpersonal conflict, 209
intimacy of real conversations, 172
isolation of children of Slings and Arrows, 90
issue, clearly stating for constructive conflict, 223–224

joyful childhoods, 36, 39–40
judgment, avoiding, 179

Kabat-Zinn, Jon, 195
Kant, Eva Margot, 94
kindness, need for when identifying blocks, 136
Kirk, Ann, 191
Kübler-Ross, Elisabeth, 148

leadership
author career in transformation of, ix–xiii
by children of In the Shadows, 63–66, 78
by children of The Matriarchy, 51–56, 60

leadership (*cont.*)
by children of The Maze, 85–87
by children of The Model Home, 44–48, 59
by children of The Nest, 37–40, 59
by children of The Nomad, 69–71, 78
by children of The Phantom Limb, 74–75, 79
by children of Slings and Arrows, 90–91
by children of Sounds of Silence, 95–97
and confronting people who hurt you, 153
and growth outside of work, 253–254
and life as three-act play, xvi–xviii
and power, xv–xvi
preparing for leading role, xviii–xxi
role of past in, xiii–xv, xxiv, xxvii–xxviii, xxx–xxxiii, xxxvi
taking next big step in, 255–256
and values, 46–48
working on in Act III, 163–164
leading role in your life, xvi–xxi
leaning in to conflict, 223
learned helplessness, 90, 213
Levatich, Matt
beliefs of, 124–125
as child of The Phantom Limb, 72, 73, 74–75
constitution of, 117–119
experience of, 123–124
implications of childhood, 113–114, 126–127
motivation of, 120–121
situation of, 125
skills of, 122–123
Levinson, Sara, 52–53
life as three-act play, xvi–xviii
life lessons, and Emotional Timeline, 9
Linebarger, Tom
360 feedback assessment of, xxiv–xxvi
as Champion of Women, 51–52
feedback for about CEO potential, xxiii–xxiv
leadership work by, xxviii–xxxv
as raised in The Matriarchy, 50
and real conversations, 167–169
listening. *See also* empathetic listening
bad, 192–193
influence of home environment on, 199–207
levels of, 188–191
levels to strive for, 191–194
Little Women (Alcott), 254–255
lone wolf, 69, 78
loneliness
of children of Slings and Arrows, 90
of children of The Nomad, 67, 68
of children of The Phantom Limb, 74
loss, dealing with feelings of, 75. *See also* The Phantom Limb
love
acting out of, 179
behind other emotions, 4
love languages, 20
loved ones, and Emotional Timeline, 9. *See also* childhood cast; parents
loyalty, 74

Manfredo Curtis Associates, LLC, xii
Manfredo Curtis, Pam
background and career of, ix–xiii
and constructive feedback, 229

creating psychological safety, 172–176
demonstrating constructive conflict, 210–211
effect of *Little Women* on, 254–255
emotions, role in childhood, 3
and emotions as data, 4
empathetic listening, 187–188, 196, 197–198
and real conversations, 168–169
studies with Jack Romano, 27
360 feedback assessment, xxiv–xxvii
work with Tom Linebarger, xxiv–xxvi, xxviii–xxxv
Martin, Sharon, 86
The Matriarchy, 50–58
blocks tied to, 139
children of as leaders, 51–56
development areas for children of, 54–57
influence on empathetic listening, 201–202
influence on giving feedback, 238, 239
versus other Homes of Stability, 35
as primary childhood environment, 51
reflection questions, 56–58
takeaways from, 58, 60
The Maze, 82–87
blocks tied to, 139–140
children of as leaders, 85–87
children raised in multiple settings, 102–104
development areas for children of, 86–87, 88
influence on empathetic listening, 204–205
influence on giving feedback, 238, 239
influence on handling of conflict, 216
versus other Homes of Trauma, 81
as primary childhood environment, 83–85
reflection questions, 87–88
takeaways from, 99, 100
MBTI (Myers-Briggs Type Indicator), 117–119
memories, spurring for Emotional Timeline, 8–11
men from The Matriarchy, 50–52, 54, 55–56, 57–58, 60
Miller, Will, xxiv
mindfulness, 178–179, 195–196
mining emotions for data, 3–5, 12–14. *See also* Emotional Timeline
mirror of truth, becoming, 181
The Model Home, 41–50
blocks tied to, 139
children of as leaders, 44–48
development areas for children of, 45–49
influence of later in life, 182
influence on empathetic listening, 200–201
influence on giving feedback, 237, 239
versus other Homes of Stability, 35
as primary childhood environment, 43–44
reflection questions, 48–50
takeaways from, 58, 59
mom, recalling and describing, 18–20. *See also* The Matriarchy; parents
motivation, 111, 120–122

multiple homes, and Emotional Timeline, 9. *See also* The Nomad
Myers-Briggs Type Indicator (MBTI), 117–119

negative emotions
on Emotional Timeline, 6–7, 12–13
forgiveness as offering relief from, 158–159
Nelson, Georgia, 102–104, 220–223
The Nest, 35–41
blocks tied to, 138
children of as leaders, 37–40
development areas for children of, 39–40, 41
influence on empathetic listening, 200
influence on giving feedback, 237, 239
influence on handling of conflict, 216–217
versus other Homes of Stability, 35
as primary childhood environment, 36–37
reflection questions, 40–41
takeaways from, 58, 59
NFL, 54
The Nomad, 67–71
blocks tied to, 139
children of as leaders, 69–71
development areas for children of, 70–71
influence on empathetic listening, 203–204
influence on giving feedback, 237–238, 239
influence on handling of conflict, 217
versus other Homes of Complexity, 61
as primary childhood environment, 69
reflection questions, 71–72
takeaways from, 77, 78
nonverbal communication, in empathetic listening, 196–197, 198
Nurturing Achievers, 37–40, 41, 59

observers
children of Slings and Arrows as, 90–91
children of Sounds of Silence as, 96, 97
children of The Maze as, 85
as role learned to play in conflict, 215–217
obstacles. *See* blocks
on edge feeling, in children of The Maze, 83, 84
other person's shoes, putting on, 196. *See also* empathetic listening; empathy
Ottino, Julio, 121
overwhelm, avoiding, 55
owning role in problems, 225

pacing conversations, 180
parents
example of impact of, 245–246, 247–248
handling of conflict by, 214–215
handling of traumatic or difficult events by, 217–218
living in shadow of, 61–62, 63, 64

in The Nest, 36–37
real conversations with, 245, 248–251
recalling and describing, 21–23
passive listening, 188–189
past. *See also* Act I; blocks; childhood; childhood cast; childhood settings
role in leadership, xiii–xv, xxiv, xxvii–xxviii, xxxvi
Tom Linebarger example, xxx–xxxiii
patience, need for when identifying blocks, 136
peers, conflict with, 213, 218–220
people-pleasing, avoiding, 39, 40
PepsiCo, xii
performance, and caring for others, 39
personality assessments, 55, 116–119, 130
The Phantom Limb, 72–76
blocks tied to, 139
children of as leaders, 74–75, 95–97
development areas for children of, 75–76
influence on empathetic listening, 203
influence on giving feedback, 238, 239
versus other Homes of Complexity, 61
as primary childhood environment, 73–74
reflection questions, 76–77
takeaways from, 77, 79
physical abuse. *See* Slings and Arrows
plan
closing constructive conflict with, 225
safety, when confronting people, 151–154
Porterfield, William, 72
positive emotions, on Emotional Timeline, 6–7, 12–13
positive intent, conveying in feedback, 230–231
positivity, 75
power, xv–xvi, 46, 163
preparation
for constructive conflict, 224
role in confronting people, 151–154
presence
in empathetic listening, 195–196
and psychological safety, 178–179
pretend listening, 189
primary childhood setting
identifying, 33
The Matriarchy as, 51
The Maze as, 83–85
The Model Home as, 43–44
The Nest as, 36–37
The Nomad as, 69
The Phantom Limb as, 73–74
In the Shadows as, 63
Slings and Arrows as, 89–90
Sounds of Silence as, 94–95
problem, clearly stating for constructive conflict, 223–224
prologue, in three-act play, xvii, xxiii–xxxvi
prosilience muscles, 74–75
psychological safety, 171–185. *See also* empathetic listening
appreciating whole person, 180
avoiding judgment, 179
becoming mirror of truth, 181

psychological safety (*cont.*)
being fully present and engaged for, 178–179
and constructive feedback, 230, 244
creating when confronting people, 153, 154, 155–156
examples of creating, 172–176, 181–184
maintaining confidentiality, 179
and meeting in informal environment, 177–178
modeling what you want to *See*, 178
pacing conversation, 180
providing unconditional support, 179
role in real conversations, 249–250
showing competence and skills, 180
steps in creating, 176–177
tips for creating, 185
purpose statements, 65
putting on other person's shoes, 196. *See also* empathetic listening; empathy

racist comments, in Slings and Arrows settings, 89, 90
rage, as preventing progress on blocks, 147, 148–149
reactions, taking responsibility for, 157
real conversations. *See also* confronting people responsible for blocks; constructive conflict; constructive feedback; empathetic listening; psychological safety
example of, 245–252
facilitating, 155–156
and forgiveness, 159, 161–162
tips for having, 165–169, 185
recognitions, and Emotional Timeline, 10
recommending solution in constructive feedback, 232–233
reconciliation, versus forgiveness, 158
reexamination, need for when identifying blocks, 136
referent power, xvi, 46, 163
refute, listening to, 190
relationships
of children of The Maze, 86–87
of children of The Nomad, 70
and Emotional Timeline, 9
impact of childhood cast on, 108
of parents, recalling and describing, 21–23
role of building in psychological safety, 178, 185
Replogle, John, 240–244
repression, 137
resilience questionnaires, 119
Resilient Committed Partners, 74–75, 77, 79
responsibilities shouldered by children of The Maze, 84
role in your life, leading, xvi–xxi
role models, in The Model Home, 44
role playing before confronting people, 153
Romano, Jack, 27
Rumsey, Jennifer, 51–52, 55

sadness, 73, 75
safety. *See also* psychological safety
creating environment of, xi, 178
lack of in children of Sounds of Silence, 94–95

planning for when confronting people, 151–154
Schacht, Henry, 62
Schacht, Jim, 61–62, 64–65
Schumacher, Amy, 54–55
secondary childhood characters, 25–28
secondary childhood setting, 33
secrets, blocks feeling like weight of, 140. *See also* Sounds of Silence
secure attachment, 36, 78
selective listening, 189
self-awareness
as breakthrough to leading better, xxviii, xxx, xxxiv
in children of In the Shadows, 65
role in improving constructive conflict, 221–222
self-blame, 72, 73
self-esteem, 90, 95
self-limiting beliefs, 40
self-reflection, when identifying blocks, 136
self-reliance, 69
self-righteousness, avoiding, 46
settings, childhood. *See* childhood settings
sexual abuse. *See* Sounds of Silence
sexual boundary crossings, 94
shadow of others, living in. *See* In the Shadows
shame, 84, 93, 95
siblings, recalling and describing, 24–25
silence, in empathetic listening, 197–198
Silence, Sounds of. *See* Sounds of Silence
situation, 112, 125–126
skills
as foundational area, 112, 122–123
showing to enhance psychological safety, 180
Slings and Arrows
blocks tied to, 140
children of as leaders, 90–91
children raised in multiple settings, 102–104
development areas for children of, 91, 92
influence on empathetic listening, 205
influence on giving feedback,
influence on handling of conflict, 217
versus other Homes of Trauma, 81
as primary childhood environment, 89–90
reflection questions, 91–93
takeaways from, 99, 100
Solso, Tim, xxiii
solution, recommending in constructive feedback, 232–233
Sounds of Silence, 93–99
blocks tied to, 140
children raised in multiple settings, 102–104
development areas for children of, 97, 98
influence on empathetic listening, 206
influence on giving feedback, 238, 240
influence on handling of conflict, 216
and need to confront people responsible, 145–146
versus other Homes of Trauma, 81
as primary childhood environment, 94–95
reflection questions, 97–99
takeaways from, 99, 100

speaking up
by children of Slings and Arrows, 91
effect of living In the Shadows on, 63
specific feedback, 228, 231. *See also* constructive feedback
Stability, Homes of. *See* Homes of Stability
Stagedoor Manor theater camp, 27
Stewart, Martha, 18–19, 20–21
strengths. *See also* strengths, of children of environments
of children of In the Shadows, 63–65, 78
of children of The Matriarchy, 51–54, 60
of children of The Maze, 85–86, 99
of children of The Model Home, 44–45, 59
of children of The Nest, 37–38, 59
of children of The Nomad, 69–70, 78
of children of The Phantom Limb, 74–75, 79
of children of Slings and Arrows, 90–91, 99
of children of Sounds of Silence, 95–97, 99
connections to Act II, 108
emergence in stable homes, 38
strengths, of children of environments
Assertive Diplomats (Slings and Arrows), 90–91, 92, 99
Chameleons (The Nomad), 69–72, 78
Champions of Women (The Matriarchy—men's strength), 51–52, 57–58, 60
Consistent Stabilizers (The Maze), 85–86, 88, 99
Drivers (The Matriarchy—women's strength), 52–54, 57,60
Illuminators (In the Shadows), 63–64, 66–67,78
Nurturing Achievers (The Nest), 37–38, 41, 59
Resilient Committed Partners (The Phantom Limb), 74–75, 77, 79
Values Champions and Values Crusaders (The Model Home), 45–45, 49,59
Vocalists (Sounds of Silence), 95–99
stress, managing proactively, 55
substance abuse. *See* The Maze
support
in The Nest, 36–37
providing unconditional, 179
supporting cast in Act 1. *See* childhood cast
suppression, 137, 148

teachers, recalling and describing, 26–27
teakettle anger, 148–149
thoughts, loudness of, 32. *See also* head, heart, and hands check-in
three-act play, life as, xvi–xviii
360 feedback assessment, xxiv–xxvii, 234–235
Timeline, Emotional. *See* Emotional Timeline
timely feedback, 228. *See also* constructive feedback
transparency, 178, 224
trauma, handling of by parents, 217–218. *See also* Homes of Trauma
trust, role in reconciliation, 158. *See also* psychological safety

truth, becoming mirror of, 181
truth tellers, 216–217

unconditional support, providing, 179
uncovering phase, in forgiveness, 147
undivided attention, in empathetic listening, 195–196
Unilever, xii
unloved, feelings of being, 74

values
  avoiding overzealousness about, 46
  of children of In the Shadows, 65–66
  and Emotional Timeline, 9
  focus on in The Model Home, 43–44, 182
  influence on empathetic listening, 201
  interest in other people's, 46
  and leadership, 46–48
  and motivation, 120–121
Values Champions, 44–45, 49, 59
Values Crusaders, 45, 49–50, 59, 182–184
venting anger, 148, 149
verbal abuse. *See* Slings and Arrows
visceral reactions. *See also* head, heart, and hands check-in
  tuning in to, 13, 185
  when checking your heart, xix
  when identifying blocks, 132, 137
Vocalists, 95–96, 98, 99
vulnerability, modeling, 178, 251

warmth, modeling, 178
Wegscheider-Cruse, Sharon, 86–87
Welling, Curt, 165–166, 181–184
whole person, appreciating, 180
women who grew up in The Matriarchy, 52–55, 56–57, 60. *See also* The Matriarchy
work environment, influence on handling of conflict, 211–213
work-related blocks, 137–138

About the Author

Pam Manfredo Curtis, PhD, is an elite executive coach to global Fortune 500 CEOs and senior leaders. She helps C-suite executives across a wide range of industries, including sports, entertainment, manufacturing, and major global brands. Of the companies she can disclose, some of her most well-known organizations include General Motors, Harley-Davidson, Cummins, and Unilever. Her proprietary approach teaches executives how to lead authentically by connecting their childhood experiences to their current leadership styles. This process has led to extraordinary results in her clients' personal and professional lives. Consequently, CEOs enthusiastically recommend her to their peers.

She is the founder and president of Manfredo Curtis Associates, LLC, and the host of SiriusXM's *Corner Office Confidential*. She holds a master's and doctorate in industrial and organizational psychology from Tulane University, as well as a bachelor's in psychology and business, magna cum laude, from Washington University in Saint Louis, Missouri.

Pam and her husband, John, live in Connecticut. They have three adult children, whom they adore. Pam has always loved to sing. In fact, after a meeting, Pam can often be found with her clients gathered around the nearest piano, belting out beloved Broadway standards.